3b23l16

Ethical Practice of Social Media in Public Relations

Given the high rate of social media use by the public, organizations are compelled to engage with key audiences through these outlets. Social media engagement requires organizations to actively participate with public groups, and this highly-interactive exchange raises a new set of ethical concerns for communicators. In this rapidly changing communications environment, the long-term implications of social media are uncertain, and this book provides the much needed research to understand its impact on audiences and organizations.

Through an examination of a broad range of ethics concepts including transparency and online identities, policies, corporate responsibility, and measurement, this book explores a variety of topics important to public relations such as diversity, non-profit communication, health communication, financial communication, public affairs, entertainment communication, environmental communication, crisis communication, and non-profit communication. The chapter authors, expert scholars within their fields of public relations, offer insights drawn from original research and case study examples of ethical dilemmas raised by social media communication.

Marcia W. DiStaso is Assistant Professor of Public Relations in the College of Communications at Pennsylvania State University, US

Denise Sevick Bortree is Associate Professor of Communications at Pennsylvania State University, US

Routledge Research in Public Relations

Ethical Practice of Social Media in Public Relations

**Edited by
Marcia W. DiStaso
and Denise Sevick Bortree**

Routledge
Taylor & Francis Group
NEW YORK   LONDON

First published 2014
by Routledge
711 Third Avenue, New York, NY 10017

and by Routledge
2 Park Square, Milton Park, Abingdon, Oxon OX14 4RN

*Routledge is an imprint of the Taylor & Francis Group,
an informa business*

Library of Congress Cataloging-in-Publication Data
Ethical practice of social media in public relations / edited by Marcia W.
DiStaso & Denise Sevick Bortree.
    pages cm — (Routledge research in public relations)
   Includes bibliographical references and index.
  1.   Social media—Moral and ethical aspects. 2.   Social responsibility
of business. 3.   Public relations. 4.   Internet—Moral and ethical
aspects. I. DiStaso, Marcia W., 1970–   II. Bortree, Denise Sevick.
  TK5105.878.E784 2014
  174'.96592—dc23
  2013033525

ISBN13: 978-0-415-72753-2 (hbk)
ISBN13: 978-1-315-85217-1 (ebk)

Typeset in Sabon
by IBT Global.

This volume was made possible
through the generous support of:

The Arthur W. Page Center for
Integrity in Public Communication

College of Communications
The Pennsylvania State University

Contents

PART II
Social Media Policies

PART III
Corporate Responsibility

PART IV
Ethical Frameworks for Communication

Figures

Tables

Foreword
Social Media is Lost
without a Social Compass

Brian Solis

Social media is not lawless. It is governed by the code of each network. At the same time however, each network is governed by the culture that develops in how people connect and communicate. The laws that we abide by in the real world influence what's right and wrong. But more so, the laws of humanity govern what we say and do whereas judgment is passed according to the law of popular society and the unsaid ethics that serve its center.

Whether it's right or wrong, what *is* right and wrong is open to interpretation. And peers often pass judgment without the benefit of a fair trial.

Ethics therefore should not go unsaid or undefined.

Ethics symbolize the code that governs actions and unlocks relationships. The question is, what type of relationships do you want to build, and have now and in the future?

Relationships?

Yes. They are the epicenter of social networks.

There's a "social" in social media for a reason. There's also a "me."

At its very core, social media is not about technology, it's about people. Connections, emotions, expression become the souls and personalities of online communities. The ties that bind them together are relationships. And it is in the value of relationships that people on either side will find value. Without value, mutual benefits, the quality of the relationship erodes.

Again I ask, what kind of relationship do you want to have with people?

Social media is a human and emotional egosystem (yes, that's an intentional word). Networks are exchanges where conversations are currency. People connect because there's value to do so.

So what is the value in a connection with you?

What do you get out of it?

What will I takeaway?

How do you want me to feel?

What do you want me to say and do?

So. Many. Questions.

It is in the answering of these questions that will govern all you do in social media.

INTENTIONS + ACTIONS = PERCEPTIONS

It's a simple formula. What you aim to do combined with what you do shape the perceptions and resulting impressions and expressions of people directly and indirectly. Opinions and dialogue are commodities. In social media, expressions are not only shared, they are also sparks for greater discussions. With momentum, conversations can create communities and communities can inspire movements.

What you say and what people hear can in fact create two or more different outcomes.

The ethical practice of social media starts with an ethical foundation. Without it, you risk falling victim to social media's relentless and unforgiving nature of real-time relevance or irrelevance. You are competing for the moment and for the future in all you do. Without a strong ethical foundation, you unintentionally make perilous decisions driven by what's right . . . right now, rather than what's truly right.

YOU HAVE NOW ENTERED THE GREY ZONE

Martin Luther King Jr. did not say, "I have an ethical dream to share." Walt Disney did not build a universe governed by morals. Instead, they challenged convention to change how we see the world. It was through their vision, words, architecture and leadership that visualized not only a new world, but they defined the roles we play in it and the advantages we'll realize for doing so.

For better or for worse, ethics is not a black and white discussion. It's often the grey-zone that sets the foundation for individual and organizational comfort zones. Much like in the legal world, what's right and wrong is often open to interpretation. Laws represent a system of rules, which carry varying penalties if they're broken. But it is in legal practice and the surrounding conversations within offices, conference rooms, and courtrooms that blur the line between meaning, understanding, and outcomes. While precedence often dictates a center to explore opportunities and consequences, contending with legal matters after a rule or law is broken is not the premise of our work together.

We must address ethics now not in the face of challenges or troubles.

This is a time for leadership.

THE ETHICAL PRACTICE OF SOCIAL MEDIA IS WHERE ACTIONS AND WORDS SPEAK LOUDER THAN SILENCE

The promise of your work and how it will affect the work of others lies in an elixir of aspiration and ambition. Indeed, ethics are the moral principles that govern behavior. It's in the intentions we have, the choices we make, the things we say, and the actions we carry out where we set the stage for reaction. But it's the grey-zone where impressions and opinions are formed. And it is this judgment that becomes truth. As we all have learned, perception is reality. Ethics are therefore open to interpretation.

For every action, there is an equal and opposite reaction . . .

Plan.

Your work must be guided by aspiration, grounded in virtues, and packaged in respect. Everything begins upon a clear ethical foundation. This means that like a vision or mission statement, your work must be governed by a manifesto that articulates hope, value, purpose, and expectations. It is guide where you, and anyone who sees is, will realize the promise and meaning of "why"—why you feel what you feel, do what you do, say what you say, and why anyone whom you touch should listen and more importantly, align with you. It's your compass, your center, and your foundation.

BE TRANSPARENT. BE AUTHENTIC

You'll hear it throughout your practice of social media. Be transparent. Be authentic. These words however, are not the only points on your compass. They are however, important pillars that stand upon your ethical foundation. Without definition though, they're just words.

Define them.

Transparency requires clarity. Authenticity requires honesty. Both are enlivened by definition and articulation in your manifesto and it is this manifesto that creates your social compass.

Your compass is more important than you may think.

A compass provides direction. It's the Google Maps for doing what's right for the moment for the good of the relationships you seek to invest in. It's the GPS for navigating what is right and what is wrong before, during, and after engagement. Your compass will define the nature of relationships and influence what people see, hear and ultimately do as a result.

YOUR SOCIAL COMPASS

A compass is a device for discovering orientation and serves as a true indicator of physical direction.

In 2009, I designed a social compass to help guide the ethical and aspirational practice of social media. It debuted in my book *Engage*[1] and was inspired by a moral compass. The Social Compass[2] was created to serve as our value system when defining strategies, initiatives, and ultimately engagement. It points a brand in a physical and experiential direction to genuinely and effectively connect with customers, peers, and influencers, where they interact and seek guidance online.

Figure 0.1 Social compass.

It was designed to guide us from the center outward. However, it can also impact how a business learns and adapts by reversing the process and listening to customers and influencers through each channel from the outside in.

When we listen and hear what's taking place in the conversational ego-system, the compass works from the outside in, moving from the edge to the center. When we engage, we move from the center to the outside edge.

CENTER: THE BRAND

At the center of the compass is the brand; essentially, everything you do will revolve around it.

HALO 1: THE PLAYERS

Fundamental to any program, the players define how, when, why, and to what extent our activity is intermediated across the Social Web. They include:

Advocates/stakeholders: Those individuals who maintain a stake in the brand and the success of the company, through emotional, strategic, or financial investment—and are usually among the first line of external champions.

Traditional media: Reporters, journalists, analysts, and other forms of mainstream and vertical media who already reach our intended audiences.

New influencers/trust agents: Individuals who focus a noteworthy portion of their updates, content, and voice on particular topics, industries, or markets.

Champions: Whereas advocates and stakeholders have skin in the game to some extent, champions are merely inspired to share their experiences and views because they are passionate, compelled, or incentivized.

Bloggers/market makers: Bloggers and market makers represent what some refer to as the "A-list." This elite group can steer, shape, and galvanize activity that moves markets based on their views.

Tastemakers/Magic Middle: Tastemakers and the magic middle are distinct from new influencers and trust agents, and, depending on the industry, serve as a subset of them. In their own way they make markets and spark trends based on their activity. Tastemakers are the trendsetters and, in the Social Web, they usually boast notable followers and connections who emulate their behavior, whether it's explicit or implicit, on behalf of the tastemaker. The term Magic Middle was coined by David Sifry, who was at the time CEO of Technorati, the world's largest blog network; he defined this group as bloggers who maintained an inbound link volume of between 20 to 1,000 links.

Now, I refer to the Magic Middle as any group of content creators who remain focused on a topic and have earned a substantial audience because of their experiences, views, and perspective.

HALO 2: PLATFORM

Every initiative, inclusive of those groups of individuals who define our markets and ensuing behavior, requires a platform upon which to connect, communicate, and congregate. These platforms represent existing and also emerging categories that are worthy of our attention today and tomorrow:

Mobile: Any network that unites groups of targeted individuals through interaction on mobile devices.

Social dashboard/microsites: As discussed previously, social dashboards and microsites aggregate distributed social presences into one experience for channeling activity, providing information, fostering community, and guiding perception and impressions.

Widgets and applications: Widgets and applications are portable services that spark interaction in a variety of networks, from mobile devices to Web-based social networks. They create an immersive experience designed to perform a dedicated function including tasks, games, interaction, learning, and other forms of entertainment and engagement within a dedicated, embeddable environment, while branding or conveying messages in the process.

Forums and groups: Web 1.0 still rules, and through research we learn that communication and influence is still widespread in forums and groups where people not only communicate with each other every day, they also organize events, manage projects, and teach and learn from one another on almost every topic imaginable and unimaginable.

Blogs: Blogs, in all of their shapes and sizes, deserve a tremendous amount of attention, as they are still among the most active and influential news sources, besides traditional media. Not only do they hit mainstream audiences, they also focus on dedicated, vertical communities and nicheworks that equally contribute to your total market.

Social networks: Of course social networks are a primary forum for today's social media interactions and therefore require a dedicated focus. As we've repeated so often in these pages, our attention is necessitated in popular networks as well as the nicheworks dedicated to our areas of interest.

Content creation: The development and syndication of social objects carries the ability to reach people in almost every medium today, and will only continue to expand as technology advances. We are now in the content publishing and distribution business.

Events (offline and online): The cultivation of communities is important online and also in the physical locales where we meet our customers, advocates, peers, and influencers. A fusion between online and offline communication is critical and therefore mandatory.

Microcommunities: While many refer to these services as microblogs, the truth is that they are not in any way, shape, or form reminiscent of blogs, nor is the behavior that they stimulate. We focus on them as dedicated platforms due to their unique interactions, communities, efficacy, and reach.

HALO 3: CHANNELS

Aggregation: The feeds, platforms, and devices that take content from multiple outlets or memes and funnel them into one branded stream.

Crowdsourced: Organizing the activity of consumers onto public stages to foster dialogue, collaboration, and glean insights.

Curation: Designing social objects to appeal to social curators extending reach and visibility.

SEO: If everything begins with search, SEO represents the enhancement of content, pages, and destinations through search engine optimization to ensure brands are readily clickable upon relevant searches.

Promotion: Even the best content requires marketing. As social objects, campaigns, and engagement strategies are introduced, they must be complemented with genuine front and backchannel support. There is no such thing as viral marketing, but information travels to the extent of our connections and investment in them.

Syndication: Whereas aggregation is about many-to-one, syndication is about one-to-many. Please note that this does not refer to the mass broadcast of information to general audiences, syndication refers to the intentional repackaging of content for different platforms and nicheworks.

SMO: Similar to SEO, Social Media Optimization (SMO) amplifies the visibility of objects within social networks by improving their "findability" through tags, descriptions, titles, conversations, and linkbacks.

Participation/Engagement: Connections are much more than the 3F's of friends, followers, and fans; they are fortified by the mutual value that is exchanged in each interaction. Engagement is measured by actions and outcomes.

Portability: Transmedia represents the ability to have stories and objects travel across multiple platforms and devices to match the behavior of the people we're trying to reach. Portability must be defined to suit their needs.

Content Streams: Streams are the windows to relevance. People discover information through attention. Appearing in streams is how we compete for attention.

UGC: Often referred to as earned media, UGC is impressionable and can be steered positively. In addition, through active engagement combined with a recipe of all things above, reach and effect are increased through the genuine voices of others.

HALO 4: EMOTIONS/SENTIMENT

The socialization of the Web is powered by people, and it is a movement that is bound by the same natural laws that govern human behavior. Successful branding is made possible when individuals can establish a human and emotional connection. In social networks, the brand is represented by you, and for that reason we must factor compassion, care, and feeling into our planning. Connect from the heart.

Reciprocation: The gesture of a response is far more powerful than we perceive. It is the act of paying it forward that actually contributes to the caliber, quality, and value of dialogue and interchanges. As influence is both democratized and equalized, giving back is a symbol of respect and gratitude.

Empathy: Understanding the sentiment of another related to material interaction and experiences, humanizes the context of an experience and conversation. You must become the very people you're trying to reach and in order to do so, our understanding must extend beyond training and embrace real-life exposure.

Recognition: Identifying the contributions of others and promoting or responding to worthy individuals and instances are parts of how we cultivate communities and build relationships. From "thank you" to "I'm sorry," the symbolic deeds of acknowledgment, admittance, and identification serve as powerful forms of validation.

Core values: The attributes that define the principles and standards of a brand are reinforced or diminished by its conduct. If we wish to attract influential peers, we must stand for something with which people can identify and associate. We must represent purpose. Our brand and our actions either encourage affinity or they don't.

Resolution: The practice of solving problems, disputes, and other correlated issues is a focus and a mission that contribute to those actions that indeed speak louder than words. And, if we're to be measured by them, then let our commitment to resolve impediments speak for itself.

Empowerment: Providing the authority to achieve something not possible before the encounter instills confidence and advocacy and sets the foundation to scale community development. Empowerment alters the balance of engagement and transforms interactions into relationships.

Humanization: Convey and embody a human voice and character in all we do in interactive media. From the creation and distribution of social objects to engagement with individuals, engagement is most effective when we personalize our approach. The Social Web is alive and powered by our ability to identify with others through direct interaction or by coming into contact with their personae, as attached to the content they interact with, share, or produce.

Honesty: Be honest and virtuous in all interactions and not misleading whatsoever in any scenario in order to achieve your objective. Be truthful. If you don't have an answer or information, say so. If what you represent doesn't measure up in a particular setting, admit it. Focus on strengths and opportunities. Do not spin or market messages.

Reward: Sometimes recognition isn't enough to satisfy someone for their contribution. The act of rewarding someone is a sign of appreciation. Rewards can span from monetary items to discounts to free products to access and special privileges. The consistent performance of rewarding community behavior fosters increased activity through positive conditioning.

Value proposition: When humanizing our stories and interactions, it is the value proposition that speaks directly to specific markets. Many times marketing either attempts to generalize features or capabilities for the masses or simply reiterates the value propositions as dictated by internal management.

Believable: Words such as transparency and authenticity are overused in any discussion related to socialized outreach and therefore lose a good deal of their essence and meaning. It is more convincing and consequential in any encounter if you are believable. This can be passionate, exuberant, and contagious, unlike transparency or authenticity. Give me something to believe in.

Sincerity: Your biggest objective moving forward is to earn and continue to gain trust. In order to do so, your actions must exclude pretense and instead enrich interactions through the exchange of genuine feelings and intentions.

DEFINE YOUR PATH—LEAD PEOPLE
ON A MEANINGFUL JOURNEY

Social media is an emotional landscape and to succeed day in and day out takes more than communication, it takes vision and purpose. Without it, what do you stand for and why would anyone wish to stand alongside you?

As you design your social media strategies, everyday content, and engagement programs, let your social compass guide you. Consider in simulation, and definitely prior to their activation in networks, how your intentions will convert to desired impressions. Doing so helps you understand how your actions will elicit the reactions you want. Use your social compass to then lead you into each network with confidence and relevance to earn relationships and spark meaningful engagement.

Remember, relationships aren't just an outcome, they're a reward for thoughtful, significant, and inspirational work.

Be strategic and thoughtful.

Be considerate.

Be empathetic.

Be approachable.

Ethics and the ethical practice of social media bridge the gaps between intentions and desired impressions and also between actions and desired reactions. You can only spark and enhance relationships as a result.

This is a time for leadership and you play a pivotal role in changing how your organization communicates and connects.

The ethical practice of social media is governed by your grey-zone. Defining what you do and what you will not do in various situations, guided by your vision in purpose, will answer what's right, right now, and what's right . . . for the future.

Give people a reason to do more than just connect or engage with you. Inspire them because you're inspired.

Preface

Marcia W. DiStaso and Denise Sevick Bortree

Since the emergence of the first social media networks some two decades ago, social media has continued to evolve and offer consumers around the world new and meaningful ways to engage with people, events, and brands that matter to them. Social media continues to rapidly grow, and has become an integral part of our daily lives. In fact, it can be argued that social networking is a global phenomenon.

Social media allows many opportunities for organizations to increase the visibility of their organization. According to Merriam-Webster (2013), social media are

> forms of electronic communication (as Web sites [sic] for social net-working and microblogging) through which users create online com-munities to share information, ideas, personal messages, and other content (as videos). (¶ 1)

Looking at its impressive impact, a Pew Internet study (Rainie, Smith, & Duggan, 2013) found that social media is in fact an important part of many people's lives. Specifically, they found that 67% of online adults use a social networking site, 67% are on Facebook, 16% are on Twitter, 15% are on Pinterest, and 13% are on Instagram. Additionally, they identified that the "typical" user is: under age 50, but 18–29 was the most likely cohort to use social media, female, and live in an urban versus rural environment.

This attests to the fact that social media is no longer in its infancy and as a result, more and more organizations are using digital platforms to reach publics. New sites continue to emerge and catch on. In addition, the popularity of mobile helps more people connect to the Internet for longer amounts of time.

While studies show that social media adoption continues to grow, most have found that organizations typically use the popular tools of Facebook, Twitter, and YouTube (see Barnes, Lescault, & Wright, 2013; Wright & Hinson, 2012). Furthermore, DiStaso, McCorkindale, and Agugliaro (Forthcoming) found that 51% of *Fortune's Most Admired Companies* had actively managed Facebook pages while 82% had Twitter accounts, and 72% had YouTube accounts.

Even when organizations have not become active in social media, it is likely that conversations are occurring about them. It is important to become a part of the conversation; however, some may argue that it is even more important for organizations to listen to the conversations. The use of social media should be strategic for both for-profit and non-profit organizations. Success in social media requires dialogue and engagement along with a commitment to transparency and authenticity by the organization. As with audiences of other channels, perception is reality, so how an organization chooses to use social media is a direct reflection of its identity.

Effective strategic use of social media requires ethical consideration. Specifically, organizations need to consider ethical equivocality with the goal of dialogic or two-way communication. As Stoker and Tusinski (2006) suggested, dialogue should be balanced with information dissemination and demanding participation may be unethical. Ulterior motives in social media are easily discovered and organizations have a responsibility to be open with their social media stakeholders. Social media should be managed with the ethic of care in mind to ensure that actions reflect a concern for others and value for the relationship.

Certain actions in social media draw ethical concerns. This includes ghost blogging (see Chapter 2), handling negative content (see Chapter 3), transparency/openness of companies (see Chapter 1), online crises (see Chapters 4, 9, and 15), communicating with diverse audiences (See Chapter 10), dialogic communication (see Chapters 1, 3, 5, and 11), astroturfing (see Chapter 15), privacy (see Chapter 5), responsible corporate social responsibility (CSR) (see Chapters 3, 7, 8, 9, and 10), and social media policies (See chapters 5 and 6).

This book is organized into parts focusing on transparency and online identities, corporate responsibility, ethical frameworks for communication, and social media policies and each of them are discussed below.

TRANSPARENCY AND ONLINE IDENTITIES

Social media allows organizations to provide transparent communication and another outlet to take responsibility for its efforts and actions. The public often demands transparency from organizations. Wright and Hinson (2012) indicated that effective social media acts as a watchdog for traditional news media and organizations, thereby advocating a transparent and ethical culture. Rawlins (2009) defined transparency as:

> The deliberate attempt to make all legally releasable information— whether positive or negative in nature—in a manner that is accurate, timely, balanced, and unequivocal, for the purpose of enhancing the

reasoning ability of publics and holding organizations accountable for their actions, policies, and practices. (p. 75)

Through transparency and all actions on social media, organizations build their online identity. While brand perception offline is important, online activities can impact opinions. Consider the analysis by Marcia W. DiStaso about how Bank of America handled their Facebook page surrounding the debit card fee crisis in 2011 in "Bank of America's Facebook Engagement Challenges it Claims of 'High Ethical Standards'", (Chapter 3). Their actions of deleting comments and trying to control conversations likely greatly impacted or minimally did not help their online identity as it is noted that Bank of America is one of the most disliked companies in America.

Similarly, when a photo accusing Kashi of deceptive advertising was posted and went viral on Facebook, Hilary Fussell Sisco found that Kashi quickly responded (see Chapter 4: "Natural or Not? A Case Study of Kashi's Viral Photo Crisis on Facebook"). While they originally tried to create a diversion, this strategy proved counterproductive. Swift action can help to minimize damage, and being transparent about products and accusations is critical to move forward.

Through interviews with communication leaders, Richard D. Waters explored perceptions of openness and disclosure to find that although some felt being open was the "cornerstone" of their business, others questioned the level necessary (Chapter 1: "Openness and Disclosure in Social Media Efforts: A Frank Discussion with *Fortune 500* and *Philanthropy 400* Communication Leaders:). Some study participants indicated their discomfort with social media, possibly explaining why openness is so difficult.

Finally, Tiffany Derville Gallicano, Thomas H. Bivins, and Yoon Y. Cho found that expectations about the ethics of ghost blogging hinged on blog reader expectations (Chapter 2: "Considerations Regarding Ghost Blogging and Ghost Commenting"). They found that although many people expected ghost blogging for CEOs and politicians, few approved of the practice.

SOCIAL MEDIA POLICIES

As more organizations are adopting social media, most are adding social media policies or guidelines to their employee handbooks and making them available on their website or social media accounts for the public. Setting expectations can encourage employees to be more aware of their social media use and provide justifications for actions with the public. For example, employees should be informed what type of content is not appropriate to discuss over social media channels.

Through interviews with social media managers at a variety of organizations, Tina McCorkindale found that the people she spoke with allowed the community to influence how social media was handled (Chapter 5: "Private Conversations on Public Forums: How Organizations are Strategically Monitoring Conversations and Engaging Stakeholders on Social Media Sites"). Most used it for customer service and to listen to and monitor what people are saying across all sites. Respondents were strategic in how they engaged and indicated that maintaining social media was a time-consuming and resource-heavy endeavor.

Non-profit organizations often have few resources to dedicate to social media, so some may say that they have to be more focused in their social media efforts. Marcus Messner found only 36% of those surveyed had a social media policy for their employees and volunteers (Chapter 6: "To Tweet or Not to Tweet: An Analysis of Ethical Guidelines for the Social Media Engagement of Nonprofit Organizations"). The reason for this low use of policies could be because most did not view social media as a likely cause for an ethical problem.

CORPORATE SOCIAL RESPONSIBILITY

Corporate social responsibility has been defined as the ethical use of corporate resources to contribute to communities, the environment, and society. Four chapters in this book looked at the ways companies are engaging in CSR communication in social media. Together, they offer a broad examination of how companies have addressed diversity, environmental issues, and crisis through their social media platforms. According to Kati Tusinski Berg and Kim Bartel Sheehan (Chapter 7: "Social Media as a CSR Communication Channel: The Current State of Practice"), the most popular brands on Facebook rarely use their pages to deliver CSR messages (less than 1%). When looking closer at the most sustainable brands, they found that less than 16% of content was CSR related. This raises questions about why organizations are not taking advantage of this channel to promote their CSR efforts.

Two other studies suggest that during crisis organizations turn to CSR content to promote their responsible actions as an image restoration strategy. Denise Sevick Bortree (Chapter 8: "Corporate Social Responsibility in Environmental Crisis: A Case Study of BP's YouTube Response to the Deepwater Horizon Crisis") found that BP posted over 300 videos to its YouTube site during the Deepwater Horizon crisis that spanned from April 2010 to October 2011. Many of these videos touted socially and environmentally responsible actions of the organization during and after the crisis occurred. W. Timothy Coombs (Chapter 9: "Nestlé and Greenpeace: The battle in Social Media for Ethical Palm Oil Sourcing") looked at a case study in which the organization's social and environment responsibility were challenged. When Nestlé was challenged by Greenpeace over its palm oil sourcing, the organization's initial response failed to meet ethical standards. Coombs examines the response and offers insights based on the theory of ethic of care.

One frequently overlooked area of CSR is diversity communication. Nneka Logan and Natalie T. J. Tindall analyze Coca-Cola's Expedition 206 campaign (Chapter 10: "Coca-Cola, Community, Diversity, and Cosmopolitanism: How Public Relations Builds Global Trust, Brand Relevance, and Diversity") to explore how the concept of happiness is used to build social community and engage with diverse audiences.

ETHICAL FRAMEWORKS FOR COMMUNICATION

The communication literature offers many frameworks for analysis of ethical content. These include dialogic loop, TARES (truthful, authentic, respectful, equitable, socially responsible), and the Arthur W. Page principles. The authors in this book explore some of these frameworks to better understand how social media communication may be following or flouting these guidelines. Angela M. Lee, Homero Gil de Zúñiga,, Renita Coleman, and Thomas J. Johnson explore the dialogic potential of Facebook and Twitter conversations on corporate pages and consider the ethical implications of the interactions based on TARES (Chapter 11: "The Dialogic Potential of Social Media: Assessing the Ethical Reasoning of Companies' Public Relations on Twitter and Facebook). They found that overall organizations did a poor job at dialogic communication, but utilized Twitter a bit more than Facebook for engagement.

In a similar vein, Päivi Tirkkonen and Vilma Luoma-aho (Chapter 13: "Authority Crisis Communication vs. Discussion Forums: Swine Flu") use the TARES model to examine online discussions of flu pandemics. They conclude that ethical online discussions with authorities would involve greater engagement than typically occurs with the public.

Social media has become a popular channel for communication between government and citizens, as Tirkkonen and Luoma-aho's chapter suggests. Kaye Sweetser also looks at government communication (Chapter 14: "Government Gone Wild? Ethics, Reputation, and Social Media"). She reviewed three case studies of government online communication including a call by government for contractors to rout out terrorism online, government engagement with Twitter accounts run by adversaries, and a smear campaign toward journalists covering the military. Backlash by the public to these missteps varied based on the degree to which the government violated norms for transparency. These case studies illustrate how difficult it can be to navigate social media when organizational risk is high.

Another popular form of social media—blogging—has been adopted by many corporations to reach specific segments of their publics. Kirsten A. Johnson and Tamara Gillis (Chapter 12: "Journalists and Corporate Blogs: Identifying Markers of Credibility") look at the media perspective on corporate blogging and offer insights into the perceived credibility of content in this channel through the eyes of journalists.

Finally, Don W. Stacks and Shannon A. Bowen consider the ethical implications and importance of research involved with social media campaigns in their evaluation of two social media misses (Chapter 15: "Understanding the Ethical and Research Implications of Social Media"). Hopefully as an industry, we can learn from the Edelman and Walmart astroturfing campaign and the Edelman Microsoft Vista third-party endorser campaign. These early mistakes in social media covered in this chapter emphasize the importance of ethics in the social media decision-making process.

CONCLUSION

The importance of social media and ethics have simultaneously arisen in the last decade as more organizations incorporate social media strategies into their communication plans and face ethical challenges in managing relationships in a virtual context. This book was developed from a call for funded grant proposals by the Arthur W. Page Center, which focuses on integrity in public communication. The authors in this book were selected to participate in a project on social media and ethics in public relations based on their expertise and their research projects. Each project became a chapter in this book, and we are pleased with the way they have come together to cover the broad spectrum of ethical concerns that organizations face today.

Chapter topics range from CSR and crisis to health, environment, and banking, in nonprofits, corporations, and government. Together, these studies illustrate how broad the adoption of social media has become in organizational communication. However, the cases and content in this book look at only the most popular social media channels, including Facebook, Twitter, YouTube, and blogging. Future studies should explore more sites in the social media space, including Instagram, Pinterest, LinkedIn, Google+ along with other emerging channels.

This book offers thoughts from some of the pre-eminent researchers in social media and public relations today. We have designed the content to provide students, scholars, and professionals with useful information to weigh decisions about an organizations' social media content. At the same time, the new concepts and cases presented in this book contribute to our theoretical understanding of ethics in the content of social media and public relations. We hope that you find our book interesting and beneficial in your work.

NOTES

1. http://www.engagingbook.com

2. http://www.briansolis.com/2011/01/the-social-compass-is-the-gps-for-the-adaptive-business/

REFERENCES

Barnes, N. G., Lescault, A. M., & Wright, S. (2013). 2013 *Fortune 500* are bullish on social media: Big companies get excited about Google+, Instagram, Foursquare and Pinterest. Retrieved from http://www.umassd.edu/media/umassd-artmouth/cmr/studiesandresearch/2013_Fortune_500.pdf

DiStaso, M. W., McCorkindale, T., & Augugliaro, A. (Forthcoming). America's Most Admired companies social media industry divide. *Journal of Promotion Management*.

Duggan, M., & Brenner, J. (2013). The demographics of social media users—2012. Pew Research Center. Retrieved from http://pewinternet.org/~/media//Files/Reports/2013/PIP_SocialMediaUsers.pdf

Rawlins, B. (2009). Give the emperor a mirror: Toward developing a stakeholder measurement of organizational transparency. Journal of Public Relations Research, 21(1), 71–99.

Stoker, K. L., & Tusinski, K. T. (2006). Reconsidering public relations' infatuation with dialogue: Why engagement and reconciliation can be more ethical than symmetry and reciprocity. *Journal of Mass Media Ethics, 21*(2–3), 156–176.

Wright, D. K., & Hinson, M. D. (2012). Examining how social and emerging media have been used in public relations between 2006 and 2012: A longitudinal analysis. *Public Relations Journal, 6*(4), 1–41.

Part I

Transparency and Online Identities

1 Openness and Disclosure in Social Media Efforts

A Frank Discussion With *Fortune 500* And *Philanthropy 400* Communication Leaders

Richard D. Waters

INTRODUCTION

Social media are internet-based applications that were created to capture the technological foundations and ideological spirit of Web 2.0, which generally focuses on openness, participation and interactivity, and collaboration (Kaplan & Haenlein, 2010). The practice of public relations has certainly expanded to include Facebook, Twitter, YouTube, blogs, and the countless other social media platforms currently in existence; however, the claim that public relations is "undergoing a revolution" (Hazleton, Harrison-Rexrode, & Kennan, 2008, p. 91) may be a slight exaggeration. Although consultants and agencies are prone to announce that social media are changing the practice of public relations, objective academic research has yet to show a major change in organizations' public relations approaches.

A multitude of studies have come forth to show that whether it be blogs (Seltzer & Mitrook, 2007), Facebook (Waters, Burnett, Lamm, & Lucas, 2009; Bortree & Seltzer, 2009), or Twitter (Bortree, 2012), organizations are still primarily using these dynamic platforms to push one-way messages out onto their stakeholders. Social media advocate Brian Solis (2008) claims that because of social media usage the organizational "monologue has given way to dialogue" (p. xviii). However, this simply has not been shown to be the case. While the Web 1.0 era is largely associated with virtual brochures in regard to organizational websites, Web 2.0 can best be summarized as virtual megaphones as for-profits, nonprofits, and government agencies are using social media platforms to broadcast their messages in direct competition with messages from individuals' personal networks. This blending of institutional commercials and interpersonal conversations and updates has resulted in massive amounts of noise, which caused Tittel (2011) to question the efficacy of social media marketing, advertising, and public relations.

Despite the proliferation of social media studies that gain traction in academic journals and conferences, critics have started to emerge. Kent (2008) encouraged the industry to use a critical eye to examine the blogosphere and its potential benefits before adding it to the organization's communication toolbox. Critics have also cautioned that although Facebook may have more than 1 billion users, it is not a warm, welcoming environment for organizations. Vorvoreanu (2009) found that individuals were apathetic to organizations attempting to establish a presence on Facebook and other social networking sites. They may not have felt strongly against organizations having a Facebook account, but they were not overly supportive. Others have questioned the mad rush to social media as the saving grace for relationship building by public relations practitioners by having more objective research to determine whether or not social media truly have long-term benefits (Hearn, Foth, & Gray, 2009). Unlike white papers and agency reports stemming from agencies and consultants who have a profit seeking motive to produce favorable social media research, strategic communication scholars need to critically examine its role and subject its practices to more theory rather than simply caving into the marketers' hype.

International consulting firm KPMG best summarized the current state of social media usage stating that "the bottom line is that it's just new for everybody . . . there are no rules, there's a lot of trial and error, there's a lot of testing, a lot of learning, and then applying it" (KPMG, 2011, p. 4). There have been several situations where organizations have had social media successes, but the rare wins must be considered in relation to the numerous campaigns that are barely hanging on and treading water. The purpose of this chapter is to explore a vital dimension of web communication, openness, and disclosure, to determine its place in social media campaigns. Although previous studies have used content analysis to gauge the level of openness and disclosure used in organizational social media profiles, this study aims to more deeply investigate the role of openness and disclosure by interviewing strategic communication leaders at *Fortune 500* and *Philanthropy 400* organizations to gather their thoughts on organizational openness in social media.

OPENNESS AND DISCLOSURE IN PUBLIC RELATIONS

As social media usage continues to increase among the users of all demographic ranges, organizations have been encouraged to secure their places in the various platforms—Twitter, Facebook, YouTube, blogs, and beyond—to tap into the community-building nature of social media. Logging into personal accounts, individuals have already been bombarded with sponsored tweets and Facebook updates from brands; those that have followed or liked a company also have the ability to interact with the company. But, what does it truly mean to send a tweet to @HomeDepot or @WaltDisneyWorld? Is the faceless entity United Way really responding to a post on its Facebook profile? Given the close, interpersonal nature of the medium has led many organizations to recognize that this cold, faceless approach to their online communication is not effective.

Figure 1.1   A screen shot of the Twitter profile, @DeltaAssist, used to help Delta Airlines customers.

Whether taking to Twitter, Facebook, or a company blog, the Web 2.0 environment has resulted in individuals taking their questions, concerns, and complaints with institutions into the public domain. Several organizations have begun updating profiles and individual messages to demonstrate greater accountability so that people know who it is at the organization speaking with them behind the computer screen—not just an institutional logo. For example, the vice president of Social Media and Community at Dell uses his name and company connection openly in his Twitter ID (@ManishatDell). Likewise, Delta Airlines encourages those employees monitoring its Twitter accounts (@Delta and @DeltaAssist) to reply using their initials to provide greater accountability to those interacting with the company online. Figure 1.1 presents the homescreen for the @DeltaAssist Twitter page, which shows a list of employees tweeting under their initials on the left side of the webpage and several examples of employees reaching out to concerned customers via personally signed tweets on the actual Twitter-stream.

Likewise, companies have taken to Facebook to provide names and contact information of employees monitoring and responding via the institutional profiles. For example, employees of Time Warner Cable reached out directly to customers who have had issues with the company. In a posting made on September 30, 2012, several customers responded to a Time Warner Cable message about a "Most Valuable Fan" contest with questions about their inability to use Time Warner Cable internet services to participate. Demonstrating elements of disclosure as to who was monitoring the accounts, Time Warner Cable employees responded personally to the complaints. An employee replied, "I would be happy to investigate your connection" and gave further offline contact information; he also signed his comment from the Time Warner Cable profile by using "—Jim" at the end of the update.

These efforts to connect organizational profiles to specific employees are examples of how institutions are trying to adapt to an environment created specifically for one-on-one interactions at the individual level. However, these attempts to connect often fail. Attempting to be helpful to customers, some institutions have used employees' names or initials to provide a point of contact for assistants and to demonstrate that individuals actually monitor the accounts. However, when organizations receive a flood of messages from various stakeholders, it may not be possible to reply to every situation in a timely manner. This lack of a response—now coming from individuals and not just a cold, faceless organization—can cause more resentment and outrage at the brand.

MEASURING OPENNESS AND DISCLOSURE

Although the provision of names can help demonstrate an organization's openness and disclosure, it is only a small portion of the topic. Scholars have grappled with how to best measure and demonstrate organizational openness and disclosure online. Various approaches have been taken, including Kent and Taylor's (1998) principles of dialogic communication and WEBQUAL (Loiacono, Watson, & Goodhue, 2002). The former approach has been conceptually defined to focus on the provision of organizational history, current news, and specific contact information of employees as elements of disclosure and openness; the latter perspective takes a similar approach as it evolved over the years to broaden its scope from simply looking at the functionality of a website to being more representative of a two-sided web-based relationship, which includes information exchanges that include information about the communicator. Organizations that take an active role in online communication, specifically social media, have an obligation to be open with their virtual stakeholders (Kelleher, 2009), and as the boundaries between institutional and interpersonal communication blur with social media the need for the revelation of identity by organizational representatives becomes increasingly important (Kelleher & Miller, 2006).

Despite the growing recognition of disclosure of personal identities online as being critical for public relations success, it has not been a mainstay of openness discussions in the realm of public relations. Instead, scholarship has focused on the provision of information at the organizational-level. Relationship management scholars have advocated that openness was an important facet of continued relationship growth. However, the conceptual definition of openness focused on an organization's willingness to communicate and answer stakeholders' questions (Hon & Grunig, 1999). It did not focus on any disclosure at the individual employee-level. Similarly, openness is a fundamental component of one of Kelly's (2001) four stewardship strategies, specifically reporting, which consists of providing full information about decisions and actions taken by an organization to stakeholders who are affected by those actions, is a fundamental behavior for ongoing relationship cultivation. Ledingham and Bruning (1998) stress that openness—disclosing organizational actions and being willing to discuss these actions with stakeholders—demonstrates a commitment to the publics. Indeed, engaging in direct conversations prompted by stakeholders concerns and questions reflects the principles of the Excellence Theory; however, it is not the full scope of openness and disclosure.

Following scandals that plagued the for-profit and nonprofit sectors, stakeholders demanded greater transparency from organizations at the same time as social media first began appearing (Bernardi & LaCross, 2005). In regard to their online communication practices, organizations seemed to respond by providing more one-way messages in corporate (Ki & Hon, 2006), nonprofit (Waters, 2007), and government (Bonsón, et al. 2012) institutions. Previous public relations scholarship has narrowly defined and discussed openness and disclosure in relation to organizational-level behaviors, and early studies of social media performance continued this narrative by examining these constructs in relation to an organization's willingness to discuss institutional dimensions outside the realm of publicity and promotion, providing information about the history and vision of the institution, and enabling the public to reach out with questions or comments by providing minimal response mechanisms online (e.g., generic email addresses, feedback forms).

Despite this narrow view of openness and disclosure, public relations scholars have stressed the power of the individual in the practice of public relations for some time. Before social media became such a major focus of public relations, Toth (2000) stressed that long-term success in public relations requires a focus on interpersonal relationships and the openness and transparency needed for such interactions. As the practice of public relations continues to experiment with social media campaigns and programming, it is becoming increasingly clear that openness and disclosure not only focus on organization-level actions but also that of individuals representing the institutions. Sweetser (2010) argues that the disclosure of personal identity in social media is key to organizational successes in social media. The nature of social media lends itself to conversations demonstrating a human tone and feeling. Insincere and cold organizational replies are easily detected in an environment that embraces genuine conversation. As such, it is as important to disclose who is representing the institution online because social media platforms reinforce the interpersonal nature of social networking (Rybalko & Seltzer, 2010).

Given the expanding nature of openness and disclosure in relation to the practice of online public relations, the current research posed three research questions to better understand how these concepts are being defined and practiced in the age of social-mediated public relations:

RQ1:   How do strategic communicators at *Fortune 500* and *Philanthropy 400* organizations define openness and disclosure?

RQ2:   To what extent do organizations value and use openness and disclosure strategies in social-mediated efforts?

RQ2:   What organizational factors influence an organization's willingness to be open to engaging in discussions and disclosing identities online?

METHOD

Given that these research questions are exploratory in nature when considering the growing scope of openness and disclosure, a qualitative methodology was chosen over quantitative surveys. Specifically, in-depth interviews were used to allow strategic communicators to discuss the concepts frankly, while discussing industry trends and examples as well as their own personal career experiences.

The interviews opened with a grand tour question that asked the participants to reflect on their definitions of openness and disclosure. From there, the researcher allowed participants to explore the concepts in an open manner, only using probing questions to keep the conversation on topic with the research questions. Direct questions were used as probes to get at the motivations and reasons for the use or disuse of openness and disclosure. Topics were pressed during the interview to uncover some opinions of public relations communicators that have not been expressed before in public relations literature.

Interviews with 25 communication leaders (ranging from vice presidents to senior directors) at both *Fortune 500* and *Philanthropy 400* organizations were conducted during from July 2011,to January 2012, and participants were purposively chosen to represent the two sectors as well as organizations that represent the continuum of openness and disclosure in their social media efforts. Prior to the interviews, participants were guaranteed anonymity and told that identifying-information would be removed from the study; generic descriptors, such as, a 54-year-old Asian female director of social media, are used to preface specific quotations in this chapter. Interviews were audio-recorded and ranged from 43 minutes to 88 minutes in length.

To allow for a more careful analysis, the researcher transcribed the recordings along with a graduate assistant rather than outsourcing the task to allow for careful thematic analysis of the more than 375 pages of transcriptions. Thematic analysis involves reading the transcriptions and comparing each one with the others while looking for similarities, which are grouped together by category. Using the Miles and Huberman's (1994) thematic conceptual matrix allowed the researcher to cluster and arrange themes to decipher patterns into a meaningful manner. Member checks occurred within two weeks of completing the interviews to ensure that the participants' words were interpreted correctly. During these validity checks, three participants did request that some information be removed because it could be used to identify specific organizations based on behaviors and processes that might be linked to the organization. Other than these changes, the transcripts were validated and left intact.

FINDINGS

The participants in this study represented a range of demographics as 14 participants were male and 11 were female; in terms of their racial/ethnic background, participants described themselves most often as Caucasian (52%), Hispanic/Latino (20%), African-American/Black (16%), and Asian/Pacific Islander (12%). The average age was 48 years of age, though it ranged from 39 to 63. The participants worked in strategic communications for an average of 20 years; additionally, they have worked for their current employer an average of 12 years and have been in their current position for an average of seven years

The study's first research question sought to determine how the participants defined openness and disclosure in relation to the expanding presence of social media in organizational communication initiatives. Nearly one-third of participants centered their definition on openness and disclosure on the traditional notions. A 57-year-old Caucasian male communication vice president noted, "Openness is simple. It's whether we talk about our internal actions with external groups. We don't have to offer information or need to talk about it when someone asks us questions or expresses concerns." Many of those who defined openness and disclosure in this manner noted that willingness to be open comes across not only through conversations with stakeholders, but also in replying to web-based queries, responding to media requests, and providing detailed reports through online news rooms. A 46-year old African-American female senior communication officer for a nonprofit added that "being open is the cornerstone of our business. If we're not open in all that we do, the public won't trust us and our funding will dry up. That happens online and offline."

Other participants realized that the two concepts were not as easy to define. A 48-year-old Caucasian female pointed out that the definition "depends on who you talk to. Does it mean disclosing financial situations to investors, disclosing new product development by discussing our R&D initiatives, or talking about our CSR work? We really have to be open about all we do." All of these types of exchanges occur online depending on the organization, but it raises interesting ethical questions concerning the defined boundaries of openness and disclosure online. Can a strategic communicator be open regarding organizational-level actions if it is not mentioned first by outsiders? Given the number of participants who used the word "willingness" in describing their discussion of organizational matters, it raises interesting contextual questions about whether an issue needs to be disclosed and addressed even if the audience does not ask for it specifically. Context clearly impacts the perceptions of openness and disclosure for these participants.

Given that a message's context was important for defining openness and disclosure, the researcher felt it was important to ask specifically about openness online and in social media platforms. The participants echoed previous sentiments, such as this 39-year-old African-American male senior public relations manager's statement that "if someone asks a question on Facebook or Twitter, you have to address it. It may be a general response to everyone rather than a direct reply, but you can't shy away from issues that people bring up." Once again, openness and disclosure were being defined solely as organizational-level discussions about actions except for six individuals, who noted that it involved open communication lines.

"We want to make sure people know how to reach us so we give our email address, our phone number, and our social media accounts in all of our messaging," said a 43-year-old Caucasian male nonprofit communicator. This perspective was largely espoused by mainstream nonprofits and customer-oriented for profits; however, it still ignored calls by recent scholars to disclose the personal identity behind the organization efforts online. Even though four of the organizations represented in the sample provided names or initials of employees monitoring and responding to customers on social media platforms, only one participant mentioned this element of disclosure:

> I know it's not mainstream, but we are as open and transparent in our online efforts. Everything is attributable to someone working here. Social media has changed how we communicate. It's more personal now, and we have decided to use our names when we tweet to someone. It may come from our organization's account, but we sign tweets. We do the same thing with Facebook. Our customers want to know who's speaking to them. It may not produce more sales, but it strengthens the connection we have to people.
> —52-year-old Caucasian male; vice president of Public Relations

While this perspective was not one that surfaced into the discussions on openness and disclosure voluntarily, it became a discussion point during the probing questions asked during the interviews. For most of the participants, it was not something that they had thought about as indicated by this reply from a 45-year-old Latina senior public relations practitioner, "We don't do that, and I'm not sure we would take that approach on Facebook but I can see where it comes across as more personal. I'm just not sure it makes a big difference to the customer with a complaint." Other participants had even more skeptical thoughts on the practice, such as "it seems that would only complicate things when they call a local affiliate or a hotline and expect to speak to the person from Twitter" (59-year-old Caucasian female corporate communications manager). One participant said, "It sounds like a nice but unrealistic practice. People have meetings, other job responsibilities; they take sick days. There's so many reasons that it just doesn't make sense to list who speaks for us on Facebook since they're not always there" (38-year-old Asian female marketing vice president).

Given the more traditional approaches to defining openness and disclosure among the participants and the mixed reactions to identity disclosure on social media platforms, the researcher was surprised to see more frank discussions about the second research question, which sought to determine the value placed on openness and disclosure strategies in online communication, specifically social media efforts. Nearly half of the participants felt that their organizations talked a lot about openness and interacting with stakeholders online, but did not practice it nearly as much. Bluntly speaking, a 44-year-old Hispanic male vice president mentioned that "we're only on social media because it's expected. I admit we don't use it to interact. It's not because we don't know how, but because we don't want to. We wouldn't miss Facebook if it weren't around." This was not the only anti-social media attitude expressed as a 42-year-old Caucasian female noted that "We're more comfortable with our blog. We control its content. More people may be on Twitter and Facebook, but those platforms have significant risks with activists being able to attack profiles. We use both of these platforms, but only to push our blog's content."

Openness on social media was met with healthy skepticism. Practitioners questioned how open you had to be with Facebook and Twitter users. "I've heard that it's great for relationship building, but all I see are extreme messages: complaints for things that are out of our control or comments that people love us. How do I manage those very different reactions and not come across as bipolar to everyone?" asked a 42-year-old African-American female corporate communications officer. This participant noted that some legitimate concerns are expressed via social media, and her staff works to address them as much as possible but she also noted that "some people don't want things resolved. They want to be able to complain. When we've tried to fix problems, our attempts have gone ignored, and we see the same complaint repeated a few hours later by the same account. We're willing to help, but it doesn't matter if they're not open to listening."

Frustrations with social media came from the nonprofit sector as well. "There are times when it would be easier not to have to deal with our stakeholders. People get hung up on the smallest things, and social media gives them a voice," said a 45-year-old Caucasian female public relations vice president, who provided an example of a campaign for child abuse being held up by online critics who were merciless in their criticism of font choices and graphic design elements.

Other practitioners recognized that these frustrations are routine in the public relations realm. "Small fires happen all the time, and social media amplifies that, but it's not a situation where I feel that I can't be open about [my company]. Some concerns are legitimate; others aren't. I don't mind stepping in and saying 'No' to those requests and concerns that we aren't going to address," said a 46-year old African-American female senior communication officer.

While these skeptical approaches to online openness and disclosure represented nearly half of the responses, the other half represented a more positive perspective. Practitioners regularly engaged in social media monitoring were able to see potential crises and problematic issues, and they were able to address them with concerned stakeholder before the issues became major headaches. "If I didn't see [an issue involving a bad product experience] in our Facebook monitoring reports, I wouldn't have known who to reach out to. I could have ignored the complaint, but I reached out, spoke directly with the consumer and took their concerns back to our development team who made minor changes to improve the product," noted one 50-year old Caucasian female marketing vice president. Similarly, a 39-year-old African-American male senior public relations manager expressed the long-term value that being open online brings, "we value the information we receive from social media. It may not be the news we always want to hear and some of it may not even be relevant to us, but ignoring it won't help anything. Long-term [relationships] require getting through short-term headaches."

It should be noted that even the skeptical voices concerning online openness and disclosure did not dismiss social media altogether. Although the 44-year-old Hispanic male vice president admitted that they would not be active contributors in social media if it weren't expected, he admitted that social media monitoring opened the organization's leadership to potential issues that needed to be addressed offline: "Facebook and Twitter have been great for pointing out *what* we need to focus on. *How* we do that is very different. We hold conversations involving our customers in private. I don't want personal details and situations mentioned in public domains."

This distinction between the private and public environments wound up being central to the factors that influence whether an employee's identity is revealed on a social media platform when representing the organization, the crux of the third research question. Not surprisingly, the four organizations that used the name or initials of employees in their social media posts were strong supporters of the organizational action. One of the youngest practitioners interviewed in the study, a 34-year-old senior marketing manager responsible for social media communication said, "Organizations can't speak. No one using Facebook or Twitter thinks that Coke or Pepsi is actually speaking to them. Those of us representing the organization have an obligation to stand up and let people know who we are." A 46-year-old Asian male strategic communication vice president commented that "I wouldn't go to a conference and participate in a discussion in front of audiences without providing my name and credentials, why is it considered acceptable online?"

For other companies, disclosing identities online was more a practical concern for managing interactions with stakeholders easier. A 52-year-old Caucasian male vice president of Public Relations noted, "our communication staff came to us wanting to put their names beside their comments to make it clear who made what comments as our customers kept referring back to previously made comments from the organization that were unsourced." The 46-year-old Asian male strategic communication vice president also noted that having employees sign their social media updates and replies "made them accountable to the Facebook user and to the organization. We were able to improve relationships with our audiences by improving our internal processes and making this a mandatory policy.

The organizations that embraced social media disclosure seemed to be more supportive of experimenting with social media. It was not that they were any more successful than the 21 companies that did not disclose identities online, but they were more open to seeing whether it made a difference in their relationship-building efforts online. The 52-year-old Caucasian male vice president said, "It's our policy now, but it may not be in the future. We have to see how things work. There's no black-or-white solution to social media. It's all grey. No one knows what works and what doesn't, but we're not going to wait for a marketing firm to tell us what to do."

Other participants were not supportive of mandated disclosure policies. One 44-year-old Hispanic male vice president said, "I understand the argument for disclosing who is behind the brand on Twitter, but I'm not going to require it. If they were public-facing employees who were out in the field working with different groups, then there's a stronger argument for people to disclose who they are. But if they're an entry-level communication staffer? That's absurd." Others did not express their feelings as strongly but indicated that they did not see it as being essential to carrying out the strategic communication efforts online. In a sense, it almost came across as the social media team in these organizations was deemed as merely that: a niche team working on social media work while more worthwhile employees were out in the field carrying out *true* public relations work.

Questions surfaced throughout some of the interviews as to whether social media was the domain of strategic communication initiatives or whether it was a customer service outlet. A 45-year-old Caucasian female public relations vice president relayed a recent conversation among her staff regarding online disclosure, specifically Twitter. The office discussion was prompted after a staff member noticed a competitor using initials in conjunction to reply messages. The story unfolded in a manner that highlighted a unique concern about full online disclosure:

> We discussed requiring people initial their replies, but decided against it. Although I doubt it would happen, if something ever were to happen with an enraged customer researching the staff member who declined a refund and sought revenge, I couldn't live with that decision. We have customer service employees who are trained to handle those situations, and quite frankly, public relations is not customer service. We're not trained to handle customer service matters, but they show up all the

time on social media and we're expected to handle it because it came to us and not the 800-number.

Another participant mocked the notion of providing employee names or initials online saying, "there may be a name or letters next to a message and that might make people feel better about receiving the message, but it doesn't really change anything. One person from a large communications team answered it, and most likely someone else will handle the next reply. It's just the nature of our offices. We're not one-person shops." A 45-year-old Latina senior public relations practitioner was even more skeptical adding that, "I don't believe the names used online are real. Even the names our customer service agents use are fake. It's just a reality for those front-line employees dealing with potentially angry mobs."

Ultimately, it seems as if an organization's willingness to be open and participate in social media conversations had little to do with their disclosure of employees' identities online. Instead, it seemed to focus on whether the organization was willing to experiment with social media and whether they really believed that social media was a public relations or marketing task and not something that should be monitored by customer service representatives.

ETHICAL IMPLICATIONS FOR THE PRACTICE OF SOCIAL MEDIA

Ethics guide individuals into making appropriate decisions about how to make decisions concerning public relations campaigns. Though participation on Twitter or Facebook as a brand rather than as an individual representing a brand may not be an apparent violation of public relations ethics, industry associations have pointed out that disclosure is vitally important to the acceptance of public relations' practice by the public.

The preamble to the most current version of PRSA's code of ethics, which was ratified in 2000, stresses the importance of honesty, which includes self-disclosure of who is communicating on behalf of the brand. In an update to the code of ethics in October 2008, PRSA issued a professional standards advisory regarding the misrepresentation of organizations and individuals as well as deceptive online practices. In this advisory, PRSA stressed that accurate, honest communication is essential for informed decision-making by the public. The association did not explicitly condemn practitioners that did not self-disclose when representing a brand online, but they did point out that this practice falls into a murky area in terms of clear-cut ethical decisions. Specifically, unnamed social media communicators posting on behalf of an organization may violate two specific provisions of their ethical code: the free flow of information and the disclosure of information; in both of these cases, the communicators may be inadvertently violating ethical codes because of the lack of accurate and truthful information, namely the lack of stating whom is representing the organization.

The Arthur W. Page Society has also expressed caution in carrying out organizational messaging in the online environment without full disclosure by the individual representing the brand. The Page Society is a professional association for senior public relations executives who seek to enrich and strengthen their profession. Unlike PRSA, the Page Society has strict membership selection criteria and is not open to everyone in the field. Since 1983, these senior industry leaders have been working to improve the reputation and management practices of public relations firms and in-house departments at nonprofits, for-profits, and government agencies. Though it has not been updated since the explosive growth of social media, the Page Society's "Principles for Public Relations on the Internet" address the role of disclosure in a social environment. Specifically, the industry's senior leaders stressed that practitioners must "disclose all participation in online chat rooms and conferences." Online chat rooms of Web 1.0 were the precursors of today's social media, and an argument can be made that the Society's leadership would argue that tweets and Facebook posts made on behalf of an organization should be clearly linked to an individual, either by initials as seen in the Delta Twitter example in Figure 1.1 or by stating the name of the poster outright.

Despite these suggestions from industry leaders, many organizations fail to disclose who maintains the brands' accounts. Research presented at the International Scientific Conference on Transparent Communication in 2013 revealed that less than 3% of Twitter updates from the *Fortune 100* and *Nonprofit Times 100* organizations disclosed who wrote the updates (Waters, 2013). Given the apparent contradictory practice to the field's guiding ethical principles, public relations scholars, practitioners, educators, and students need to revisit the importance of social media disclosure.

Ultimately, public relations ethics are not clearly defined with simple yes or no answers. PRSA's updated advisories and emerging guidelines, such as the Arthur W. Page Society's "Principles for Public Relations on the Internet," help address situations that are not addressed specifically in ethical codes, but they may not always provide practitioners with a clear decision. Ultimately, an individual's personal ethics will guide what they do as a practitioner. However, it may be most helpful to approach the situation with the mindset of the public: Who would you rather communicate with on social media platforms, a named individual, or a brand's name?

CONCLUSION

Public relations practitioners and scholars have long advocated that public relations is not simply "relating with the public" in a customer service manner. Significant time and research has been dedicated into molding the profession into one of organization counselors who are able to manage communication efforts and campaigns to build strong reputations and respected brands while also aiding senior officials with decision-making assistance in wake of potential and real crises. Social media advocates have argued that platforms, such as Facebook, Twitter, and YouTube, provide outlets to accomplish these goals; however, a majority of examples shown as being exemplars in social media focus on customer service responsibilities. Indeed, many of the leading social media advocates have argued that the customer service focus brought about by social media platforms is revolutionizing the public relations practice (Li & Bernoff, 2008; Solis & Breakenridge, 2009). Whether the change in the practice of public relations is an evolution to a greater place inside an organization or a devolution into primarily being responsible for customer service is worthy of future academic inquiry. Only time will be able to gauge its impact on the field; however, this study found that social media are beginning to impact how organizations' view openness and disclosure.

Through 25 in-depth interviews with senior communication leaders, ranging from senior public relations directors to vice presidents of marketing and public relations, this study found that openness although one-third of practitioners still define openness and disclosure by demonstrating a willingness to discuss organizational-level matters, there is increasing recognition that social media are aiding in organizational openness. Disclosure, on the other hand, remains a sensitive situation in regard to their social media presence. Two concepts that have been closely linked in public relations practice are now showing signs of separation in social media.

Through frank discussions about their social media efforts, a handful of participants indicated that organizational participation in social media make them uncomfortable—not because of failure to understand the platforms, but because the space is an interpersonal one created without corporate, nonprofit, and government institutions' presence. Although the platforms have grown to accommodate these institutions, the public's reaction has been mixed with some wishing that faceless corporations would leave the space while others acknowledging occasional marketing benefits from their presence (Vorvoreanu, 2009). Those responsible for social media efforts have noticed the hit-or-miss strategies with social media audiences.

However, there was a general mood of support for social media monitoring, especially in regards to providing a foundation for opening discussions about experiences external audiences had. Several participants noted that daily reports on social media conversations helped identify people to reach out to for more information on potential crises so they could be resolved before major harm came to the organization. In these situations, social media proved to be useful. There were other participants, however, who dwelled on the problems of having social media audiences offer critical and sometimes misdirected complaints and commentaries that were irresolvable for a myriad of reasons. These practitioners noted that they were either forced into conversations that they knew would not end in solutions simply to demonstrate organizational response or risk backlash from a social media community if they chose to ignore someone's ranting.

Rarely did organizations readily define openness and disclosure to include the voluntarily disclosure of the account administrators or employees representing the organization in the social media landscape. Only one of the four companies using this strategy that were represented in this study mentioned the practice without probing. As the interviews revealed, this is an area of concern for many of the practitioners. While they recognize the value of having a human voice online, the risk of having a human name associated with that voice is considerable. Although to many the possibilities of a customer seeking revenge against a named employee may sound outlandish, the concerns were real to these participants. Whether they feared physical harm or social embarrassment at a perceived mishandling of a situation, many participants did not consider it worthwhile to place their names or initials alongside corporate responses in the social media landscape.

Others perceived that social media was not the environment for such required disclosure. Names and credentials appeared to be relegated to offline stakeholder actions where such provision was an expected norm. To summarize one participant, an entry-level staffer working on social media would not have the expectation of self-disclosure since they are only doing customer service work on Facebook. Though the researcher may not share this participant's belief, it is worth noting that he was not alone in his thoughts. Others expressed similar concerns—namely that public relations was held to a higher standard and these employees were not really working in public relations. Although social media fell under their responsibilities in the organization, it really was being used for customer service processes.

The four organizations that mandated the provision of initials or names in relation to social media posts onto the organizational Twitter or Facebook account had an entirely different view of social media. They recognized the value of community building even though the acknowledged it was an intangible benefit that could not directly be linked to revenues. This distinction over the role of social media as a public relations function or a customer service function helped create a separation of openness and disclosure as complementary concepts, a finding that was eye opening and surprising. It should be noted that, unlike the figure displayed in the chapter, the participants in this study did not work at *Fortune 500* or *Philanthropy 400* organizations that used their social media efforts as being primarily customer-service focused. Instead, a handful of participants saw that social media was more suited to handle customer service matters and began moving staff to accommodate this shift.

Reflecting the previously mentioned KMPG (2011) study, the participants in this study indicated that their social media experiences and current usage patterns are run the gamut from methods of pushing one-way messaging to responding to customer concerns and complaints to genuine conversation over common situations. Although not the intent of this study, the schism that emerged between social media as a public relations function or a tool of customer service warrants further exploration. Observationally, it seems that there is a relationship between openness and disclosure and one's view as to social media's place in the communication toolkit. If the skepticism concerning social media does stem from views of it being a customer service rather than public relations function, then the multitude of studies showing dismal social media performance regarding traditional public relations measures begins to make more sense and raise new questions about the future of public relations practice.

DISCUSSION QUESTIONS

1. Given that public relations practitioners sign op-ed letters, position papers, and articles in newsletters and annual reports as well as disclosing their names on news releases, why would a practitioner not want to acknowledge writing an organizational message in the social media environment?
2. As a general consumer of social media messages, how would you respond differently to a message created by Delta Airlines on Twitter compared to ^GW (i.e. Twitter updater's initials) or Glenn Wickman (i.e. Twitter updater's name)?
3. After reviewing the codes of ethics from Public Relations Society of America and the International Association of Business Communicators, do current codes need to be revised to address disclosure and transparent communication more explicitly in social media?

SUGGESTED READINGS

Breakenridge, D. K. (2012). *Social media and public relations: Eight new practices for the PR professional.* Upper Saddle River, NJ: FT Press.
Fuchs, C., Boersma, K., & Albrechtslund, A. (2012). *Internet and surveillance: The challenges of Web 2.0 and social media.* New York: Routledge.
Gillin, P. (2009). *The new influencers: A marketer's guide to the new social media.* Denver, CO: Quill Driver Books.
Macnamara, J. (2010). Public relations and the social: How practitioners are using, or abusing, social media. *Asia Pacific Public Relations Journal, 11,* 21–39.
Sweetser, K. (2010). A losing strategy: The impact of nondisclosure in social media on relationships. *Journal of Public Relations Research, 22*(3), 288–312.

REFERENCES

Bernardi, R. A., & LaCross, C. C. (2005). Corporate transparency: Codes of ethics disclosure. *The CPA Journal, 75,* 34–37.
Bonsón, E., Torres, L., Royo, S., & Flores, F. (2012). Local e-government 2.0: Social media and corporate transparency in municipalities. *Government Information Quarterly, 29,* 123–132.

Bortree, D. S. (2012). Pro-environmental behaviors through social media: An analysis of Twitter communication. In Ahern, L. A, & Bortree, D. S. (Eds.) *Talking green: Exploring contemporary issues in environmental communication* (pp. 147–170). Peter Lang: New York.

Bortree, D. S., & Seltzer, T. (2009). Dialogic strategies and outcomes: An analysis of environmental advocacy groups' Facebook profiles. *Public Relations Review, 35,* 317–319.

Hazelton, V., Harrison-Rexrode, J., & Keenan, W. (2008). New technologies in the formation of personal and public relations; Social capital and social media. In S. Duhe (Ed.), *New media and public relations* (pp. 91–105). New York: Peter Lang.

Hearn, G., Foth, M., & Gray, H. (2009). Applications and implementations of new media in corporate communications: An action research approach. *Corporate Communications: An International Journal, 14*(1), 49–61.

Hon, L. C., & Grunig, J. E. (1999). *Guidelines for measuring relationships in public relations.* Gainesville, FL: Institute for Public Relations.

Kaplan, R., & Haenlein, M. (2010). Users of the world, unite! The challenges and opportunities of social media. *Business Horizons, 53*(1), 59–68.

Kelleher, T. (2009). Conversational voice, communicated commitment, and public relations outcomes in interactive online communication. *Journal of Communication, 59*(1), 172–188.

Kelleher, T., & Miller, B. M. (2006). Organizational blogs and the human voice: Relational strategies and relational outcomes. *Journal of Computer-Mediated Communication, 11*(2), 395–414.

Kelly, K. S. (2001). Stewardship: The fifth step in the public relations process. In R. Heath (Ed.), *Handbook of public relations* (pp. 279–289). Thousand Oaks, CA: Sage.

Kent, M. L. (2008). Critical analysis of blogging in public relations. *Public Relations Review, 34*(1), 32–40.

Kent, M. L., & Taylor, M. (1998). Building dialogic relationships through the World Wide Web. *Public Relations Review, 24,* 321–334

Ki, E.-J., & Hon, L. C. (2006). Relationship maintenance strategies on *Fortune 500* company websites. *Journal of Communication Management, 10*(1), 27–43.

KPMG. (2011, July). *Social media: The voyage of discovery for business.* Retrieved from http://www.kpmg.com/AU/en/IssuesAndInsights/ArticlesPublications/Documents/social-media-the-voyage-of-discovery-for-business.pdf

Ledingham, J. A., & Bruning, S. D. (1998). Relationship management and public relations: Dimensions of an organization–public relationship. *Public Relations Review, 24,* 55–65.

Li, C., & Bernoff, J. (2008). *Groundswell: Winning in a world transformed by social technologies.* Boston: Harvard Business Press.

Loiacono, E. T., Watson, R. T., & Goodhue, D. L. (2002). WebQual: A measure of web site quality. *Proceedings of the AMA Winter Educators' Conference* (American Marketing Association, Chicago, IL), February 22–25, pp. 432–438.

Miles, M. B., & Huberman, A. M. (1994). *Qualitative data analysis: An expanded sourcebook.* Thousand Oaks, CA: Sage Publications.

Rybalko, S., & Seltzer, T. (2010). Dialogic communication in 140 characters or less: How *Fortune 500* companies engage stakeholders using Twitter. *Public Relations Review, 36,* 336–341.

Seltzer, T. & Mitrook, M. A. (2007). The dialogic potential of weblogs in relationship building. *Public Relations Review, 33,* 227–229.

Solis, B. (2008). Foreword. In D. Breakenridge, *PR 2.0: New media, new tools, new audiences* (pp. xvii–xx). Upper Saddle River, NJ: FT Press.

Solis, B., & Breakenridge, D. (2009). *Putting the public back in public relations: How social media is reinventing the aging business of PR*. Upper Saddle River, NJ: FT Press.

Sweetser, K. D. (2010). A losing strategy: The impact of nondisclosure in social media on relationships. *Journal of Public Relations Research, 22*, 288–312.

Tittel, M. (2011, December 6). Turn off the social media noise. *Forbes Online*. Retrieved from http://www.forbes.com/sites/gyro/2011/12/06/turn-off-the-social-media-noise/

Toth, E. (2000). From personal influence to interpersonal influence: A model for relationship management. In J. A. Ledingham & S. D. Bruning (Eds.), *Public relations as relationship management: A relational approach to the study and practice of public relations* (pp. 205–220). Mahwah, NJ: Lawrence Erlbaum Associates

Vorvoreanu, M. (2009). Perceptions of corporations on Facebook: An analysis of Facebook social norms. *Journal of New Communications Research, 4*(1), 67–86.

Waters, R . D. (2007). Nonprofit organizations' use of the internet: A content analysis of communication trends on the internet sites of the *Philanthropy 400*. *Nonrprofit Management & Leadership, 18*(1), 59–76.

Waters, R. D. (2013, November). *The impact of transparent communication on Twitter: Disclosing authorship of tweets by Nonprofit Times 100 and Fortune 100 public relations practitioners*. Presented at the International Scientific Conference on Transparent Communication, Brussels, Belgium.

Waters, R. D., Burnett, E., Lamm, A., & Lucas, J. (2009). Stakeholder engagement and social networking sites: How nonprofit organizations are using Facebook. *Public Relations Review, 35*, 102–106.

2 Considerations Regarding Ghost Blogging and Ghost Commenting

Tiffany Derville Gallicano,
Thomas H. Bivins, and Yoon Y. Cho

INTRODUCTION

This chapter is focused on the ghostwriting of *organizational blogs*, which are blogs that officially represent organizations, such as Sea Views, the blog by Royal Caribbean President and CEO Adam Goldstein (Defren, 2010; Gallicano, Brett, & Hopp, 2012). By contrast, a *personal, organization-aligned blog* is a blog that is meant to only represent the writer's opinions and not necessarily the employer's positions, even though the writer's employer is disclosed on the blog (Defren, 2010; Gallicano, Brett et al., 2012). IBM (n.d.), for example, has a web page that lists IBM bloggers and explains:

> As they'll tell you themselves, the opinions and interests expressed on IBMers' blogs are their own and don't necessarily represent this company's positions, strategies or views. But that doesn't mean we don't want you to read them! Because they do represent lots of business and technology expertise you can't get from anyone else. (¶ 1)

Key conversations about ghost blogging have occurred on the following thought leaders' blogs:

- Todd Defren (2010), principal at SHIFT Communications, argued that organizational ghost blogging without disclosure in a corporate context is ethical if the stated author provides final approval of the content.
- Bill Sledzik (2009), associate professor at Kent State University, also defended undisclosed ghost blogging, provided that the ideas for the content come from the stated author and the stated author provides content approval.
- However, Dave Fleet (2009), vice president of Edelman Digital, insisted that undisclosed ghost blogging is unethical.
- Beth Harte (2009), director of marketing for Advent Global Solutions, also advocated against undisclosed ghost blogging.

Combined, these blog posts resulted in more than 200 comments in which people continued to debate the topic.

The Public Relations Society of America, the Word of Mouth Marketing Association, and the Social Media Business Council do not specifically approve or prohibit the practice, although they do emphasize disclosure as a generic ethical principle. Given the need for additional guidance regarding this matter, this chapter provides a significant contribution by sharing the results of a nationwide survey of people who read corporate blogs, politicians' blogs, and nonprofit blogs (see Gallicano, Cho, & Bivins, 2012, for the study). The chapter concludes with recommendations about ghost blogging and ghost commenting.

CONCEPTUALIZATION

Arguments in Favor of Undisclosed Ghost Blogging and Commenting

The strongest arguments in defense of undisclosed ghost blogging and commenting are based on the position that the stated author provides the content and then edits and approves the final blog post or blog comment (e.g., Gallicano, Brett et al., 2012; Sledzik, 2009; Subveri, 2010). This was the position assumed in a discussion of the topic in Tactics, a publication by PRSA (Subveri, 2010). In a study of PRSA members by Gallicano, Brett et al. (2012) that Katie Paine (2012) characterized as "Most Disturbing to Bloggers," 71.1% of 291 respondents approved of undisclosed ghost blogging, as long as the stated author would provide the ideas for the content and give final content approval (Gallicano, Brett et al., 2012). Although there is not enough research to identify how common the practice is, preliminary research suggests that it is not an unusual practice. In one study, about 41% of the survey respondents had at least one executive blog, and a little more than half of these respondents expressed that their executive blogs were ghostwritten (Gallicano, Brett et al., 2012). In addition, a content analysis of 40 CEO blogs revealed that five of the blogs contained disclosure statements about assistance from other writers or editors (Terilli & Arnorsdottir, 2008). Of course, the sample size was small, and it's possible that CEOs actually authored the blogs that did not have disclosure statements.

The reasons offered in favor of undisclosed ghost blogging parallel the justifications for ghostwriting other public relations tactics, such as speeches. Executives and politicians commonly lack the time and skills to write a blog, and authenticity can be accomplished by having them share the main ideas and provide final approval (see Gallicano, Brett et al., 2012; Sledzik, 2009; Subveri, 2010, for ghost blogging and see Auer, 1984; Einhorn, 1981; Riley & Brown, 1996, for speechwriting). An organizational blog or speech is more about the organization than the author, writers tend to have at least as much core knowledge about the topic as the stated author, and an executive or politician should delegate writing responsibilities to a communications professional, just as he or she uses other specialists for running the organization (see Defren, 2010; Gallicano, Brett et al., 2012; Nerad, 2010, for ghost blogging and see Einhorn, 1991, for speechwriting). Also, audiences are sophisticated and are not likely to be deceived by thinking that the executive or politician actually wrote the blog (see Gallicano, Brett et al., 2012; Nerad, 2010, for ghost blogging and see Riley & Brown, 1996, for speechwriting).

Arguments against Undisclosed Ghost Blogging and Commenting

Critics of undisclosed ghost blogging believe that social media should not be compared to traditional tactics (Gallicano, Brett et al., 2012; Fleet, 2009; Harte, 2009). Writers use blogs to cultivate personal relationships. As Fleet (2009) quipped, "When did outsourcing your relationships become okay?" (¶ 5). Scholarship supports the argument that social media is a relationship-building channel. Specifically, interactivity—a key distinction of social media—has a major impact on relationship building (Bortree & Seltzer, 2009; Kent & Taylor, 2002; Seltzer & Mitrook, 2007). Another concern is that ghost blogging could result in overestimating an executive's skills and the organization's future (Terilli & Arnorsdottir, 2008). Also, most case studies regarding unethical practices online involve covering up information (Martin & Smith, 2008), and there are concerns that not revealing that a blog is ghostwritten could be perceived as deceptive, especially if audiences do not expect ghost blogging (see Gallicano, Brett et al., 2012; Fleet, 2009; Harte, 2009, for ghost blogging and Bormann, 1956, for speechwriting). Public relations professionals recognize that if they ever have to wonder, "What if people find out?" the practice should be avoided because anything that needs a cover-up is unethical.

RADICAL TRANSPARENCY

The philosophy of radical transparency has been rising in popularity with the digital age and the consequent demands for unprecedented levels of transparency (Beal & Strauss, 2008). The concept has been championed by thought leaders such as Richard Edelman (2011, 2012), Ketchum president Rob Flaherty (2011), and Bob Pickard, president and CEO of Burson-Marsteller Asia Pacific (de Vera, 2011). In public relations, the concept of *radical transparency* refers to "a philosophy for doing business that refers to prioritizing transparency above all other competing values, with the exception of disclosing information that violates regulations or ethical principles" (Gallicano, Brett et al., 2012, p. 6). Communication professionals can use radical transparency to build trust, which can help an organization cultivate relationships with its stakeholders. This idea is salient in the context of blogging, given that corporate blogs are trusted by only 16% of the people who read them (Bernoff, 2008). This percentage rises to 39% for readers who have blogs themselves; however, this percentage is still low. Radical transparency, of course, will hurt an organization that acts unethically and is not competitive in the marketplace (Gallicano, Brett et al., 2012). In such cases, people would avoid the organization due to its unethical practices or because it is a poor investment. When an organization is ethical and competitive, however, showing areas of improvement is viewed as a strength. As described by Denise Hollingsworth (2012), brand strategy director for HMH agency,

> It's OK to show your human, imperfect side. As a matter of fact, your customers will like you better if you do. . . . If it seems unnatural to not try to hide your company's blemishes, ask yourself this: Do you trust someone who tries to project perfection? Or do you distrust them and wonder what they are hiding? (¶ 1–3)

Hollingsworth also points out that anything negative about an organization will surface on various social media sites anyway, so it's best to adopt a strategy that is compatible with this reality by embracing the level of transparency that stakeholders expect.

Examples of actions that fit within the radical transparency philosophy include "spill[ing] information in torrents, posting internal memos and strategy goals, [and] letting everyone from the top dog to shop-floor workers blog publicly about what their firm is doing right—and wrong" (Thompson, 2007, ¶ 8). In addition, radical transparency includes sharing policies for the organization's operations (Anderson, 2006), which includes addressing the practices behind executive blogs. An excellent example of blog disclosure is by Bill Marriott (2012) for Marriott on the Move (note that he was born in 1932):

> I sometimes handwrite my blogs because I don't know how to type. An assistant from our global communications team helps me with all the technical aspects of my blog. When I want to do a blog, they come to my office with a digital recorder and record what I say.
>
> Sometimes I write it out, sometimes I use notes and sometimes I speak off the top of my head. I come up with a lot of the ideas, but people in our company also have topics for me to consider. When I'm through recording, it's transcribed and the text and the audio file are uploaded. The comments are viewed and printed out for me to read. If there are any I feel I should respond to, I dictate what to say.
>
> As you can see, being a technophobe like me adds a lot of steps, but I make it work because I know that it's a great way to communicate with our customers and stakeholders in this day and age. When your

family's name is on the building or you are the person clearly identified with the company, everything you say or do affects the business, good or bad. In this fascinating information age, you have to be transparent.

I'm Bill Marriott and thanks for helping me keep Marriott on the move. (¶ 1–4. Further discussion of the Marriott blog can be found in Gallicano, 2014.)

ALTERNATIVES TO UNDISCLOSED GHOST BLOGGING

An obvious way to avoid undisclosed ghost blogging is to disclose it. Shel Holtz (2011) provided a hypothetical example of ghost blogging disclosure:

> Welcome to my blog. Several times each week, I articulate my thoughts to Mary Jones, who runs communications for the company, and she posts them here ensuring that I make the points I want to make. But rest assured, while Mary makes me sound better, the messages you read are mine; they come from my heart and I read all the comments myself. (¶ 3)

Another option is to have several employees jointly author the blog, rather than having the CEO as the sole author. Graco's Heart to Heart blog is an example of this. A third option is for executives to only use social media channels that are less time consuming and involve less writing than full-length blogs.

RESEARCH INQUIRY

For our study (Gallicano, Cho et al., 2012), we conducted audience research to explore the extent to which blog readers expect ghostwriting on the corporate, politician, and nonprofit blogs they read. Also, to determine whether readers approve of ghostwritten content on professional blogs, we also studied the extent to which blog readers approve of ghostwriting on the blogs of companies, politicians, and nonprofit organizations. We separated the categories of corporate blog readers, readers of politicians' blogs, and nonprofit blog readers because we thought that the context might affect expectations and opinions about undisclosed ghost blogging.

METHOD

Qualtrics, a research company, randomly selected participants from a U.S. Census-representative population for an online survey that included 507 corporate blog readers, 501 nonprofit blog readers, and 510 readers of politicians' blogs. Participants expressed their opinions about the extent to which they expect ghost blogging to occur and the extent to which they find various ghost blogging practices acceptable, provided that the content comes from the stated author and the stated author provides content approval.

We created a version of the survey for the three contexts: corporate executive, politician, and nonprofit executive. Participants answered a screening question about whether they read a particular type of blog at least monthly (the type of blog was a company's blog, politician's blog, or nonprofit's blog, depending on the survey). If qualified, respondents were asked to answer the main questions about their expectations and acceptance or rejection of ghost blogging.

Participants rated their agreement or disagreement with statements on a 5-point Likert scale. For example, we examined expectations about ghost blogging on a politician's blog by the extent to which respondents agreed or disagreed with statements such as, "I think it's common if a politician is listed as the author of a blog, even though it's really written by someone else—as long as the ideas come from the politician and this person approves the message." An example of a question about the acceptance or rejection of ghost blogging in the nonprofit area was, "I think it's okay if a nonprofit's president or executive director is listed as the author of a blog, even though it's really written by someone else—as long as the ideas come from the president or executive director and this person approves the message." We used SPSS 18.0 as the statistical package to analyze the survey data.

Our study has a significant number of randomly selected participants; however, the results could be compromised if survey volunteers fundamentally differ from blog readers who do not volunteer with research firms. Of course, there are drawbacks with any method, and the design of our study is comparatively strong given the sample size and random sampling method from a U.S. Census-representative population. The findings can only be generalized to U.S. blog readers due to the sample.

RESULTS

Ghost Blogging Expectations

For a question that asked respondents about the extent to which they agreed or disagreed that it is common for a [company/politician/nonprofit] to have a blog that lists the [president or CEO/politician/president or executive director] as the author, even though it's really written by someone else,

- Nearly 60% of corporate blog readers agreed or strongly agreed that they expected a CEO blog post to be written by someone else.
- Just over half of the readers of politicians' blogs agreed or strongly agreed that they expected a politician's blog post to be written by someone else.

- A little more than a third of nonprofit readers agreed or strongly agreed that they expected an executive director's blog post to be written by someone else.

Ghost Blogging Permissibility

For the next question, participants were asked about the extent to which they agreed or disagreed that it was okay if a [company president or CEO/politician/nonprofit president or executive director] is listed as the author of a blog, even though it's really written by someone else—as long as the ideas come from the stated author and the stated author approves the message. The survey results showed that

- Nearly 40% of corporate blog readers agreed or strongly agreed that it was okay for a CEO blog to be written by someone else, as long as the ideas come from the stated author and the stated author approves the message.
- A little more than 30% of the people who read politicians' blogs agreed or strongly agreed that it was okay for a politician's blog to be written by someone else, as long as the ideas come from the stated author and the stated author approves the message.
- About 35% of nonprofit blog readers agreed or strongly agreed that it was okay for an executive director's blog to be written by someone else, as long as the ideas come from the stated author and the stated author approves the message.

Expectations of Ghost Commenting on the Stated Author's Blog

Next, respondents answered a question about the extent to which they agreed or disagreed that it was common for the [corporate executive/politician/nonprofit executive] to have a staff member write comments in reply to readers' comments on the blog of the [corporate executive/politician/nonprofit executive] without a disclosure statement that it was a staff member responding on behalf of the [corporate executive/politician/nonprofit executive]. The survey results showed that

- Nearly 65% of corporate blog readers agreed or strongly agreed that it is common for the CEO to have a staff member write comments in reply to readers' comments on the CEO's blog on his or her behalf.
- Nearly 65% of the respondents who read politicians' blogs agreed or strongly agreed that it is common for the politician to have a staff member write comments in reply to readers' comments on the politician's blog on his or her behalf.
- Nearly 53% of the nonprofit blog readers agreed or strongly agreed that it is common for the executive director to have a staff member

write comments in reply to readers' comments on the executive director's blog on his or her behalf.

Permissibility of Ghost Commenting on the Stated Author's Blog

For the subsequent question, participants expressed the extent to which they thought it was acceptable or unacceptable for a staff member to write comments in reply to readers' comments on the executive or politician's blog on behalf of the stated author, provided that the ideas came from the stated author and the stated author approved the message. The beliefs of the three groups were similar:

- About 40% of the readers from the corporate survey agreed or strongly agreed that it is permissible for the CEO to have a staff member write comments in reply to readers' comments on the CEO's blog on his or her behalf, as long as the ideas come from the stated author and the stated author approves the message.
- About 37% of the readers of politicians' blogs agreed or strongly agreed that it is permissible for the politician to have a staff member write comments in reply to readers' comments on the politician's blog on his or her behalf, as long as the ideas come from the stated author and the stated author approves the message.
- About 35% of the readers from the nonprofit survey agreed or strongly agreed that it is permissible for the executive director to have a staff member write comments in reply to readers' comments on the executive director's blog on his or her behalf, as long as the ideas come from the stated author and the stated author approves the message.

Expectations of Ghost Commenting on Others' Blogs

After answering questions about ghost commenting on the stated author's blog, respondents expressed their opinions about how common it is for a [corporate executive/politician/nonprofit executive] to have a staff member write comments in reply to other people's blogs without a disclosure statement that it is a staff member commenting on behalf of the [corporate executive/politician/nonprofit executive]:

- A little more than half of the corporate blog readers agreed or strongly agreed that they think it's common for a CEO to have a staff member write comments in reply to other people's blogs without a disclosure statement that it is a staff member commenting on behalf of the CEO.
- About half of the readers of politicians' blogs agreed or strongly agreed that they think it's common for a politician to have a staff member write comments in reply to other people's blogs without a

disclosure statement that it is a staff member commenting on behalf of the politician.

- Almost 45% of nonprofit blog readers agreed or strongly agreed that they think it's common for an executive director to have a staff member write comments in reply to other people's blogs without a disclosure statement that it is a staff member commenting on behalf of the executive director.

Permissibility of Ghost Commenting on Others' Blogs

Finally, participants expressed their opinions about how acceptable or unacceptable it is for a [corporate executive/politician/nonprofit executive] to have a staff member write comments in reply to other people's blogs without a disclosure statement that it is a staff member commenting on behalf of the [corporate executive/politician/nonprofit executive]:

- About 33% of corporate blog readers agreed or strongly agreed that it's okay for a CEO to have a staff member write comments in reply to other people's blogs without a disclosure statement that it is a staff member commenting on behalf of the CEO, as long as the ideas come from the stated author and the stated author approves the message.
- Nearly 30% of readers of politicians' blogs agreed or strongly agreed that it's okay for a politician to have a staff member write comments in reply to other people's blogs without a disclosure statement that it is a staff member commenting on behalf of the politician, as long as the ideas come from the stated author and the stated author approves the message.
- About 30% of nonprofit blog readers agreed or strongly agreed that it's okay for an executive director to have a staff member write comments in reply to other people's blogs without a disclosure statement that it is a staff member commenting on behalf of the executive director, as long as the ideas come from the stated author and the stated author approves the message.

DISCUSSION

Although a fair number of blog readers expected ghost blogging for CEOs and politicians, not many blog readers approved of the practice, even under the conditions that the stated author would provide the ideas for the content and give final approval of the blog posts. A small percentage of people who read nonprofit blogs expected ghost blogging, and a large number disapproved of the practice. Interestingly, blog readers were more likely to expect an executive or politician to delegate the commenting than the actual writing of the blog posts. Nevertheless, ghost commenting on the author's own blog did not receive the support of even half of the participants in any context, and ghost commenting on other people's blogs received even less support, even with the assurance that the stated author provided the ideas and gave final approval of the comments.

Ethical Implications for the Practice of Social Media

Given the disapproval for undisclosed ghost blogging and ghost commenting, executives and politicians should choose alternatives to these practices. Public relations professionals should avoid placing themselves in a situation in which they would be concerned about readers finding out that the blog or comments are not drafted by the stated author, given the amount of disapproval for these practices. As such, any ghostwritten blog and comments on the blog should contain a disclosure statement. It is not realistic to have a disclosure statement for comments posted to other blogs unless the disclosure is included in the comments, so we suggest that executives and politicians avoid the practice of ghost commenting on other blogs.

Public relations practitioners who are concerned that a disclosure statement would constrain readers' engagement with the blog should recognize that this reaction is motivated by an intention to deceive audiences into believing that the stated author is the real author, which is ethically questionable. Moreover, our results show that many readers expect ghost blogging and commenting on the stated author's blog anyway (at least in the contexts of CEO's and politicians' blogs); consequently, a disclosure statement could actually increase a blog's credibility, particularly considering the scholarship that suggests that most people who read corporate blogs do not trust them (see Bernoff, 2008). Alternatives to a disclosure statement would include having an organizational blog that is authentically authored by one or more employees who have time to draft the blog posts, or an executive or politician could choose to participate in social media channels that require less time than blogs.

Discussion questions

1. Why do you think people were more likely to be deceived by undisclosed ghost blogging in the context of nonprofit organizations, as opposed to the context of companies and politicians?
2. Think of one of your favorite blogs. How would you react if the stated author announced that he or she has decided to get some help writing the blog posts by sharing the content each week with a PR person and having that person draft the blog post? The stated author would provide reassurance that all blog posts would be edited by himself or herself, and he or she would respond to all comments without assistance.
3. What do you think about undisclosed ghost blogging? What about disclosed ghost blogging? Make your best argument in favor of the one you think is best, arguing, at the same time, against the other one.

SUGGESTED READINGS

Bivins, T. (2009). Mixed media: Moral distinctions in advertising, public relations, and journalism. New York: Routledge.

Gallicano , T. D. (2014). Marriott on the Move cultivates relationships and increases profit. In Center, A. H., Jackson, P. J., Smith, S., & Stansberry, F. (Authors), Public relations practices: Managerial case studies and problems (8th ed.). Upper Saddle River, NJ: Prentice Hall.

Gallicano, T. D., Brett, K., & Hopp, T. (2012, March). Is ghost blogging like speechwriting ? A survey of practitioners about the ethics of ghost blogging. Proceedings of the International Public Relations Research Conference, 15, 137–160. Retrieved from http://iprrc.org/docs/IPRRC_15_Proceedings.pdf

Gallicano, T. D., Cho, Y. Y., & Bivins, T. H. (2012, August). What do blog readers think ? A survey to assess ghost blogging and ghost commenting. Paper presented at the meeting of the Association for Education in Journalism and Mass Communication, Chicago, IL.

Terilli, S. A., & Arnorsdottir, L. I. (2008). The CEO as celebrity blogger: Is there a ghost or ghostwriter in the machine? Public Relations Journal, 2(4). Retrieved from http://www.prsa.org/SearchResults/view/6D-020404/0/The_CEO_as_Celebrity_Blogger_Is_There_a_Ghost_or_G

REFERENCES

Anderson, C. (2006, November 26). In praise of radical transparency [Web log message].
Retrieved from http://www.longtail.com/the_long_tail/2006/11/in_praise_of_ra.html

Auer, J. J. (1984). Ghostwriting and the cult of leadership response. Communication Education, 33(4), 306–307.

Beal, A., & Strauss, J. (2008). Radically transparent: Monitoring and managing reputations online. Indianapolis, IN: Wiley.

Bernoff, J. (2008, December 9). People don't trust company blogs: What you should do about it. Retrieved from http://forrester.typepad.com/groundswell/2008/12/people-dont-tru.html

Bormann, E. G. (1956). Ghostwriting agencies. Today's Speech, 4(3), 20–23.

Bortree, D. S., & Seltzer, T. (2009). Dialogic strategies and outcomes: An analysis of environmental advocacy groups' Facebook profiles. Public Relations Review, 35(3), 317–319.

de Vera, I.J.M. (2011, November 24). Survey: PH firms slow to adopt social media. Retrieved from http://www.entrepreneurship.org.ph/index.php?option=com_content&view=article&id=94:survey-ph-firms-slow-to-adopt-social-media&catid=5:entreprenews

Defren, T. (2010, January 28). In defense of ghostblogging: Social media ethical dilemmas [Web log message]. Retrieved from http://www.pr-squared.com/index.php/2010/01/ghostblogging-social-media-ethical-dilemmas

Edelman, R. (2011, November 10). Reimagining PR in the age of complexity. Retrieved from http://www.edelman.com/speak_up/blog/archives/2011/11/reimagining_pr.html

Edelman, R. (2012, April). Earning license to lead. Speech presented at the Marquette Corporate Communications Summit, Milwaukee, WI.

Einhorn, L. J. (1981). The ghosts unmasked: A review of literature on speechwriting. Communication Quarterly, 30(1), 41–47.

Einhorn, L. J. (1991). Ghostwriting: Two famous ghosts speak on its nature and its ethical implications. In R. E. Denton (Ed.) Ethical Dimensions of Political Communication (pp. 115–144). New York: Praeger.

Flaherty, R. (2011, February 4). *Lessons from the frontiers of radical transparency.* Retrieved from http://www.ketchum.com/files/Rob_Flaherty_Lessons_From_Frontiers_of_Radical_Transparency_Article_2–11.pdf

Fleet, D. (2009, February 24). Why ghost blogging is wrong [Web log message]. Retrieved from http://davefleet.com/2009/02/ghost-blogging-wrong/

Gallicano, T. D., Brett, K., & Hopp, T. (2012, March). *Is ghost blogging like speechwriting? A survey of practitioners about the ethics of ghost blogging.* Paper presented at the meeting of the International Public Relations Research Conference, Miami, FL. Available at http://www.instituteforpr.org/iprwp/wp-content/uploads/15th-IPRRC-Proceedings.pdf

Gallicano, T. D., Cho, Y. Y., & Bivins, T. H. (2012, August). *What do blog readers think? A survey to assess ghost blogging and ghost commenting.* Paper presented at the meeting of the Association for Education in Journalism and Mass Communication, Chicago, IL.

Harte, B. (2009, February 23). Social media ghostwriting: The great marketing/PR debate [Web log message]. Retrieved from http://www.theharteofmarketing.com/2009/02/social-media-ghostwriting-the-great-marketingpr-debate.html

Hollingsworth, D. (2012, March 22). Imperfection IS perfection [Web log message]. Retrieved from http://www.hmhagency.com/culture/feed/denise-hollingsworth/imperfection-perfection

Holtz, S. (2011). A ghost-blogging cartoon from Noise to Signal [Web log message]. Retrieved from http://shelholtz.com/a-ghost-blogging-cartoon-from-noise-to-signal

IBM. (n.d.). IBM syndicated feeds. Retrieved from http://www.ibm.com/blogs/zz/en

Kent, M. L., & Taylor, M. (2002). Toward a dialogic theory of public relations. *Public Relations Review, 28*(1), 21–37.

Marriott, B. (2012, January 1). About my blog [Web log message]. Retrieved from http://www.blogs.marriott.com/marriott-on-the-move//about-marriott-blog.html

Martin, K. D., & Smith, N. C. (2008). Commercializing social interaction: The ethics of stealth marketing. *Journal of Public Policy & Marketing, 27*(1), 45–56.

Nerad, S. (2010, February 6). Blog ghost writing amplifies authentic voices [Web log message]. Retrieved from http://usefularts.us/2010/02/06/ghost-write-blogs-ethics-shava-nerad/

Paine, K. (2012, March 22). Katie Paine's 13 favorite papers from IPRRC 2012. *The Measurement Standard.* Retrieved from http://kdpaine.blogs.com/themeasurementstandard/2012/03/iprrc-2012-wrap-up-by-katie-paine-the-consensus-on-this-years-iprrc-is-that-the-quality-of-discussions-and-papers-has.html

Riley, L. A., & Brown, S. C. (1996). Crafting a public image: An empirical study of the ethics of ghostwriting. *Journal of Business Ethics, 15*(7), 711–720.

Seltzer, T., & Mitrook, M. A. (2007). The dialogic potential of weblogs in relationship building. *Public Relations Review, 33*(2), 227–229.

Sledzik, B. (2009, March 1). Ghostwriting and blogs: Let's take a closer look [Web log message]. Retrieved from http://toughsledding.wordpress.com/2009/03/01/ghostwriting-and-blogs-lets-take-a-closer-look/

Subveri, A. (2010, April). Is it right to ghostwrite? *Tactics, 17*(4), p. 6.

Terilli, S. A., & Arnorsdottir, L. I. (2008). The CEO as celebrity blogger: Is there a ghost or ghostwriter in the machine? *Public Relations Journal, 2*(4). Retrieved from http://www.prsa.org/SearchResults/view/6D-020404/0/The_CEO_as_Celebrity_Blogger_Is_There_a_Ghost_or_G

Thompson, C. (2007). The see-through CEO [Web log message]. Retrieved from http://www.wired.com/wired/archive/15.04/wired40_ceo.html

3 Bank of America's Facebook Engagement Challenges its Claims of "High Ethical Standards"

Marcia W. DiStaso

INTRODUCTION

In the 2013 Bank of America Code of Ethics, CEO Brian T. Moynihan begins his letter stating,

> Every day, millions of individuals, households, families and businesses of every size trust us to help make opportunity possible for them. That trust is at the heart of what we do, and is crucial to the value we provide. Our customers and clients want to know that all our employees will treat them fairly, communicate forthrightly, and make clear, honest and ethical decisions. (p. ii)

He also states that Bank of America employees are, "accountable for upholding the highest ethical standards as we execute our responsibilities" (p. ii).

Unfortunately, its actions do not always match what is promised. Many customers and people around the country hate Bank of America, resulting in their making the list of The 10 Most Hated Companies in America list for most of the twenty-first century (Tracey, 2013). This feeling is generated from excessive fees, impenetrable call centers, abominable customer service, high executive compensation, government bailout, and/or foreclosure horror stories (Giang & Lubin, 2011). The 2012 Harris Poll Annual RQ found that financial services companies suffered greater reputation losses than other industries in 2011, and Bank of America was the company with the greatest decline. In fact, Bank of America, AIG, and Goldman Sachs were in the range that companies such as Enron, Adelphia, and WorldCom once occupied; "dangerous territory" (p. 3).

Facebook provides companies with a tool to connect with the public and build a community. Simply having a Facebook page does not build relationships, but it does provide an opportunity for dialogic communication.

Given Bank of America's commitment to high ethical standards and the opportunities social media provide companies, the purpose of this study is to analyze the way the Bank of America managed its Facebook page during

2011 when they had a large outpouring of public discontent with their announcement of a $5 debit card fee for account holders.

LITERATURE REVIEW

Corporate Social Reporting

Corporate social behavior has become an important aspect of society. In fact, for companies to be successful today, they must be involved in more than profit seeking behavior (Yeung, 2011). The intent of business, therefore, is not just about creating wealth alone, but doing it responsibly.

According to Werther and Chandler (2006), corporate social responsibility is concerned about what companies do and how their actions impact the environment and society. Corporate social responsibility (CSR) is defined as, "the voluntary actions that a corporation implements as it pursues its mission and fulfills its perceived obligations to stakeholders, including employees, communities, the environment, and society as a whole (Coombs & Holladay, 2012, p. 8). It can also be considered the relationship between business and the larger society.

Many organizations approach CSR as "doing good to do well" (Vogel, 2005, p. 19).

Carroll (2009) identified four components of CSR: economic, legal, ethical, and discretionary or philanthropic. The economic component is a company's fundamental responsibility to make a profit. The legal component is its duty to obey rules and the law. The ethical component is the company's responsibility to respect the rights of others and to meet the obligations placed on it by society; to do what is right, fair, and just. Finally, the discretionary component involves being a good corporate citizen.

Companies can use their CSR efforts as a way of differentiating themselves as well as a means to gain competitive advantage. Besides strengthening core corporate capabilities, CSR is often used as a means to build positive attitudes towards companies among consumers. Therefore, publicizing CSR efforts is done to affect the public's perception of the company (Hooghiemstra, 2000).

The reporting of CSR efforts is called corporate social reporting. According to legitimacy theory, corporate social reporting is aimed at providing information that legitimizes company behavior by intending to influence stakeholders and eventually society's perceptions about the company so it is regarded a "good corporate citizen" and its continued existence is justified (DiStaso & Scandura, 2009; Guthrie & Parker, 1989; Neu, Warsame & Pedwell, 1998).

The way that companies gain legitimacy is through impression management. Impression management is defined as, "any behavior by a person that has the purpose of controlling or manipulating attributions and impressions formed of that person by others" (Tedeschi & Riess, 1981, p. 3). Essentially, it is a self-presentation aimed at insuring stakeholder satisfaction with the company's behavior. While on the surface, there is nothing wrong with impression management; companies have an ethical responsibility to stakeholders to provide an accurate and complete picture of the company (DiStaso, 2012).

Social Media & CSR

Companies historically have used traditional mass media as the preferred communication channel, but today, online mediums such as websites and social media are becoming more frequently utilized. The 2010 Social Media Influence study (Custom Communications, 2010), found that only 23% of companies used social media to inform the public about CSR efforts.

The advantage of using social media to communicate about CSR efforts is its ability for interaction and the creation of relational capital (Etter & Fieseler, 2010). Social media provides an opportunity for companies to have a dialogue that was otherwise impossible before. According to Kent and Taylor (1998), dialogue refers to "any negotiated exchange of ideas and opinions" and it represents efforts by parties to engage in an honest, open, and ethically based give and take.

Currently, not all companies are on social media, and of those that are not all use it as communication channels for CSR efforts. McCorkindale (2010) found that 22% of the 55 Facebook pages for *Fortune 50* companies had CSR content. Angeles and Capriotti (2009) and Etter (2013) found that companies are hesitant to engage with stakeholders about CSR on Twitter. Etter (2013) postulated that this may be due to the sensitivity of CSR topics and the impact it can have on reputation and legitimacy. He also indicated that by openly engaging companies risk possible criticism and attracting additional critics.

Social Media Engagement

Social media can be viewed as a two-way form of media that empowers the public relations function (Porter & Sallot, 2005) by helping humanize a company. Today, public relations has shifted from focusing primarily on one-way asymmetrical strategies of the past to two-way symmetrical strategies for building relationships (Rawlins, 2009).

According to Kent and Taylor (1998), dialogic communication is "any negotiated exchange of ideas and opinions" (p. 325). This requires that both parties are willing to be open and listen to the other even if there is disagreement and the communication should be focused on intersubjectivity. Most public relations scholars agree that dialogue is a necessary, ethical form of communication (DiStaso & McCorkindale, 2013; Gilmore & Pine, 2007; Gilpin, 2010; Henderson, 2010; Kent & Taylor, 1998;

McCorkindale, 2012). Dialogue must be ethical, honest, forthright, and authentic (Gilpin, 2010; Henderson, 2010).

Dialogue for public relations efforts relies on the idea of embedded ethics—an ideal towards which many practitioners and scholars strive, but whereas the process of dialogue can promote ethical behavior, it cannot compel companies to behave ethically (Kent & Taylor, 2002). It also cannot force companies to engage in dialogue with stakeholders.

While dialogue is what is sought in social media, engagement is typically seen as the next best thing. According to Paine (2011), "engagement means that someone has taken an additional step beyond just viewing what you tossed out there" (¶ 5). This includes actions such as "Liking," "Sharing," or commenting on Facebook posts.

Engagement is beneficial to companies for a variety of reasons and it is often linked to loyalty (Bowden, 2009; Roberts & Alpert, 2010). Brodie and Hollebeek (2011) state that customer engagement is positively related to brand relationship outcomes such as satisfaction, trust, and loyalty. Customers who participate in social media conversations with companies are believed to already have a baseline relationship with the company, which is then further influenced by their participation (Algesheimer, Dholakia, & Herrmann, 2005).

Social media sites like Facebook and Twitter are typically considered to be tools best suited for facilitating dialogic communication and engagement (Avery, Lariscy, Amador, Ickowitz, Primm, & Taylor, 2010). DiStaso and McCorkindale (2013) found that 46% of companies had Facebook pages and 73% had Twitter accounts. On Twitter, users can ask questions and receive responses from the company. On Facebook, organizations can allow users post information on their wall. This public openness indicates the company's willingness to receive feedback and their desire for a dialogue.

Through an analysis of candidate use of Facebook in the 2006 election, Sweetser and Lariscy (2008) identified the vast potential for dialogic communication in Facebook. Bortree and Seltzer (2009) looked at environmental advocacy group Facebook pages and found that they were missing the opportunity to build relationships because they were not participating in dialogue.

How companies handle negative comments is critical to the success of the social media site. Dekay (2012) studies the Facebook pages for the ten largest companies in banking, retail, software/services, and household/personal product industries. Of the 40 companies, 25 had a Facebook page. Of these, 48% participated in the practice of deleting negative comments. Whereas broad censorship is not suggested, companies should have a policy that stipulates what will be censored such as profanity or discriminatory comments (Dekay, 2012; DiStaso & McCorkindale, 2013).

In his study, Dekay (2012) found that 60% of companies responded to negative comments (n=15), and this included only one of the four banks in his study. He also found that negative comments appeared to be primarily in response to explicit marketing efforts by the company. The type of content least likely to receive negative comments was "fun" posts. Ultimately, Dekay (2012) suggested that negative comments on social media sites should be treated as opportunities to resolve problems.

Banks, CSR, and Social Media

As a result of the 2008 global financial crisis, there has been a steep decline in trust in banks, financial institutions, and big businesses. The 2012 Edelman Trust Barometer found that the banking and financial services sectors were the least trusted industries for the second year.

The 2011 Ernst & Young Global Banking Survey of more than 20,500 individuals across the globe identified that confidence in banking continued to decrease. Their findings led to their suggestions that the following four steps are necessary to restore brand confidence in banks: (1) innovative marketing of customer experiences, (2) personalized products and services, (3) creating brand ambassadors through transparency and incentives, and (4) adopt "a coherent social media approach will help improve brand perceptions and leverage the benefits of online advocacy" (p. 18). Bottom line, they suggested that banks should rebuild trust by "refocusing on the customer relationship" (p. 31).

In her series of surveys, DiStaso (2013) found the media felt that CSR efforts could help 'fix' trust in U.S. banks. In an effort to require banks to contribute to their communities, Congress adopted The Community Reinvestment Act in 1977. The purpose of this Act is to encourage meeting the credit needs of the communities in which the banks operate (CRA, 2013). Other efforts by banks often include philanthropy, employee volunteerism, nonprofit partnerships, arts, cultural programs, and environmental business initiatives.

Each year the American Bankers Association awards their members for the "innovative and high impact contributions banks of all sizes make to the communities they serve" (ABA Community Commitment Awards, 2013, ¶ 1).

Another opportunity to improve trust in banking is through social media. As Frank Eliason, Citi's SVP of social media said, "We look to social media to try to change that perception, and we try to do it in a very human way" (as quoted in Fox, 2011).

According to Michael Versace, global research director, IDC Financial Insights, "social media will continue to force service industries like banking to find ways to engage with customers" (quoted in Adams, 2013, ¶ 2). In an American Banker article (Adams, 2013), social media experts identified five major ways banks can use and benefit from social media:

1. Build a community and get product or service ideas from it by including customers into the creative process.

2. Monitor content to learn about needs and preferences. This includes using information available on Facebook like favorite shows, relationship status, etc. to target communication and make it more relevant.
3. Use personal information gleaned to properly advertise. For example, learn what shows their Facebook followers watch and advertise there.
4. Use social media data in making credit decisions.
5. Include social media in reward and loyalty programs.

More specifically, a Mashable article by Zoe Fox (2011) listed five ways for financial institutions to "loosen their neckties, roll up their sleeves and show some personality" (2011, ¶ 1) on Facebook:

1. Use it to build a community not just talk about banking.
2. Host contests.
3. Provide career advice.
4. Loosen up and provide more conversational tone than typical press release wording.
5. Show off community involvement.

With the highly regulated industry of finance, many banks have been hesitant to open accounts. There is currently no regulatory guidance on social media, but in January 2013, the Federal Financial Institutions Examination Council (FFIEC) proposed guidance on social media (FFIEC, 2013) and as an industry, formal regulations are eventually expected. Still, many financial institutions have ventured into the social media arena; even the FDIC has its own Facebook page. Banking compliance requires that negative comments received in social media are handled similarly as in-person or in-writing complaints. This means responding and retaining a copy of the complaint along with the response for audit purposes.

Before establishing a Facebook page, Bank of America conducted research with 418 consumers under 50 (Yarow, 2011). They found that 96% of their respondents used Facebook and were interested in learning more about local deals and businesses.

Bank of America

Bank of America's history dates back more than 200 years (BOA, 2013). Throughout the years they have played central roles in the "development of economies, nations and communities" (¶ 10). Currently, Bank of America is one of the largest banks in the United States. They were listed fifth on the *Fortune 500* list in 2010, this decreased to 9th in 2011, 13th in 2012 and 21st in 2013. Although the global financial crisis had much to do with this decrease, other factors greatly impacted Bank of America's backslide.

Customer service problems led to its receiving the lowest scores compared to its peers in 2011 and 2012 on the American Customer Satisfaction

Index and the worst score for customer service for all companies in an MSN Money online survey (Alix, 2012). However, customer service has not been its only problem recently. Just 33 days after announcing their plans to begin charging a $5 monthly debit card fee Bank of America announced canceling it. In the official statement David Darnell, co-chief operating officer, said,

> We have listened to our customers very closely over the last few weeks and recognize their concern with our proposed debit usage fee. Our customers' voices are most important to us. As a result, we are not currently charging the fee and will not be moving forward with any additional plans to do so (as quoted in Kim & Gutman, 2011).

Bank fees were a common complaint among Occupy Wall Street protesters, and the Bank of America $5 fee was the focus of an online protest that garnered over 300,000 signatures. Even President Obama criticized the fee (Kim & Gutman, 2011). Many people across the country pulled their money from the "big banks" and moved it to local banks or credit unions, with credit unions indicating an increase each year since 2008 (Smith, 2013). The online movements Move Your Money Day and Bank Transfer Day in 2011 encouraged such shifts and were credited for more than 650,000 people transferring their money from Bank of America to community banks (Anderson, 2013).

Research Questions

Based on the preceding review of literature, the following research questions were explored:

RQ1: Did Bank of America seek to engage the public on their Facebook page in 2011, and what was the result?

RQ2: Did Bank of America participate in dialogic communication on their Facebook page in 2011, and what was the result?

RQ3: Did Bank of America post about non-self-serving content on their Facebook page in 2011, and what was the result?

RQ4: Did Bank of America delete negative comments on their Facebook page in 2011?

RQ5: Did Bank of America handle their Facebook account differently before and after their $5 fee crisis?

METHOD

With Bank of America's reputation under attack in 2011, their social media presence provided them with an opportunity to listen and engage. The purpose of this chapter was to explore how Bank of America handled their CSR focused Facebook account in 2011.

A content analysis on the Bank of America Facebook page was conducted for 2011. Each post by the company and the subsequent comments were analyzed. This resulted in an analysis of 85 company posts with 1,573 comments. Posts were analyzed for likes, comments, shares, negative comments, deleted comments, Bank of America responses, engagement, and topic focus. Engagement seeking was coded as posts that sought action such as comments, liking or sharing. Participating in dialogic communication was determined by responding to comments. Self-serving content included posts about Bank of America. Negative comments included any comment that was negative, insulting, or complaining about Bank of America policies or services. Scores ranged from 93% to 100% with Scott's Pi and 98% to 100% with Holsti.

Bank of America created their Facebook page on June 7, 2011 and their first post was on June 22, 2011. As of July 19, 2013, the Facebook page had 1,072,919 people who "Like" it.

On October 11, 2011, Bank of America opened a tab on their wall for public posts. This content was not coded because it is not easy to locate and the average Facebook user does not typically go looking for a "Posts by Others" page. However, it is important to note that a cursory analysis found that this tab was managed similarly to how their Wall was managed.

To identify if Bank of America handled their account differently before and after the $5 fee crisis that began on September 29, 2011, the analysis was broken into two groups: June through September 28 and September 29 through December.

During the seven-month analysis, Bank of America posted 85 times. This was an average of 12 posts per month, or about three a week. Their posts had an average of 93 likes, 19 comments, 3 shares, 7 negative comments, 2 deleted comments, and one Bank of America reply per post. There were a total of 1,573 comments.

Research question one analyzed Bank of America's engagement seeking behavior, and found that 44% of the posts were engagement seeking. Examples include:

- Questions such as: "How do you feel about arts education in elementary and high schools?"
- Used fill-in-the-blank statements like: When kids have a mentor, they have the opportunity to _____.
- Providing engagement directions such as: Like this post if you know chef Elizabeth Falkner (owner of Citizen Cake in Hayes Valley, a participant on Bravo's Top Chef and Food Network's Iron Chef America). She's helping us end hunger by volunteering at the Second Harvest Food Bank in Silicon Valley.
- Polls like: How many people do you think volunteered in the US in 2010?

Engagement seeking posts (M=53.68, SD=64.06) received a less "Likes" than non-engagement seeking posts (M=122.8, SD=105.44; $t(83) = 9.53$, $p \leq .001$); less shares (M=1.51, SD=6.0) than non-engagement seeking posts (M=4.54, SD=7.27; $t(83) = -2.052$, $p \leq .05$); and fewer negative comments (M=2.78, SD=5.86) than non-engagement seeking posts (M=10.17, SD=26.65; $t(83) = 1.02$, $p \leq .001$).

For research question two, it was found that Bank of America responded to 42% of the posts, and 94% of those responses contained dialogic communication, so in the end, 40% of their posts contained dialogic communication. Simply commenting on their posts was not considered dialogic; specific replies mentioning a person was coded as dialogic. Many of the posts in September contained a "form" message

> Thanks folks, we appreciate all of the active commentary on this thread. For future reference we have opened our Wall for other topics. Be sure to see our Info tab for our community guidelines. Thanks. ^cs

This was posted on October 6, and it was common for replies to be a day or week after the post was written. When people complained about deleted comments this, "form" message was posted:

> We're sorry that your comments are no longer visible. We manage posts if they violate our community guidelines or are off-topic of the original post. In the case of being off-topic, we have opened the Wall for you to be able to start a new topic. Be sure to see our Info tab for our community guidelines. Thanks.^nl

Note that neither of these messages were dialogic but simply just Bank of America talking to everyone. When they were called out for the "form" messages they replied messages like:

> @Wandeline Calderon We're reading your comments. Keep the posts coming. ^cs

and

> @Kathy Appreciate all the comments and we do hear that folks are upset. We only ask that everyone stay on topic on our posts around volunteering and community efforts. Our wall is open and we're there listening and sharing issues and concerns with folks across the bank. ^nl

At times they simply seemed to mostly ignore what people were saying or gloss over it in their response, such as in this dialogue:

> Rebecca Prince Tabert: How dare you Bank of America, you run veterans right into the ditch every day they are overseas fighting for this

country!!!! I cant [sic] reach an intelligent person when I call from the U.S., how is a soldier from Afghanistan supposed to stop you from stealing thier [sic] lives right from under them???

Bank of America: @Rebecca. We understand your concerns. We have set up a special Military Assistance unit that handles military customers in distress. For mortgage inquiries, please call (1–877–430–5434); the team is available 24/7. If it is difficult to reach us by phone, we also have an official social media servicing platform on Twitter that can answer all other account questions. This team is reachable at @BofA_Help. If you have a friend or family member in the military that needs assistance, please pass this information along to them. ^cw

Another common response was to send people to Twitter.

@Barbara Haynes The team managing this Facebook page unfortunately does not have access to customer information so we aren't able to answer any questions about your account. We do have an official social media servicing platform on Twitter. This team is reachable at @BofA_Help. They are ready and standing by to assist. ^cw

Some of the deleted comments received replies, and most of time they were similar to:

@Jessie we're sorry to hear you're having an issue. Unfortunately, we aren't able to provide customer service through this page but we do have a number of options that can quickly direct you to an employee who can help you. If you're on Twitter, you can tweet us @BofA_Help or you can reach someone via online chat at http://go.bofa.com/contact. If phone works best, our contact number is 1.800.432.1000 ^cs

Some people accused them of using the Facebook page about CSR as PR stunts such as with this dialogue:

Gayle Asher: I would be embarrassed to share anything from BoA! How dare you cheat people out of their homes and then throw them a bone in the name of Green Energy! This is just a PR stunt.

Bank of America @Gayle We appreciate your comment. While the bank's energy efficiency finance program is designed to help address critical issues of energy efficiency, it will also help serve low income communities by creating jobs and reducing utility costs for people who own, live and work in older buildings. It's important that we find ways to address the critical issues affecting the communities we serve, and we are committed to doing that through partnerships with leading community organizations and our lending, investing and giving programs. Here is a link to show you our commitment to this topic http://go.bofa.com/qa5p

An analysis of the content for research question three found that almost half of the posts in 2011 were specific to Bank of America (48%, n=41). Examples include posts with pictures about Bank of America Career Day and content such as, "Bank of America is working to help revitalize neighborhoods in East New York through financing affordable and sustainable housing projects like Dumont Green in Brooklyn."

Negative comments were more common on posts that contained Bank of America specific content (M=11.59, SD=28.76) than those that had nothing to do with Bank of America (M=2.64, SD=4.75; $t(83) = 2.04$, $p \leq .05$).

In regard to research question four it was found that over the seven-month period, 51% of the posts had comments deleted from them. There were a total of 160 comments deleted for an average of 9% of all comments. As they stated, they removed comments that violate their "community guidelines or are off-topic of the original post." Many comments remained that were off-topic, so it is likely that they primarily deleted comments that were profane, obscene, or inappropriate as they indicate would be removed in their guidelines.

Research question five looked at differences before and after the announcement of the $5 fee. Quite a few differences were noted. The number of "Likes" was much higher after the $5 fee announcement ($t(83) = -5.56$, $p \leq .001$). Before the announcement had an average of 41 "Likes" per post (SD=70.57) and after it increased to an average of 141 "Likes" per post (SD=91.74).

The total number of comments slightly increased after the announcement ($t(83) = -2.07$, $p \leq .05$) slightly (from an average of 12.9 comments per post before (SD=17.48) to 23.7 after(SD=28.96)), but the number of negative comments increased substantially ($t(83) = -2.17$, $p \leq .05$). The average number of negative comments before the fee announcement was 2.0 per post (SD=6.6) and it jumped to an average of 11.55 negative comments per post after the announcement (SD=27.32). Along with this, there was an increase in dialogic communication ($t(83) = -3.37$, $p \leq .001$), with less than one comment per post from Bank of America before the announcement (M=0.39, SD=0.77) to more than one comment per post after it (M=1.27, SD=1.5). There was not a significant difference in the number of deleted comments.

The amount of posts seeking engagement substantially decreased from 78% before the announcement to 22% after it ($\chi^2(1, N=85) = 23.84$, p<.001).

The amount of posts with self-serving content markedly increased as well from 24% before the announcement to 76% after ($\chi^2(1, N=85) = 18.04$, p<.001).

DISCUSSION AND CONCLUSIONS

One of the biggest lessons to be gleaned from this chapter is that using a Facebook page about CSR does not shield companies from public outrage. Another lesson is that companies should treat Facebook comments as they would personal communication with customers and strive for dialogue that is ethical, honest, forthright, and authentic.

Ethical Implications for the Practice of Social Media

Simply having a Facebook page that solely focuses on CSR can be considered a form of impression management. This is especially obvious by reviewing the comments on the page and through consideration of what was occurring with Bank of America during the time of the analysis. By removing comments that are "off-topic" when they are not related to the CSR post indicates to the public that Bank of America does not care about what is important to them. Companies cannot script what topics the public wants to discuss and force everyone to play by the rules. By sending such a message, people go elsewhere and in this case many moved their money to another bank and found a community they felt comfortable with on the Facebook page, "Bank of America Sucks." It is important to note that Bank of America broadened the focus of their Facebook page from solely about CSR to including content to help customers with their "financial lives." Whereas the name changed from "Building Opportunity from Bank of America" to "Bank of America," the content did not change much.

How Bank of America handled their Facebook account during 2011 surrounding the $5 fee announcement crisis sheds light on the challenges and opportunities companies have with managing their accounts. The high frequency of negative comments should not have been surprising to them, but they appeared unprepared to fully handle the negativity.

Although comments with profanity or those that are obscene, defamatory, abusive or such should be deleted, but it is important to let the community know why the comment was deleted such as: "@XYZ person: Your post was deleted because it violated our community guidelines. Please see http://go.bofa.com/Facebook for details." Bank of America did occasionally make similar comments, but they often were not to specific people and did not provide the link for easy access to the policy. They also indicate that they delete off-topic posts and that was not necessary because it is stated in the guidelines.

It is also important to truly pay attention to what is being asked and not simply reply with "form" comments as was done in almost all cases in this analysis. Simply putting someone's name at the start of a comment does not personalize it. Ethical dialogic communication requires that both parties are willing to be open and listen to the other even when there is disagreement (Kent & Taylor, 1998), and not addressing the actual comment in a reply indicates a breakdown in listening, or possibly caring. Although this analysis was of the Facebook page in 2011, truly listening remains a problem for Bank of America in 2013. This time they received media attention for the use of their Twitter account because of "form" replies to Tweets. For example, @OccupyLA tweeted "@BoA_Help you can help by stop stealing people's houses!!!!" and Bank of America replied, "@OccupyLA We'd be happy to review your account with you to discuss any concerns. Please let us know if you need assistance.^sa"

This study found that the public was much more likely to post their negative comments when the content in posts was related to Bank of America and less likely when they were engagement seeking. This is a strong message for companies—keep your Facebook page fun and not self-serving. This also provides an opportunity to include the community in the creative process as was suggested in the American Banker article (Adams, 2013), and loosen up as the Mashable article suggested (Fox, 2011).

Bottom line, identities cannot be controlled in social media and are a creation built on interaction. Instead of trying to force control, companies should use Facebook to listen, participate, and respect the community. Doing so can help the social media team at Bank of America uphold the highest ethical standards for which they claim to strive.

Limitations and Future Research

As with all research, this study was bounded by limitations. This study assumed that the missing comments had been deleted by Bank of America, however, it is possible that they were deleted by the person who made the comment. This is unlikely, because many of the people who had comments deleted went back and commented about it being deleted. This analysis took place long after the posts were made so it was not possible to see deleted posts. Future research could include a live analysis to catch posts before they are deleted to identify their content. The Facebook account was not analyzed past 2011, so it is unclear if Bank of America has learned from the mistakes discussed in this research, so future research could be conducted to identify any changes.

Although Bank of America's actions with their Facebook page may not be directly unethical, they certainly walk the line and future research should address perceptions of their focus on CSR, their propensity/guidelines to delete off-topic posts, and their reliance on "form" dialogue.

Discussion Questions

1. What are the ethical responsibilities of social media managers with negative comments?
2. How should companies engage in dialogic communication when they are under attack as Bank of America was with the $5 fee?

3. What should companies do to be prepared for potential backlash in social media?

SUGGESTED READINGS

Carroll, A. B., & Buchholtz, A. K. (2009). *Business and society: Ethics and stakeholder management*, 7th ed. Mason, OH: South-Western Cengage Learning.

DiStaso, M. W. & McCorkindale, T. (2013). A benchmark analysis of the strategic use of social media for Fortune's Most Admired U.S. companies on Facebook, Twitter and YouTube. *Public Relations Journal, 7*(1), 1–33.

Ernst & Young Global Banking Survey (2011). Retrieved from http://emergingmarkets.ey.com/global-consumer-banking-survey-2011/

Kent, M. L., & Taylor, M. (1998). Building dialogic relationships through the World Wide Web. *Public Relations Review, 24*(3), 321.

McCorkindale, T. (2010). Can you see the writing on my wall? A content analysis of the *Fortune 500*'s Facebook social networking sites. *Public Relations Journal, 4*(3), 1–13.

REFERENCES

ABA Community Commitment Awards (2013). Retrieved from http://www.aba.com/About/Pages/CommunityCommitmentAwards.aspx

Adams, J. (2013, February 1). Five ways banks should be using social media. *American Banker*. Retrieved from http://www.americanbanker.com/issues/178_23/five-ways-banks-can-use-social-media-1056408–1.html

Alix, A. (2012, December, 13). Bank of America's crummy report card. *The Motley Fool*. Retrieved from http://www.fool.com/investing/general/2012/12/13/bank-of-americas-crummy-report-card.aspx

Algesheimer, R., Dholakia, U. M., & Herrmann, A. (2005). The social influence of brand community: Evidence from European car clubs. *Journal of Marketing, 69*, 19–34.

Anderson, G. E. (2013, July 19). Reputation risk: More important than ever. *ABA Banking Journal*. Retrieved from http://www.ababj.com/briefing/reputation-risk-more-important-than-ever-4115.html

Angeles, M., & Capriotti, M. (2009). Communicating CSR, citizenship and sustainability on the web. *Journal of Communication Management, 13*, 157–175.

Avery, E., Lariscy, R., Amador, E., Ickowitz, T., Primm, C., & Taylor, A. (2010). Diffusion of social media among public relations practitioners in health departments across various community population sizes. *Journal of Public Relations Research, 22*(3), 336–358.

Bank of America Our History. (2013). Retrieved from http://about.bankofamerica.com/en-us/our-story/our-history-and-heritage.html#fbid=3Rhfyla4oie

Bortree, D. S., & Seltzer, T. (2009). Dialogic strategies and outcomes: An analysis of environmental advocacy groups' Facebook profiles. *Public Relations Review, 35*(30), 317–319.

Bowden, J. L. (2009). The process of customer engagement: A conceptual framework. *Journal of Marketing Theory and Practice, 17*(1), 63–74.

Brodie, R. J. and Hollebeek, L.D. (2011), Advancing and consolidating knowledge about customer engagement. *Journal of Service Research, 14*(3), 283–284.

Carroll, A. B., & Buchholtz, A. K. (2009). *Business and society: Ethics and stakeholder management*, 7th ed. Mason, OH: South-Western Cengage Learning.

Community Reinvestment Act (CRA) (2013). Retrieved from http://www.ffiec.gov/cra/

Coombs, W. T., & Holladay, S. J. (2012). *Managing corporate social responsibility: A communication approach*. Malden, MA: Blackwell Publishing.

Custom Communications (2010). *SMI special report: Social Media Sustainability Index*. Retrieved from http://socialmediainfluence.com/SMI-Wizness/

Dekay, S. H. (2012). How large companies react to negative Facebook comments. *Corporate Communications: An International Journal*, 17(3), 289–299.

DiStaso, M. W. (2012). The annual earnings press release's dual role: An examination of relationships with local and national media coverage and reputation. *Journal of Public Relations Research*, 24(2), 123–143.

DiStaso, M. W. (2014). The impact of Occupy Wall Street on the business media's perceptions of banks. *Corporate Reputation Review*, 9(Forthcoming).

DiStaso, M. W. & McCorkindale, T. (2013). A benchmark analysis of the strategic use of social media for Fortune's Most Admired U.S. companies on Facebook, Twitter and YouTube. *Public Relations Journal*, 7(1), 1–33.

DiStaso, M. W., & Scandura, T. A. (2009). Organizational legitimacy: Lessons learned from financial scandals. In D. W. Stacks & M. B. Salwen (Eds.), *An integrated approach to communication theory and research* (2nd ed.). Mahwah, NJ: Lawrence Erlbaum Associates, Inc.

Edelman Trust Barometer (2012). Retrieved from http://www.scribd.com/doc/79026497/2012-Edelman-Trust-Barometer-Executive-Summary

Ernst & Young Global Banking Survey (2011). Retrieved from http://emergingmarkets.ey.com/global-consumer-banking-survey-2011/

Etter, M. (2013). Reasons for low levels of interactivity. (Non-)interactive CSR communication in Twitter. *Public Relations Review*, 1–3.

Etter, M., & Fieseler, C. (2010). On relational capital in social media. *Studies in Communication Sciences*, 10(2), 167–189.

Federal Financial Institutions Examination Council (FFIEC). (2013, January 22). Social media: Consumer compliance risk management guidance. Retrieved from http://www.ffiec.gov/press/Doc/FFIEC%20social%20media%20guidelines%20FR%20Notice.pdf

Fox, Z. (2011, October, 24). 5 Best Practices for Financial Institutions on Facebook. *Mashable*. Retrieved from http://mashable.com/2011/10/24/banks-facebook/

Ciang, V., & Lubin, G. (2011). The 19 most hated companies in America. *The Atlantic* Retrieved from http://www.theatlantic.com/business/archive/2011/07/the-19-most-hated-companies-in-america/241344/

Gilmore, J. H., & Pine, J. B. (2007). *What consumers really want: Authenticity*. Boston: Harvard Business School Press.

Gilpin, D. R. (2010). Socially mediated authenticity. *Journal of Communication Management*, 14(3), 258–278.

Guthrie, J., & L. D. Parker (1989) Corporate social reporting: A rebuttal of legitimacy theory. *Accounting and Business Research*, 19(76), 343–352.

Henderson, A. (2010). Authentic dialogue? The role of "friendship" in a social media recruitment campaign. *Journal of Communication Management*, 14(3), 237–257.

Hooghiemstra, R. (2000). Corporate communication and impression management—new perspectives why companies engage in corporate social reporting. *Journal of Business Ethics*, 27, 55–68.

Kent, M. L., & Taylor, M. (1998). Building dialogic relationships through the World Wide Web. *Public Relations Review*, 24(3), 321.

Kent, M. L., & Taylor, M. (2002). Toward a dialogic theory of public relations. *Public Relations review, 28*, 21–37.

Kim, S., & Gutman, M. (2011, November 1). Bank of America cancels $5 fee. ABC World News. Retrieved from http://abcnews.go.com/Business/bank-america-drops-plan-debit-card-fee/story?id=14857970

McCorkindale, T. (2010). Can you see the writing on my wall? A content analysis of the Fortune 50's Facebook social networking sites. *Public Relations Journal, 4*(3), 1–13.

McCorkindale, T. (2012). Follow me or be my friend: How organizations are using Twitter and Facebook to build relationships and to communicate transparently and authentically. In S. Duhe (Ed.), *New Media and Public Relations* (2nd ed.) Peter Lang.

Neu, D., Warsame H., & Pedwell, K. (1998). Managing public impressions: Environmental disclosures in annual reports. *Accounting, Organisations, and Society, 23*(3), 265–282.

Paine, K. D. (2011). Lies and consequences in KD Paine's PR Measurement Blog. Retrieved from http://kdpaine.blogs.com/

Porter, L. V., & Sallot, L. M. (2005). Web power: A survey of practitioners' worldwide web use and their perception of its effects on their decision-making power. *Public Relations Review, 31*, 111–119.

Rawlins, B. (2009). Give the emperor a mirror: Toward developing a stakeholder measurement of organizational transparency. *Journal of Public Relations Research, 21*(1), 71–99.

Roberts, C., & Alpert, F. (2010). Total customer engagement: Designing and aligning key strategic elements to achieve growth. *Journal of Product & Brand Management, 19*(3), 198–209.

Smith, R. (2013, January 9). Americans keep fleeing banks, flock to credit unions instead. *Daily Finance.* Retrieved from http://www.dailyfinance.com/2013/01/09/credit-union-growth-bank-transfer/

Sweetser, K. D., & Lariscy R. W. (2008). Candidates make good friends: An analysis of candidates' uses of Facebook. *International Journal of Strategic Communication, 2*, 175–198.

Tedeschi, J. T., & Riess, M. (1981). *Verbal strategies in impression management.* In C. Antakki (Ed.) The psychology of ordinary explanations of social behavior, (pp. 271–309). London: Academic Press.

Tracy, C. (2013). The 10 most hated companies in America. *Street Authority.* Retrieved from http://finance.yahoo.com/news/10-most-hated-companies-america-163000649.html

Vogel, D. (2005). *The market for virtue.* Washington, DC: Brookings Institution.

Werther, W. B., & Chandler, D. (2006), *The strategic context of CSR, strategic corporate social responsibility: Stakeholders in a global environment.* London: Sage.

Yarow, J. (2011, May 31). The TRUTH about Facebook: Bank of America's new report. *Business Insider.* Retrieved from http://www.businessinsider.com/facebook-charts-2011-5

Yeung, S. (2011). The role of banks in corporate social responsibility. *Journal of Applied Economics and Business Research, 1*(2), 103–115.

4 Natural or Not?

A Case Study Of Kashi's Viral Photo Crisis On Facebook

Hilary Fussell Sisco

INTRODUCTION

The use of social media like Facebook, Twitter, and YouTube allows companies to communicate directly with their publics. They can promote new products, gain feedback on current campaigns, and interact with consumers instantly. On the other hand, social media also allow consumers to voice both their praise of and their complaints about an organization in front of a potentially vast audience at virtually no cost and with little accountability for the accuracy or fairness of their comments.

What is the responsible and ethical thing to do if a consumer questions the integrity of your organization through social media channels? What can be ethically done through social media to correct any misinformation and reassure your publics of the company's good intentions?

In 2012, a photo posted on Facebook accused a prominent health food company of providing false and deceptive information about its products, prompting a huge backlash from consumers. This chapter examines how consumers used social media in order to question the transparency and ethical actions of the company and the ethical implications of the ways the company used social media to respond to its critics.

LITERATURE REVIEW

Practitioners and scholars have reiterated the value of reputation management. A strong reputation can increase customer loyalty, economic success, and a positive attitude toward the organization (Lyon & Cameron, 2004). Reputations are most in peril when an organization is faced with a crisis; the manner in which they respond will shape the organization's character in the eyes of the public.

Professional Ethics in Public Relations

According to the Member Code of Ethics of the Public Relations Society of America (2013), it is the ethical obligation of public relations practitioners to be forthright in providing accurate information through social media. In a crisis, ethics should help to determine response to the situation.

The PRSA Member Code of Ethics outlines core values for public relations practitioners. It encourages professionals to value honesty, fairness, and to serve as advocates for stakeholders. In addition to these general values, the PRSA Provisions of Conduct suggest specific provisions arguably applicable to the Kashi situation.

First, PRSA suggests that practitioners should advance the "free flow of accurate and truthful information" (PRSA, 2013, ¶ 13). The guidelines under this provision urge practitioners to:

- Preserve the integrity of the process of communication.
- Be honest and accurate in all communications.
- Act promptly to correct erroneous communications for which the practitioner is responsible.

Another provision advises the practitioner to disclose information that helps to "build trust with the public by revealing all information needed for responsible decision making" (PRSA, 2013, ¶ 7–12). Therefore, practitioners should:

- Be honest and accurate in all communications.
- Act promptly to correct erroneous communications for which the member is responsible.
- Investigate the truthfulness and accuracy of information released on behalf of those represented.
- Reveal the sponsors for causes and interests represented.
- Avoid deceptive practices.

These provisions, as well as the general guidelines outlined by PRSA, help to guide practitioners to avoid ethically ambiguous situations. The Member Code of Ethics for PRSA offers a professional standard to help mold the practice of public relations for all practitioners. It is a suggested code for the profession that can easily lend itself to any company facing an ethical decision.

Organizational History

Kashi, a subsidiary of the Kellogg Company, is a producer of a well-known "natural" and "organic" brand of healthy foods. In 2012, sparked by a posting on a Facebook page, the company faced a social media assault from consumers when the company was reported to be using genetically modified organisms in some of its products.

There long has been much controversy about the use of genetically modified organisms (GMOs). The disputes about the use of GMOs stem from basic arguments about the potential of genetically modified foods to harm consumers, the need for broad labels to alert consumers and the impact of the use of GMOs on the environment and agricultural practices.

GMOs are commonly plants or animals that have been modified by employing genetic engineering. The resulting experimental combinations of genes from different types of species do not occur in nature on their own. Agriculturally, GMOs are used to strengthen crops by increasing plant yields, help withstand the application of herbicides and pesticides, and allow plants to better tolerate drought. GMOs are the bases of genetically modified foods, which are in as much as 80% of conventional processed food in the U.S.

The opponents of genetically modified foods worry about the lack of regulation of crops and ingredients for human consumption. They would like genetically modified foods banned, or at least labeled, so that consumers can avoid these products. Opponents also have ecological concerns about genetically modified foods contaminating non-genetically modified foods and economic concerns about the food supply being controlled by companies that produce GMOs. The supporters of genetically modified foods claim these foods are as safe as any other food and that labeling genetically modified foods will alarm consumers unnecessarily.

The U.S. does not currently require GMO labeling, but countries like the India, Australia, New Zealand, China, and the European Union do require labels for all foods that use any genetically modified ingredients. A study (Gruère & Rao, 2007) on the effect of labeling laws in India found that once labeling went into effect, companies reduced the use of genetically modified ingredients in their products. Further, the study reported that businesses stopped carrying products once they were labeled as containing GMOs. Consumers who want to buy non-genetically modified food already have a clearly labeled option, they can purchase USDA certified organic foods that are labeled "100% Organic," which by definition cannot be produced with non-organic ingredients. The arguments about mandatory labeling are some of the fiercest for consumer activists because many consumers may not realize there is a very strict labeling process in place for organic products.

According to the Cornucopia Institute, a farming watchdog group, "unlike the organic label, no government agency, certification group or other independent entity defines the term "natural" on food packages or ensures that the claim has merit (other than meat, where the USDA has created some extremely modest requirements)" (2011, p.5). Because companies are able to define "natural" without a universal definition of what that might entail, "natural" can be used in promotional materials without any evidence or regulation.

METHOD

In the *Sage Handbook of Qualitative Research* (2011), Bent Flyvbjerg suggests that the straightforward definition of case study found in Merriam-Webster's dictionary (2009) as "an intensive analysis of an individual unit (as a person or community) stressing developmental factors in relation to environment" (p. 301) is an appropriate, commonsensical definition of the methodology. According to Flyvbjerg, "[t]he main strength of the case study is depth—detail, richness, completeness, and within-case variance . . ." compared to more traditional quantitative statistical methods (2011, p. 301).

According to Donaldson and Gini (1996), the case study approach is especially appropriate when used to examine ethical issues because "the end or aim of ethical enquiry is different from that of empirical enquiry. Whereas the goal of empirical enquiry is factual or empirical knowledge, the goal of ethical enquiry is ethical insight" (p. 14). A case study "emphasizes practical reasoning, which is a crucial component of ethical reasoning" (p. 16).

The case study discussed in this chapter examined artifacts, including social media comments on Facebook, Twitter, and YouTube, involved in an organizational response by a major health food company to a social media controversy. The approach is from an ethical perspective, with particular regard to the management of accuracy, transparency, and misinformation. Therefore, the following research question was posed:

RQ1:   How did Kashi utilize social media to respond to an unethical accusation?

RESULTS

Kashi's Predicament

Kashi was founded in 1984 by Philip and Gayle Tauber in La Jolla, California ("What we believe," 2012). The company's goal was to provide cereal and other breakfast items that incorporate whole grains. In 2000 Kashi was purchased by the Kellog Company, another maker of popular cereals. Today, Kashi specializes in breakfast cereals and other breakfast foods, frozen entrées including pizza as well as snack foods. The company advertises its products as a blend of seven whole grains and emphasizes high protein and fiber content. The advertising and promotion of Kashi products is centered on a company that uses "natural" and "simple" ingredients to provide "real" food for consumers.

In April 2012, the owner of a grocery store in Rhode Island pulled Kashi products from his shelves and posted a sign to explain the missing products. The sign on the shelf of the Green Grocer said:

> You might be wondering where your favorite Kashi cereals have gone. It has recently come to our attention that 100% of the soy used in Kashi products is genetically modified, and that when the USDA tested

the grains used there were found to be pesticides that are known car-
cinogens and hormone disruptors. (Where's my Kashi?, 2011)

The photo was posted on Facebook and Twitter by the owner of the Green
Grocer and then went viral even making its way back to a posting on
Kashi's Facebook page. Customers quickly began to post their outrage over
this "deception" and "betrayal" on Kashi's social media platforms. In one
week, the photo had been shared more than 12,000 times on Facebook.

This was not the first time that Kashi's statements had been questioned.
In August 2011, a class action lawsuit was filed against Kashi/ Kellogg
for allegedly misleading consumers with its "natural" claims. The suit
alleged Kashi's act of printing "All Natural" or "Nothing Artificial" on
its packages violated federal and California laws protecting consumers
from false or misleading advertising. Plaintiffs in the class action lawsuit
claimed Kashi mislabeled its products as free of artificial ingredients, even
although some of its products were "composed almost entirely of synthetic
and unnaturally processed ingredients" (*Bates v. Kashi Co.*, 2011).

Furthermore, the Cornucopia Institute affirmed some of these claims
in its October 2011 report "*Cereal Crimes*," in which it compared several
cereals with the "organic" and "natural" labels to inform consumers about
false labeling. The report claimed the presence of GMOs in several Kashi
cereals despite the "natural" label. These two incidents occurred prior to
the Green Grocer incident and received some publicity, but did not spark
anything like the volume of scrutiny that began with a single photo spread
through social media.

The social media backlash toward Kashi caused a flurry of mass media
attention as well because Kashi had been using a very broad mass media
approach to advertise its products. The company regularly placed advertising in magazines, ran television commercials, and created website content
that was heavily focused on the holistic philosophy of the company and
the natural ingredients in its products. The controversy was reported in
The Huffington Post, USA Today, and on various nutrition and wellness
organization websites.

In addition to the possible loss of sales for the company's products,
the Kashi viral photo situation created an ethical issue raised by accusations of consumers and Non-GMO advocates that Kashi had purposefully
employed deceptive advertising. Employing the word "natural" in labels
on food products could give the impression that only wholesome ingredients are being used and that the products do not contain any processed
additives or elements. The use of GMOs technically may not be unnatural
and therefore their use in products described as "natural" is defensible.
Unfortunately for Kashi, based on comments on Facebook, many consumers equate the term "natural" with an "organic" product.

Perhaps Kashi cannot be held responsible for educating all consumers
about the differences between the terms "natural" and "organic" in their

food, but the company's heavy use of the "natural" label in advertisements and other branding efforts clearly seem to have been designed to influence consumer behavior. If Kashi's branding practices led consumers to believe that its products were more natural and holistic than other similar food options, ethically, is the company guilty of making deceptive claims even if they were within the letter of the law? Do consumers have a legitimate right to feel betrayed by Kashi's use of GMOs in its products?

Kashi's Response

Because the accusations spurred mounting critical social media commentary as well as traditional media attention, Kashi decided to respond directly to consumers through its own social media platforms. On April 23, 2012, Kashi posted a short note on its Facebook page with the Green Grocer's photo:

> Thanks for your posts about the information in the photo recently shared on our page. We're committed to providing food you're proud to share with your family. We believe the credible way to provide information about GMOs is through USDA Organic certification and Non-GMO Project Verification. On store shelves now you can find seven of our foods with Non-GMO Project Verification, several others are USDA Organic certified and many more that contain organic ingredients. To learn more, check out Kashi.com/non-gmo

In the following days, two videos were posted on Kashi's YouTube site and then shared through Facebook and Twitter. The videos featured Keegan, a Kashi team member and nutritionist, who suggested that the publicity about GMOs in the company's products portrayed the company inaccurately. In one of the videos, Keegan claimed that GMO use is unavoidable and that Kashi could not control all of the ingredients used in its cereals:

> While it's likely that some of our foods contain GMOs, the main reason for that is because in North America, well over 80% of many crops, including soybeans, are grown using GMOs. Factors outside our control such as pollen drift from nearby crops, and current practices in agricultural storage, handling, and shipping have led to an environment where GMOS are not sufficiently controlled.

Keegan, later in the video, described the efforts that Kashi had made in partnership with the Non-GMO Project, an independent verifier of non-GMO foods, and the only third-party verification system in the U.S. She confirmed that currently seven Kashi products had been verified to be free of GMOs and that those particular products carry the Non-GMO Project Verified seal.

The videos spurred an enormous response by consumers on Facebook. The posting of the first post, in which Kashi acknowledged the photo posted on its page, received 310 responses in the first week. Of those, 85% were negative and the predominant theme of the comments focused on the perceived unethical actions of Kashi in deceiving the public. The second post, in which consumers were able to view the video with Keegan, drew 445 comments in the first week. Again, an overwhelming majority of those responses were negative, primarily accusing Kashi of unethical actions, and criticizing the company for using GMOs. Some examples of consumer comments included:

> "I ate your products for years but will never again buy a Kashi or Kellog product. Hopefully the publicity of your dishonesty will be your ultimate undoing."

> "I appreciate that you are addressing this issue, but I don't know if I want to continue to purchase Kashi Products anymore. I don't mind spending extra money for food products that contain no gmos and are organic, but I feel truly misled."

> "you look like a natural healthy LIAR!!!"

> "So, how long will Kashi keep claiming no research was done, and maybe produce some proof of their own to back up their claim. Love how you shut your customer service lines down while you got your story together"

> "I will wait for more info. before I decide if my kids can eat this safely. I hope this more than just damage control."

> "I will never buy another Kashi product again."

Most of those leaving negative comments expressed outraged about the discrepancies between the advertisements for products and the news about GMO use. The Cornucopia Institute, that produced the report that Keegan was refuting as "inaccurate," issued an immediate response verifying its testing and the presence of GMOs in Kashi cereals.

In a final attempt to restore its battered reputation, Kashi General Manager David DeSouza publicly denied any wrongdoing. In a statement to *USA Today*, DeSouza stated that "Kashi has done nothing wrong" and that "the FDA has chosen not to regulate the term 'natural'" (Weise, 2011, ¶ 4). As further justification, he added as further justification that Kashi provides its own definition of natural on its website: "food that's minimally processed, made with no artificial colors, flavors, preservatives or sweeteners" ("Our food," 2012).

DISCUSSION

Reputation Management

Virtually all organizations are susceptible to a crisis that has the ability to cause not only physical damage and financial loss, but harm to reputation as well. Because an organization's reputation is primarily based on its relations with its key publics, crisis management has become a focus of both public relations academics and professionals. A controversy like this can easily cause reputational damage for an organization. Crisis management is hinged on a timely and accurate response. Organizations have an ethical obligation to respond to their stakeholders (Coombs, 2002) to assure them that there is no possibility of physical or psychological harm to them. Then, organizations can begin to repair their reputation through either corrective action or acknowledgement of the accusations against them. Depending on the degree of responsibility the organization hold for the situation, the response to the stakeholders will be varied. The more control the organization has in a situation the more responsibility one would attribute to that organization in a crisis. A swift and accurate response to consumers can help to minimize reputational damage and uphold the ethical standpoint of the organization.

Kashi was able to use their social media channels to quickly respond to consumers. They acknowledged the Green Grocer photo that was posted to their wall and they gathered a nutritional expert to help justify the findings of GMOs in their products. They also tried to clarify that there were seven products that have been certified as organic and do not contain GMOs. Despite the quick response by Kashi to the concerns of their consumers, the ethics of the organization were still in question due to the intense emotional response from consumers as shown through social media. In contrast to traditional organizational crises, a social media controversy like this one can rapidly intensify. The pace in which information spreads and the formation of groups of dissent from consumers is unique to social media crisis situations.

Moving Forward

In June 2012, just two months after the Facebook photo went viral, Kashi announced two new certified organic cereals: *Simply Maize* and *Indigo Morning*. These two cereals added to the seven other certified "organic" cereals already in Kashi's line. As an additional effort to win back customer support, at the end of 2012, the company launched 'The Kashi Real Project,' a program designed to raise money for nonprofit organizations that promotes natural food and healthy meals for children and families.

These new initiatives were followed by an even bigger announcement in early 2013. Kashi publicly pledged that by the end of 2014, all of its existing products will be Non-GMO Project Verified and, starting in 2015, all new Kashi foods will contain at least 70% organic ingredients and will also be Non-GMO Project Verified.

Despite its initial claims, there was no wrongdoing in labeling its products as "natural," the introduction of new certified organic products and the pledge to stop using GMO ingredients in existing products apparently in response to the social media controversy give credence to complaints that the company's initial social media responses were ethically questionable at best. Furthermore, the initial responses and videos concerning the Kashi viral photo situation in 2012 have been removed from all of Kashi's social media platforms. In fact, as of 2013, Kashi no longer has a YouTube channel.

Social Media Ethical Issues

The ethical issues specific to this case involve the integral role that social media played in every phase of the crisis, particularly the public relations response by Kashi. Stoll (2009) outlines specific criteria for companies when trying to engage in ethical decision-making. He first suggests that companies must pause to gather critical information in order to make good moral decisions. Organizations are then able to listen intently to moral critiques whether they feel they are guilty of the incident or not. Given the amount of attention given to the Kashi controversy and the rapid spread of the Green Grocer photo, it would appear as although Kashi should have given more consideration to the public's perception before responding.

Stoll also suggests that what "corporate moral decision makers must bear in mind [is] the importance of considering the cultural role of the company in question" (p. 8). Kashi very clearly presented an image of being a natural and holistic brand featuring "whole grains" and "real" food. Therefore, the discovery of GMOs in its products was understandably perceived as a betrayal of that image by consumers.

Finally, Stoll stresses that throughout the "decision-making process, company leaders must be attentive to the likely consequences of its decisions upon both the public's sense of corporate character and on the company's ability to meet its other duties to shareholders, employees, and consumers" (p. 6). This process of moral decision-making provides organizations a step-by step guide to ethical decision-making. The public can then be better assured that the organization is considering the ethical implications of its actions and they are portrayed to their publics. In the present case, Kashi displayed an image that many may well have considered false or deceptive; therefore consumers felt that the company was operating unethically by deceiving them.

The information about Kashi's use of GMOs was readily available in the report by the Cornucopia Institute for months. Diligent consumers worried about genetically modified foods and active in the disputes about labeling

GMO products were probably already aware of Kashi's discrepancy, but it was only when the Green Grocer's photo spread throughout social media that the controversy became truly public.

Ethical Implications for the Practice of Social Media

Kashi's initial response was to create a diversion away from the full accusation in the Green Grocer photo. Company spokespersons clearly stated that the credible way to verify whether a product contains non-organic ingredients is through USDA Organic certification and Non-GMO Project Verification. The company highlighted the seven products that fit these guidelines but did not name which products these were. This course of action did not directly address the issues raised by the Green Grocer photo but added more confusion and misinformation that would eventually only anger consumers more as reflected by the Facebook comments.

In the subsequent YouTube video posted on Facebook and Twitter, Kashi did little to reassure the public of its good intentions, but instead claimed that neither it (nor anyone) could control the influx of Non-GMO ingredients into their products because of existing agricultural practices. This response did little to reassure consumers that Kashi was working to improve its use of Non-GMO ingredients, nor did it directly address the claims reported in the Cornucopia Institute report and Green Grocer photo that specifically talked about GMO soy ingredients in Kashi cereals. Could Kashi have addressed the accusations more directly? Would this have helped minimize the negative impact on their reputation with consumers?

Social media provides a unique and instantaneous platform for consumers to communicate with brands and vice versa but this case exemplifies some of the cautions of social media for public relations practitioners. One must always evaluate the accuracy of the information being spread. The photo posted by the Green Grocer was in fact accurate according to the report by the Cornucopia Institute but the photo does not give the source of this information or even reference the "*Cereal Crimes*" report that did the analysis. In contrast, Kashi questioned the science behind that report's testing and even initially said that the information reported was inaccurate. It is important to evaluate information like this with care so that misinformation can be avoided.

In this particular situation, it was even more important to be a little skeptical because the information that was being spread was through a visual image. Images can easily be manipulated and transformed to misrepresent facts. The first step for any consumer or organization should be to verify this information from other sources. There have been many instances where organizations and consumers have been misled because of information traveling too quickly without the correct authentication.

Second, when information is being circulated through channels like Facebook and Twitter, one must be aware of their own accountability for spreading information. Social media is a public space where information remains permanent and easily accessible. One must be careful to avoid involvement in any defamatory or inaccurate rumors.

In the case of Kashi, there were several commenters who were very upset over the use of GMOs and were calling for monetary retribution and legal action against the brand. Legally, Kashi had not been found guilty of false advertising for using the "natural" label on their products. It is important not to get swept up in the fast pace of a social media controversy without due diligence to check for facts. Always try to attribute information to the original sources so that the accountability for information spread is clear.

CONCLUSION

In this case study, the ethics and morals of a corporation were called into question through the channels of social media. Kashi's initial response to consumers on its Facebook page fit all the recommended criteria of crisis management "best practices," but may not have been thought through enough from an ethical perspective to minimize the mounting social media backlash.

It should be emphasized that the Kashi example is not an obvious, outrageous, violation of ethical conduct in terms of public harm. Kirk Hallahan (2006) notes that companies have been guilty of such practices online as using "false-front organizations [where the real identity of sponsors is purposefully withheld]" (p.122) to attack an organization's critics, accessing and taking an active role in chat rooms about a topic but not identifying themselves as company spokespeople, creating confusing look-a-like websites to "divert traffic from legitimate site operators"(p.123), and attempting to hamper searches for information by flooding search engines with "positive" information that reduces the likelihood that negative comments or criticism will be found.

By comparison, the social media controversy involving Kashi might be considered as benign or even trivial by some. That would be an error. This case study looking at the social media ethical issues raised by the actions taken by Kashi was purposely chosen to illustrate the more day-to-day situations that can compromise an organization by raising complex ethical concerns that can arrive without warning. It is vital that public relations practitioners prepare for ethical situations of all shapes and sizes.

In order to minimize reputational damage with consumers, Kashi could have provided more assurance and accurate information in order to clarify the information posted in the Green Grocer photo. In its initial responses, Kashi highlighted the minimal use of non-GMO products and organic cereals, but did not address the deception or betrayal felt by consumers. Therefore, consumers felt that the brand had clearly misrepresented itself as a healthy company using natural ingredients.

Even when industry standards may not regulate the use of a term like "natural" in branding, it is important for companies like Kashi to consider the ethical issues involved in the perceptions given to consumers by that label. Kashi clearly denies doing anything wrong because it did not legally deceive consumers. That definition of wrongdoing may not be enough to appease consumers, creating a social media controversy in which allegations and misinformation spread at an alarmingly rapid rate.

Discussion Questions

1. How should companies such as Kashi be held accountable for deceptive claims?
2. What alternative actions, if any, should Kashi have taken regarding the deceptive claims?
3. Do Kashi's actions create doubt in regard to claims by other "natural" companies?

SUGGESTED READINGS

Carroll, D. (2012). *United breaks guitars: The power of one voice in the age of social media.* New York, New York: Hay House.
Ethical Guidance for Public Relations Practitioners. (n.d.) Retrieved from http://www.prsa.org/AboutPRSA/Ethics
Kang, J. (2012). A Volatile public: The 2009 Whole Foods boycott on Facebook. *Journal of Broadcasting & Electronic Media, 56*(4), 562–577
Lim, M. (2012). Clicks, cabs, and coffee houses: Social media and oppositional movements in Egypt (2004–2011). *Journal of Communication, 62*(2), 231–248.
Wojcieszak, M., & Mutz, D. (2009). Online groups and political discourse: Do online discussion spaces facilitate exposure to political disagreement? *Journal of Communication, 59*, 40–56.

REFERENCES

Bates v. Kashi Co., (2011) No. 11-cv-01967 (S.D. Cal.)
Coombs, T. (2002). Protecting Organization Reputations During a Crisis: The Development and Application of Situational Crisis Communication Theory. *Corporate Reputation Review, 10*(3), 163–176.
Cornucopia Institute. (2011).*Cereal Crimes*. Retrieved from http://cornucopia.org/cereal-scorecard/docs/Cornucopia_Cereal_Report.pdf
Donaldson, T., & Gini, A. (1996). *Case Studies in Business Ethics.* New Jersey: Prentice Hall.
Flyvbjerg, B. (2011). Case Study. In N.K. Denzin & Y.S. Lincoln (Eds.), *Handbook of qualitative research* (pp.301–316). Thousand Oaks, CA: Sage.
Gruère, G. P, & Rao, S. R. (2007). A review of international labeling policies of genetically modified food to evaluate India's proposed rule. *AgBioForum, 10*(1), 51–64.

Hallahan, K. (2006). Responsible Online Communication. In K. Fitzpatrick & C. Bronstein (Eds.) *Ethics In Public Relations: Responsible Advocacy.* (pp. 107–130*)*. Thousand Oaks, CA: Sage.

Lyon, L., & Cameron, G. T. (2004). A relational approach examining the interplay of prior reputation and immediate response to a crisis. *Journal of Public Relations Research*, 16(3), 213–241

Member Code of Ethics. (2012). Public Relations Society of America, Retrieved from http://www.prsa.org/AboutPRSA/Ethics/CodeEnglish

Merriam-Webster's Collegiate Dictionary (11th ed.). (2009). Springfield, MA: Merriam-Webster.

Our food. (2012). Kashi. Retrieved from https://www.kashi.com/our-food

Public Relations Society of America (PRSA) (2012). Code of ethics. Retrieved from http://www.prsa.org/AboutPRSA/Ethics/CodeEnglish/

Stoll, M. (2009) Boycott Basics: Moral Guidelines for Corporate Decision Making. *Journal of Business Ethics*, 84, pp. 3–10.

Weise, E. (2012). Kashi cereal's 'natural' claims stir anger. *USA Today.* Retrieved from http://usatoday30.usatoday.com/money/industries/food/story/2012–04–29/kashi-natural-claims/54616576/1

What we believe. (2012). Kashi, Retrieved from https://www.kashi.com/what-we-believe.

Where's My Kashi? (2011). [Photo] Retrieved from http://healthfulmama.com/2012/04/kashi-the-truth-about-gmos/

Part II
Social Media Policies

5 Private Conversations on Public Forums

How Organizations are Strategically Monitoring Conversations and Engaging Stakeholders on Social Media Sites

Tina McCorkindale

INTRODUCTION

Social Media and Relationships

In 2012, Pew Research Center's Internet and American Life Project reported that 65% of American adults who are online use social networking sites (e.g., Facebook). In 2012, the research center reported 13% of all Americans used Twitter compared to only 8% in 2010. With the increasing popularity of social media, organizations are becoming concerned with how their employees are using these sites both personally and professionally, and are implementing policies to manage the use of social media. Of the organizations that have a social media policy in place, some give much leeway to their employees whereas others restrict the ability of their employees to communicate especially with increased concerns of violating laws such as the Stored Communications Act, National Labor Relations Act, or HIPAA policies, just to name a few (Gevertz & Greenwood, 2010). According to Gevertz and Greenwood, if employers do not develop adequate policies and train employees about these policies, then they may be held liable for the conduct of their employees, which in turn negatively impacts reputation. Many public relations researchers advocate transparency, authenticity, and open communication on social media sites in an effort to improve relationships with various stakeholders. However, the need to protect proprietary information while trying to be open and transparent with various stakeholders, as recommended by many public relations scholars, may create a contradiction.

To build relationships, research indicates practitioners should engage in dialogic communication (Kent & Taylor, 1998; McCorkindale, 2012), but determining how to do so appropriately may be challenging. Although private conversations take place on public forums, there may be a question of ethics in terms of monitoring conversations as well as publicly engaging stakeholders, which may include customers, employees, suppliers, and community members. Few scholars have addressed the ethical issues of "forcing" stakeholders to engage in dialogue (Stoker & Tusinski, 2006) or listening to online conversations. To date, no one has addressed the circumstances under which organizations will engage or not engage with stakeholders.

Solis (2011) stipulates that in order for organizations to engage, they must have the resources and policies, as well as be able to monitor and listen to what their stakeholders are saying online. Failing to appropriately monitor conversations and take appropriate action, if needed, may affect an organization's reputation. As evidenced in recent case studies, so many organizations are placing increased emphasis on their communication efforts on social media outlets (Qualman, 2010). Listening or responding to those who do not think anyone is listening may be an issue in terms of expectations of privacy. Also, according to Chris Boudreaux, Global Social Media Architect at Accenture, brands in highly regulated industries have to be careful in how they respond (personal interview, April 12, 2012).

Transparency in Social Media

With social media come the opportunity for organizations to engage with a wide variety of publics, both from an internal and an external standpoint. Tapscott and Ticoll (2003) posit organizations need to be transparent to facilitate relationship building and boost employee morale. Rawlins (2009) developed a stakeholder measure of organizational transparency, which includes a set of reputation traits (integrity, respect, and openness) and communication efforts (participation, substantial information, accountability, and secrecy). Social media allow organizations to display an authentic and transparent side of communication where individuals can be responsible for an organization's communication efforts. Also, transparency may help restore trust and improve an organization's reputation (Gower, 2006).

Rawlins (2009) defined transparency as having three important elements: "information that is truthful, substantial, or useful; participation of stakeholders in identifying information they need; and objective, balanced reporting of an organization's activities and policies that holds the organization accountable" (p. 74). However, transparency does not mean an organization should disseminate more information; rather, information must meet standards of openness, responsibility, and accountability (Gower, 2006).

In 2007, the Arthur W. Page Society published the *Authentic Enterprise Report*, which indicated one of the most significant challenges facing organizations today is the issue of trust. Moreover, corporations must demonstrate authenticity in "radically open environments" with integrated stakeholders, especially in the face of new media (p. 3). While scholars and public relations practitioners suggest transparent, open, and authentic communication should guide an organization's social media strategy, this notion may be contradicted by an organization's social media policies or mission. Therefore, determining how social managers engage with stakeholders in an ethical context is important for answering these questions.

Ethical Considerations

Few researchers have studied ethics in social media. However, specific ethical approaches that may impact how organizations respond or interact with stakeholders can be applied to social media sites. The concept of *ethic of care* focuses on doing what is right using the principles of care and concern. According to Coombs and Holladay (2007), "The ethic of care's focus on interdependence, mutuality, and reciprocity mirrors our perspective on public relations . . . We cannot choose to ignore a relationship with a stakeholder simply because it is not that important to us" (p. 32). The ethic of care revolves around the understanding that self and others are interdependent (Stoker & Walton, 2009). Considering the core of public relations is building and maintaining mutually beneficial relationships, Stoker and Walton wrote, "The ethic of care moves beyond thinking about the relationship in terms of organizational or personal rights and places an emphasis on relationships and an organizations responsibility to relationships created under its care" (p. 11). However, organizations may violate this principle if they choose to focus on certain social media users such as those with a high number of followers.

Corporations are now creating tools to identify the most important online influencers. Because of the public nature and manner in which information is disseminated among social networks, if organizations choose to solely focus on these individuals without focusing on others who need help then this would violate the ethic of care. Similarly, resource dependency theory states that organizations are more likely to pay attention to stakeholders who control resources critical to the organization than those who do not control resources (Rogers & Gago, 2004). With social media, this resource could be reputation. According to Jones, Felps, and Bigley (2007), companies should be attentive to both salient stakeholders as well as discretionary (legitimate but not urgent) because of the long-term benefits associated with moral behavior. With instrumental stakeholder theory, social media managers must balance the interests of all stakeholders (Shankman, 1999). Research has not examined whether organizations are more likely to pay attention to some stakeholders than others.

One area that has received a great deal of attention in the organizational literature is corporate social responsibility (also referred to as social responsibility and corporate citizenship). According to L'Etang (1994), one justification for these types of programs is "enlightened self-interest," which suggests both the corporation and community benefit. When an organization is motivated by their self-interest, then they may in fact engage in an exploitative relationship by not considering the needs of the stakeholder.

Researchers have argued that scholarship in applied ethics has focused on the importance of other-regarding rather than self-regarding in decision-making processes and behavior (Jones et al., 2007). Kant's deontological approach suggested that an act performed for reasons of personal benefit may not be as moral as an act performed out of duty. Organizations experience a tension where their self-regard may conflict with their regard for other (Jones et al., 2007). Therefore, stakeholders should be treated as ends in themselves and not means to an end (Jones et al., 2007; Shankman, 1999). Social media users who interact on behalf of the organization must be sensitive to the needs and the concerns of the stakeholders (Murphy, Laczniak, & Wood, 2007).

Research Questions

Understanding how organizations engage and interact with stakeholders using social media is important. With social media sites becoming more prevalent in the public domain, organizations may have to proactively or reactively communicate with stakeholders. Therefore, determining how an organization decides to engage or not with stakeholders should be explored.

Therefore, this study will answer the following research questions:

RQ1: How are organizations generally using social media and how important is it to their organization?
RQ2: What is the extent to which social media managers monitor conversations on social media?
RQ3: Under what conditions do organizations engage with stakeholders on social media sites?
RQ4: What is the potential backlash or negative effects of engagement?
RQ5: What conditions influence the organization to respond to stakeholders or not?

METHODOLOGY

Semi-structured interviews of 16 individuals who manage some aspect of social media in their organizations were conducted from January 2012 to May 2012. An additional expert in social media governance was also chosen to participate for a total of 17 interviews. Participants were selected based on the number of fans/followers and the perception of their organization's success in social media. Participants were given the option to participate without releasing their name or their organization's name. For these four participants, a pseudonym and a white-label organizational description were given. Participants were also given the option of receiving a $50 gift card for their participation. Participants were asked questions regarding their organization's philosophy and use as well as their personal approach to social media to support their organization's strategy. The length of interviews ranged from 18 minutes to one hour, with an average interview length of 30 minutes. Participants were also given the option of reviewing this chapter prior to publication. The organizations included nine corporations, four nonprofits, a public relations firm, a military organization, and an expert in social media governance. Specifically, this included: Kraft Foods, Dell, Doctors Without Borders, Conservation International, charity: water, UPS, Army, Ketchum Digital, Alcoa, Discern Digital (representing a multinational mass media company), a multinational aerospace company, a national insurance company, a multinational networking company, a global consumer and commercial products organization, and an arts and entertainment nonprofit.

RESULTS

Usage and Importance of Social Media

The importance of social media to the organizations the interview participants represented cannot be understated. Not surprisingly due to the selective nature of the interview participants, social media were critical for all organizations and all felt the need to participate. Nearly all the participants emphasized the importance of social media for engaging and driving conversations as opposed to using the platforms as channels for information dissemination. Robert Anderson, vice president of Digital Marketing and eCommerce for a global consumer and commercial products organization, said even if a company is not on social media, conversations are happening. For his organization, "the conversation was loud and large and once we entered we gave it a home."

In terms of use, customer service tended to be the most frequent external use. Debbie Curtis-Magley, UPS's social media manager, said UPS's customer service team is very active in responding to customer service issues on both Facebook and Twitter. Customer service also extended to receiving praise from satisfied customers. In some cases, this praise was recognized or retweeted. An unnamed senior manager of social media with a national insurance company, also said if a stakeholder said something great, then they may retweet as well.

However, not all companies had a customer service aspect because of the nature of their business may not be consumer-focused. Mark Kasperowicz, global manager for Digital Brand Marketing and Social Media at Alcoa, said shareholders, analysts, and financial journalists communicate often with their company as Alcoa tweets and posts earnings on social media as they are released. Listening and investor relations are a "big part" of what they do on social media.

The organizations frequently interacted with stakeholders who were not customers on social media sites. Several interview participants mentioned they received questions regarding job opportunities at their organizations. Participants also mentioned the importance of social media for internal use. Dell were extensively educates their employees about properly using social media with extensive training programs for all its employees to help them use social media effectively.

The Army uses social media sites for both their internal and external stakeholders, including the soldiers' families. Staff Sergeant Dale Sweetnam, of the Online and Social Media Division in the Office of the Chief of Public Affairs of the Army, said the Army has developed best practices based on what they learned from using social media channels in the past. He said although they may have some "naysayers," as a whole, the work of the Army has been "incredibly productive" on social media sites. In fact, the Army's foray into Pinterest was highlighted in a February 2012 article in *Mashable* (see Fitzpatrick, 2012). According to Sweetnam:

> We've taken our communication and distributed to a much broader audience than we could have possibly imagined seven to eight years ago. We know that instead of hoping that the media or the press goes to the Army website and picks up a press release that these 1.4 million on Facebook can see the content we put out there on our news feed . . .There's a great deal of value and the senior leadership can see the value. They're using it also.

Jonathan Kopp, partner and global director at Ketchum Digital, said with the social web, all lines are blurred. According to Kopp, there is an important opportunity for every organization whether for profit or not, regulated or not, B2B or B2C, with social media. Every organization can be social and he said that if they are not, they are missing opportunities. He said, "We're blurring the line between sales and service. Everyone's business is customer service. We counsel our clients that they must listen and monitor, as well as engage and create relationships."

Monitoring

The majority of organizations in this study were listening and monitoring their social media channels. One of the challenges organizations face is the public nature of the conversation. Robert Anderson (global consumer and commercial products organization) said individuals may not realize the extent to which organizations are monitoring. For example, one job applicant applied for two brands and said on a social media site that he wanted to work for this brand, but not the other. Anderson said, "If someone is doing this now online, what will they say after they are hired?" Similarly, Marcia Morgan, senior manager of Strategic Marketing for a multinational networking company, said her company had the same experience. A potential applicant tweeted they thought a recently offered job may be "boring," which sparked a conversation online about how companies are listening.

Several participants emphasized the importance of listening in online conversations. Chris Coletta online engagement coordinator with

Conservation International, said Conservation International "listens before we speak. If we aren't listening, then we aren't participating in a conversation." Sweetnam (Army) said by listening to conversations he has learned that the audience loves videos and photos and his group typically limits the postings to two per day. He said, "The only way to determine what the audience wants is to listen."

Sue Sonday, president of Discern Digital, said listening and monitoring helps the multinational mass media company she represents to strengthen their marketing plan. On social media sites, her client's overall goal is to generate buzz and increase awareness prior to her client's film opening to increase the number of viewers who go see the movie.

All interview participants monitored and listened to at least one social media site. Paull Young, director of Digital Engagement for charity: water, said, "I don't think we miss a tweet. We read all of them." The nonprofit does so organically and Young says the organization is "glued" to social media sites. Sweetnam said the Army does listen to stakeholders, but thought "monitor" was a tricky word. He said the Army does not monitor, but instead reviews what is posted on their Facebook wall, which is one of their strongest social media channels.

Although the majority of interview participants carefully monitored social media sites for mentions of their organizations, some said that when they contacted stakeholders who had talked about their respective organizations, the stakeholders were surprised. Cory Edwards, director of Social Media and Online Reputation with Dell, said his team's philosophy is to respond to those who publicly say they have issues on social media. He states that customers are "shocked" that Dell is proactively monitoring and are "surprised and delighted" when Dell engages.

Frequency of Interaction

The overwhelming answer as to the conditions in which organizations interact with various stakeholders was "it depends on the situation." A senior manager (national insurance company) echoed the sentiment of most interview participants when they said, "While we don't respond to everything, we do review everything on our company branded assets."

Although most organizations in this study monitored social media, some responded to nearly everyone but others responded infrequently. Donna Sitkiewicz, director of Corporate Employee and Online Communications with Kraft Foods, said on the corporate side, the company responds to almost everyone, but in some cases a person does not need or expect a response. Whether to respond or not depends on the situation. She said:

> What is the right action? If it's a product issue we respond. If someone is inflammatory, then we may not respond. If we have already responded, and if we have already replied, are they trying to start up

again? In social media, so much is about judgment and assessing context. It's hard to be cut and dry.

On Twitter, Curtis-Magley (UPS) said the company interacts with most of the individuals who mention them. But, UPS does not have to respond to everything because it is a community. "We chime in and thank people for feedback. We respond to a lot of comments on the blog, which provides us an opportunity to add additional insight." This also depends on the social media site. Although UPS is engaging at YouTube, the nature of commentary at the channel does not necessitate that same level of support that customers at Twitter and Facebook expect.

Kasperowicz (Alcoa) said if someone says something positive or inquisitive, he will engage by retweeting or thanking the individual for the mention. Also, when a member of the media asks a question, Alcoa engages. "Engaging outside the community is par for the course," he said.

Some of the organizations tried to answer all questions or respond to all mentions even if it is a daunting task. Anderson (global consumer and commercial products organization) said it would be too overwhelming for his organization to respond to every time someone mentioned his organization. Instead, his group scours for customer service issues and then sends them to the appropriate team. The organization joins conversations where they think they can add value. He said, "You have to make choices as to when you're going to step in."

Similarly, Morgan (multinational networking company) said they do not respond to every mention because of the sheer volume. Morgan, as well as other organizations, allowed the community to dictate the social media use. Her company uses it more for customer service and according to her, responding to these issues are "no brainers." Their social media use is more customer-service related because that is what the community has dictated.

According to Sonday (Discern Digital), her client's goal is primarily monitoring and amplifying although they do engage in dialogue. Positive comments may be retweeted and some questions answered, but not all questions are answered. On the other hand, Lynn Williams, senior manager of new media with a multinational aerospace company, said her company does try to respond to everyone and rarely ever ignores a question or post. Depending on the situation, the company may respond with a direct message versus a public message.

Edwards (Dell) said if anyone publicly states an issue with Dell on a community forum that is public and searchable, the Social Outreach Services team will proactively reach out to them offering for Dell to jump in to help. He said:

> If you think about traditional customer technical support, usually it's a very reactive model. We give you software, we give you hardware, and if you have a problem, you tell us and we'll help you. In this case we're

looking for people who have a problem and proactively reaching out to people to fix it.

Compared to corporations, nonprofits typically have fewer resources available to them, but there was not a reported difference in how the interview participants from nonprofits used social media accounts. Coletta (Conservation International) said his organization tries and responds to everyone under the premise that if someone is interested enough to ask a question, then Conservation International will try to answer. He added, "We're not perfect but we try. . . . Otherwise, you're staring at them with a blank face. We try to participate with others and be included in the conversation." Conservational International also thanks their followers and fans for posting about them.

Social media has also allowed nonprofits to have an additional space where they can receive donations. Julie Whitaker, social media strategist for Doctors Without Borders, said they may thank someone who donated, but it's more on a limited basis depending on time. She added, "We don't put great pressure on ourselves to respond to everything." Paull Young (charity: water) said his nonprofit does not solicit donations on social media sites.

Williams (multinational aerospace company) said what is different about her organization on social media sites is it is not consumer-oriented although they have many fans of their business. She said many of their posters frequently ask about employment opportunities. Other interview participants also said their organization received a significant number of employment-related inquiries so knowing the right channels to direct those inquiries is important.

Negative Comments or Criticism

One of the challenges for many of the organizations in this study was how to respond to comments online, especially those that may not portray the organization is a positive light. Some research (McCorkindale, 2010) has suggested organizations may sanitize their Facebook pages, meaning they remove non-offensive comments that portray the organization negatively, but this was not the case with any of the organizations interviewed in this study. All the organizations had received negative comments in some form or another and none of them deleted comments based merely on the negative tone of the post but rather if the comment was offensive or inflammatory. Those dealing with customers or activist groups had more negative comments than other organizations. It should be noted that some negative comments were not necessarily directed to the organization, but rather a poster venting about an issue.

Most said they would remove offensive comments, but they also reported their organizations had guidelines for their social media communities about the right to remove these types of comments. For the most part, participants in this study reported their respective organizations received little criticism. Some participants were surprised by this, and expected their organizations to receive more criticism.

Delia Hamilton, manager of marketing with an arts and entertainment nonprofit, is selective about how she interacts with those on social media because of the time issue. She said she responds to negative comments because she "wants to be honest and transparent." Coletta (Conservation International) said criticism of his organization is welcome, and he believes it contributes to the discussion:

> We don't respond to anything that is personal, uncivil, or hateful. Some people don't agree with our model. We just say we have a difference in opinion. We respect their opinion, and we agree or disagree. Sometimes backlash is a good thing. If you show that you have a willingness to have a discussion, then that becomes part of the brand.

Stakeholders who had issues or complaints typically received attention from the organizations, but posters who were rude, offensive, or disrespectful were either ignored or were reminded about policies. Hamilton (an arts and entertainment nonprofit) said if in a rare case someone on Facebook is being rude or inappropriate, her organization responds publicly or privately depending on the situation, provides the individual with their policy, and tells them that they appreciate the input but they expect people to be responsible on social sites.

Other times, negative reactions from stakeholders may have positive results. Whitaker (Doctors Without Borders) said whereas her organization may have advocacy campaigns over which a couple people may disagree, these typically end positively. Sometimes stakeholders just want the organization to listen to their concerns.

For the most part, the interview participants' reported that their organizations reached out to customers who were having issues to hopefully find a resolution. Curtis-Magley (UPS) said most people were pretty receptive about engaging whereas sometimes people just wanted to be angry or chose not to engage. She added, "People are generally respectful, and how and if we engage depends on the community. While we do monitor, we may not give input in all circumstances because it's not appropriate."

With other organizations that faced crises, responding on social media channels is extremely important. According to Kasperowicz (Alcoa), "We'll have our share of what we refer to as "crises" where we may have a situation at one of our facilities. The community may be wondering what happened. We can proactively communicate and correct information that is inaccurate."

In some cases, organizations expect to get criticism on social media sites, and must be prepared to deal with it. In April 2012, Kraft Foods (along with other Fortune 100 companies), left the conservative lobbying group, American Legislative Exchange Council (ALEC). After their departure,

Kraft Foods received criticism for their decision but Sitkiewicz said they asked themselves, "Where do we want to want to stand on this issue and can we support it over time?" She said this philosophy has helped Kraft build a strong reputation by making sure they do the right thing.

Cory Edwards (Dell) said the company has not received much negative backlash when contacting a customer about an issue that he or she discussed on a public forum:

> It's not like we're getting on the phone and calling them. It's that we saw a tweet. It's a pretty nonthreatening thing. It's a comment to a blog post, it's a reply to a tweet, it's just a simple touchpoint offering to help them out.

This strategy has been extremely successful for Dell. He continued:

> One out of every three people we engage online who expresses dissatisfaction with a product, end up posting something positive after we engage with them. They will turn around and post back to the same medium used previously about how thrilled they were with their support experience. They go from being demoters to promoters.

To Respond or Not to Respond

Similar to how an organization responds to negative comments, it is also important to understand the circumstances in which an organization may or may not respond. Although trade publications may discuss the importance of influentials on social media sites, to most of the interview participants, the number of followers or friends did not make a difference in terms of how likely the organization was to respond. An unnamed senior manager (national insurance company) said:

> We don't just respond to people who only have a large number of followers. Everyone deserves assistance if needed. For those that need help, we contact them and ask what we can do. Sometimes they respond and sometimes they don't. We want to get them to a place where things can be resolved to their satisfaction.

There were mixed results as to whether organizations would retweet positive comments or respond to praise from a follower or fan. To demonstrate listening, some organizations retweeted their stakeholders' tweets especially if there was positive praise for the organization. Others did not. What was consistent across the board was all organizations were listening and monitoring social media.

Whitaker (Doctors Without Borders) said her organization listens and if someone needs help, they will direct them to the appropriate person. If someone complains, which she said they rarely do, they will respond on Facebook or Twitter usually directing them to email or call one of the teams.

Some organizations discussed how their stakeholders may use the social media sites to air their frustrations. Anderson (global consumer and commercial products organization) said he believes:

> Sometimes it's best to let people have conversations and sometimes you have to let the conversation flow and not be the Big Brother on top of it. Some people who had something happened or if we try and can't do something, we let them vent.

Several participants also said with issues relating to lawsuits or financial performance, the organization typically listened to the conversations, but did not respond. For example, Morgan (multinational networking company) said although her organization keeps track of financially-related postings, they are careful with how they respond to not violate any laws or regulations.

Similarly, Curtis-Magley said UPS steers away from conversations dealing with financial performance. Also, in UPS's case, they had a plane crash several years ago in Dubai. During this time, the company had limited ability to comment or discuss due to the regulatory authorities' investigations. She said, "In this case, we monitored conversations closely. We refrained from responding to commentary related to the investigation, but we did reply to those who offered their condolences."

For some participants, they said a "no response" approach may be their best approach. Robert Anderson (global consumer and commercial products organization) told a story that his company had an issue on their Facebook page with money his company donates to a specific cause. In one instance, a group of moms posted nearly every hour for a week on the company's Facebook page trying to pressure the organization into giving money to a different charity. Anderson said he felt bad the company could not give to this charity as well, but the company thought if they opened the door to one, then other groups may follow suit. Ultimately, the organization chose not to respond. In this case, the community supported the organization and told the posters that their tactic of continuously posting on the organization's Facebook page was not appropriate. It was the community that provided guidance for how to handle the situation. Understanding the role the community plays in dictating social media use is crucial.

Multiple organizations reported the community also maintains order and will respond to stakeholder issues. For example, Hamilton (arts and entertainment nonprofit) said many times the community will respond or answer questions so the organization does not always have to. Some of the tech organizations interviewed said their community is extremely helpful on technical support issues.

Williams (multinational aerospace company) said because of the nature of her organization, the company has many activists. Although they do not post directly, they do tweet about the organization on their own Twitter account. Generally, the organization does not engage with activists because they view this as a "no-win" situation. This sentiment was echoed with many interview participants; only a couple conversed with activists on social media sites.

CONCLUSION

Compared to previous research that suggests organizations are still using one-way communication without a strategy, this was not the case with the organizations represented by the interview participants. All organizations were very strategic in how they monitored and engaged on social media. Although there were differences among the participants in terms of when they would or would not engage in conversations on social media sites, it was clear that every organization was listening and monitoring conversations. They all saw the value in gathering insight from the social media communities. Considering the sheer number of mentions most of these organizations receive in a given day, this was surprising. Overall, every organization was focused on monitoring and listening to conversations on social media sites, although some organizations were not engaging as much as others. Interview participants also mentioned stakeholders' surprise the organization was listening. It seemed that some stakeholders regarded their interactions on public sites as private conversations in public forums. However, this conversation interruption to help the stakeholder if needed was well received the vast majority of the time.

Organizations seemed to know at what point they should respond to stakeholders who mentioned them on social media, but it was based more on personal judgment rather than organization protocol. Some organizations chose to respond and have conversations with more stakeholders than others. If a stakeholder had a question or a customer had an issue, then for the most part, the organization responded. Some tried to respond to nearly every social media post, but others used an "it depends" approach. However, if the individual was offensive in their post, then the organization was less likely to respond and more apt to delete the post.

Organizations differed as to whether they responded to positive comments from individuals who were not necessarily seeking a response. Some simply replied with "thanks", whereas others retweeted the posts to their followers. However, none of the organizations retweeted every post. There were mixed results in terms of the frequency of interaction. Overall, the organizations were strategic as to how they engaged and under what circumstances. It appeared that most organizations' response to stakeholders was situational. They all saw the value of social media in terms of how it can benefit both the organization and its public.

The majority of interview participants appeared to truly care about their communities and wanted to ensure their stakeholders' needs were met. They wanted to provide information and satisfaction to the various stakeholders who engaged. They also used the information received from monitoring to improve their communication, thereby imbibing a two-way symmetrical communication strategy. When organizations interjected themselves into the conversation, they did so with the perspective that they were helping out the stakeholder. Most of the interviewees focused on providing stakeholder value as opposed to driving organizational needs. Relating to Kant's deontological perspective (Jones et al., 2007), only one organization regarded the stakeholders as a means to an end, rather than an end, but this appeared to be situational. However, this may not be representative of other organizations, as these organizations were chosen specifically for their social media usage.

Also, all organizations faced some sort of negative comments or backlash from participating on social media sites, but some were just from activist groups or trolls. Most of the organizations indicated that they respond to negative consumer comments if they thought engaging could help the person. Organizations were less likely to engage with activist groups because they did not think it would be productive.

Ethical Implications for the Practice of Social Media

From an ethical standpoint, many adopted the *ethic of care* to do what was right for their stakeholders. Organizations did not report giving more attention to those stakeholders who had more clout or influence than others. For the most part, the organizations felt an obligation to respond to the public. Therefore, organizations did not adhere to the resource dependency theory. However, the exception to this was with activist groups. A couple organizations chose not to engage because they did not think it would do any good. Therefore, this was an ethical egoist approach, in that "it is necessary and sufficient for an action to be morally right that it maximize one's self-interest" (Stanford Encyclopedia of Philosophy, 2010, p. 1).

Most of the organizations were strategic in how they engaged. They used value judgments to determine what was appropriate or inappropriate. The interview participants also mentioned the evolutionary nature of social media. They tried to stay on top of the latest trends as much as possible, but most pointed to how difficult it is to keep up, and to educate their employees on best practices in terms of use.

According to the participants, managing social media is time consuming and resource heavy. A couple organizations had only one person devoted to managing social media. Overall, social media management was a team effort, which included members from multiple departments in the organization. Participants also said they worked with other departments on social media strategy to ensure it benefited the entire organization, and not just one specific function, such as customer service. As Boudreaux (personal interview, April 12, 2012) maintained, one area alone cannot be responsible for social media because other areas, such as the supply chain, customer service, and marketing, are all impacted by social media. He added:

> You can't expect one person to determine how to use social media throughout your business. You have to involve people from each functional area and business unit to collectively determine how you use social media across your organization. It's a lot like IT, in that way.

Limitations

Limitations of this research include the limited and purposive nature of the sample. All the participants were willing to share best practices and talk about what their organization was doing, even if they chose not to disclose their name or organization. Approximately 30% of the organizations I contacted did not want to participate or did not respond to my interview requests.

There was no right or wrong way as to how the organizations interacted and engaged on social media sites. The organizations tended to behave in terms of what best fit the organization's overall strategy. Although they all employed the recommended two-way communication and engagement model, how they engaged was unique to each organization. In some cases, what best fit was the result of trial and error to find out what worked and what did not. There appeared to be a fine line that organizations must decide whether or not to cross when engaging or not engaging with stakeholders. In closing, Paull Young (charity: water) said it best, "We're social. It's in the core of how we operate. It's how we do business." The different organizations may have different styles, but they are all doing what works best for them. Regardless, all organizations appeared to be "uniquely" strategic in their social media use, and they all understand the importance of engaging and building relationships with stakeholders.

Discussion Questions

1. What are the ethical implications of only engaging with stakeholders who have clout or influence?
2. How may the size and type of organization affect social media use?
3. How important is monitoring and measuring social media?

SUGGESTED READINGS

DiStaso, M. W., & McCorkindale, T. M. (2013). A benchmark analysis of the strategic use of social media for Fortune's most admired U.S. companies on Facebook, Twitter, and YouTube. *Public Relations Journal, 7*(1), 1–33

Li, C., & Bernoff, J. (2011). *Groundswell: Winning in a world transformed by social technologies.* Boston: Harvard Business School Press.

Rawlins, B. (2009). Giving the emperor a mirror: Toward developing a stakeholder measurement of organizational transparency. *Journal of Public Relations Research, 21*(1), 71–99.

Solis, B. (2011). *Engage: The complete guide for brands and businesses to build, cultivate, and measure success in the new web.* Hoboken, NJ: Wiley.

Stoker, K. L., & Tusinski, K. A. (2006). Reconsidering public relations' infatuation with dialogue: Why engagement and reconciliation can be more ethical than symmetry and reciprocity. *Journal of Mass Media Ethics, 21*(2–3), 156–176.

REFERENCES

Arthur W. Page Society. (2007). The authentic enterprise report summary. Retrieved from http://www.awpagesociety.com/images/uploads/AE_Summary_4.pdf

Coombs, W. T., & Holladay, S. J. (2007). *It's not just PR: Public relations in society.* Malden, MA: Blackwell.

Fitzpatrick, A. (2012, February 16). The U.S. Army uses Pinterest? Sir, yes sir. Retrieved from http://mashable.com/2012/02/16/army-uses-pinterest/

Gevertz, D., & Greenwood, G. (2010). Crafting an effective social media policy for healthcare employees. *Health Lawyer, 22*(6), 28–33.

Gower, K. K. (2006). Truth and transparency. In K. Fitzpatrick & C. Bronstein (Eds.), *Ethics in public relations: A responsible advocacy* (pp. 89–106). Thousand Oaks, CA: Sage.

Jones, T. M., Felps, W., & Bigley, G. A. (2007). Ethical theory and stakeholder related decisions: The role of stakeholder culture. *Academy of Management Review, 32*(1), 137–155.

Kent, M., & Taylor, M. (1998). Building dialogic relationships through the World Wide Web. *Public Relations Review, 24*(3), 321–334.

L'Etang, J. (1994). Public relations and corporate social responsibility: Some issues arising. *Journal of Business Ethics, 13,* 111–123.

McCorkindale, T. (2010). Can you see the writing on my wall? A content analysis of the Fortune 50's Facebook social networking sites. *Public Relations Journal, 4*(3). Retrieved from http://www.prsa.org/Intelligence/PRJournal/Documents/content_analysis
_of_the_fortune_50s_facebook.pdf

McCorkindale, T. (2012). Twitter me this, Twitter me that: A quantitative content analysis of the 40 Best Twitter Brands. *Journal of New Communications Research 2011 Anthology,* 43–60.

Murphy, P. E., Laczniak, G. R., & Wood, G. (2007). An ethical basis for relationship marketing: A virtue ethics perspective. *European Journal of Marketing, 41*(1–2), 37–57.

Pew Internet and American Life Research Project. (January 2012). What Americans do online. Retrieved from: http://www.pewinternet.org/Trend-Data/Online-Activites-Total.aspx

Qualman, E. (2010). *Socialnomics: How social media transfer the way we live and do business.* Westford, MA: Courier Westford.

Rawlins, B. (2009). Giving the emperor a mirror: Toward developing a stakeholder measurement of organizational transparency. *Journal of Public Relations Research, 21*(1), 71–99.

Rodgers, W., & Gago, S. (2004). Stakeholder influence on corporate strategies over time. *Journal of Business Ethics, 52,* 349–363.

Shankman, N. A. (1999). Reframing the debate between agency and stakeholder theories of the firm. *Journal of Business Ethics, 19,* 319–334.

Solis, B. (2011). *Engage: The complete guide for brands and businesses to build, cultivate, and measure success in the new web.* Wiley.

Stanford Encyclopedia of Philosophy. (2010). Ethical egoism. Retrieved from http://plato.stanford.edu/entries/egoism/

Stoker, K. L., & Tusinski, K. A. (2006). Reconsidering public relations' infatuation with dialogue: Why engagement and reconciliation can be more ethical than symmetry and reciprocity. *Journal of Mass Media Ethics, 21*(2–3), 156–176.

Stoker, K., & Walton, S. (2009). *Corporate compassion in a time of downsizing: The role of public relations in cultivating and maintaining corporate alumni social networks.* Institute for Public Relations. Retrieved from: http://www.instituteforpr.org/topics/corporate-compassion/

Tapscott, D., & Ticoll, D. (2003). *The naked corporation: How the age of transparency will revolutionize business.* New York: Free Press.

6   To Tweet or Not to Tweet

An Analysis of Ethical Guidelines for the Social Media Engagement of Nonprofit Organizations

Marcus Messner

INTRODUCTION

Leading nonprofit organizations in the United States are setting the pace for social media adoption among public relations practitioners. As early studies on the use of Facebook, Twitter, and other social media platforms have shown, large nonprofit organizations utilized these new communication platforms early on for community engagement, fundraising, and to monitor their brands. According to Barnes and Mattson (2009), the 200 largest charities in the U.S. had outpaced the business community with a 97% usage rate for social media in 2009.

As nonprofit organizations play an important role in American society to provide services from health care and community education to youth development and crime prevention, it is essential to study the social media use and strategies of this growing sector of the U.S. economy.

Nonprofits constitute about 10% of the American economy with 13 million employees and around $300 billion in revenues (Kanter & Fine, 2010), and the adoption of social media allows organizations to directly communicate with their audiences as well as allows their audiences to directly communicate with them. Whereas this new two-way communication environment presents great opportunities for nonprofit organizations to circumvent traditional media channels and their gatekeepers, it also creates new challenges in the direct engagement of employees with their audiences on social media platforms.

The goal of the study presented in this chapter was to analyze the development and implementation of social media policies and guidelines at nonprofit organizations that guide their engagement and provide best practices for public relations practitioners. The study first evaluated the frequency and duration of the social media engagement and in a second step the policy and guideline implementations. The study broadened the approach in this area through a national survey of nonprofit organizations of all sizes and in a broad spectrum of nonprofit sectors with a focus on social media engagement on six leading platforms.

LITERATURE REVIEW

Nonprofit Organizations and Social Media

Social media platforms such as Facebook, Twitter, and YouTube have gained great popularity among Internet users as well as media professionals. Other platforms such as Google+, Tumblr, and LinkedIn have also secured a following of millions of users. Subsequently, most news organizations are now disseminating their content via these platforms, and public relations practitioners have been quick in their adoption as well. Wright and Hinson (2011) found that 84% of practitioners believe that social networks like Facebook are important to the public relations efforts of their organization; 72% believe the same for microblogging sites like Twitter, and 71% for video sharing sites like YouTube. In addition, McCorkindale (2010) found a strong engagement of major corporations on Facebook. However, the findings of the study also showed that engagement still lacked effectiveness.

Due to the implications of social media on public relations practice, the body of research in this area has been continuously growing over last few years (Avery, Lariscy, Amador, Ickowitz, Primm, & Taylor, 2010; Waters, Tindall, & Morton, 2010; Vorvoreanu, 2009). One of the largest sectors within the field of public relations in the U.S. consists of more than 1.5 million nonprofit organizations. Nonprofit organizations have also been at the forefront of social media adoption and outpaced the corporate sector between 2007 and 2009 (Barnes & Mattson, 2009). Nah and Saxton (2012) found that organizational features, capacities, governance features, and external pressures impact the adoption and use of social media by nonprofit organizations. Curtis, Edwards, Fraser, Gudelsky, Holmquist, Thornton, and Sweetser (2010) also found that an organization with a public relations department was more likely to adopt social media. However, recent studies have also shown that current social media engagement of nonprofit organizations mainly constitutes a one-way communication strategy (Greenberg & MacAulay, 2009; Muralidharan, Rasmussen, Patterson, & Shin, 2011; Lovejoy, Waters, & Saxton, 2012; Messner, Jin, Medina-Messner, Meganck, Quarforth, & Norton, 2013).

Much of current research in this area focuses on the adoption and use of a specific social media platform by nonprofit organizations. Lovejoy and Saxton (2012), for instance, analyzed the functions of different categories of Twitter updates. Waters and Lo (2012) and Lo and Waters (2012), on the other hand, explored the behavior and communication patterns by nonprofit organizations on Facebook. However, research on the engagement of nonprofit organizations on other popular social media platforms besides Facebook and Twitter has been limited at this point. This is surprising in so far as platforms like YouTube, Google+, and LinkedIn rank among the most popular websites in the U.S. (Alexa. com, 2012), and vastly growing platforms such as the microblogging site Tumblr are increasingly popular among teenagers and educated users in urban areas (Duggan & Brenner, 2012). This study, therefore, attempted to first analyze the level of engagement of nonprofit organizations across various popular social media platforms.

Social Media Engagement and Ethical Guidelines

The widespread adoption of social media has changed how the public communicates about and with organizations. The old one-way communication model of mass communication is replaced by the need to engage the public through two-way communication. This presents challenges for hierarchical organizations that have structured lines of communication (Kanter & Fine, 2010). As shown by the example of the widely popular viral video Kony 2012 and its disappointing effect on actual audience action, social media engagement can only be successful if organizations maintain a continuous communication with their audiences and their ethics remain unquestioned by audiences that are likely to move quickly on to other topics (Greenblatt, 2012a, 2012b). As Henderson and Bowley (2010) pointed out, it is important for nonprofit organizations that audiences perceive the organizations' social media engagement as authentic, which in turn leads to questions about organizations' control over the engagement and the formulation of ethical guidelines for their employees.

Up to this point, very little attention has been paid to ethical issues surrounding the use of social media by nonprofit organizations. Much more attention has been paid to such guidelines in corporations, especially in professional publications. Hay (2010) wrote that "Having clear guidelines in place to promote good practice and encourage a positive use of social media can help safeguard any business from negative feedback and potential bad publicity" (n.p.). Hallett (2013) also distinguished between social media policies and guidelines as follows: "Corporate policies should focus on behavior that can get an employee disciplined or terminated. Social media netiquette guides and best practices are another discussion" (n.p.).

The lack of attention to the nonprofit sector is surprising in so far as many scholars have focused on ethics and new media public relations for several years, especially involving new media formats such as blogs (Burns, 2008; Craig, 2007). As engagement in social media demands transparency and credibility, many news media organizations have also developed and implemented ethical guidelines for social media (Bell, 2010). Although there is no current research on ethical social media guidelines for nonprofit organizations, Liu (2012) found that communicators at nonprofit organizations in the U.S. see laws and regulations, along with employee engagement among the main challenges of their social media engagement. Kanter (2013) stressed that "in some nonprofits the relationship between in-house legal counsel or the organization's lawyers is based on fear and control" (n.p.). Kanter (2013) points out, however, that it is important that the social media policy of an organization "is a living document that reflects current practice" (n.p.) and that various legal and ethical issues are addressed in the document.

Ward and Wasserman (2010) have argued that social media engagement for media organizations needs to be conducted through the creation of "an 'open media ethics' and offers an exploration of how these developments encourage a transition from a closed professional ethics to an ethics that is the concern of all citizens" (p. 275). Nonprofit organizations are faced with the same ethical challenges of social media engagement and are thereby important subjects for the study of social media uses as well as campaign and ethical guideline implementations. Kanter and Fine (2010) stress that as nonprofit organizations mature in their social media engagement, they can ensure by developing social media policies that "senior staff has fully embraced and taken responsibility for social media use. It also provides direction for individual staffers to know what they can and cannot do" (p. 55). This study, therefore, attempts to analyze the state of social media policies and guidelines in the nonprofit sector and evaluate how implementation and development are connected to the maturity of the social media engagement.

Research Questions

Based on the above literature review the following research questions were derived:

RQ1:   How frequently do nonprofit organizations engage on popular social media platforms?

RQ2:   How do nonprofit organizations develop and implement ethical guidelines for their engagement on social media?

RQ3:   How does the duration and frequency of social media engagement impact the implementation of ethical guidelines at nonprofit organizations?

METHODOLOGY

This study used a national web-based survey that targeted 1,915 non-profit organizations in the U.S. The organizations were sampled from the "200 Largest U.S. Charities" list by Forbes magazine as well as the website Nonprofitlist.org, which allowed sampling from all 50 states and the District of Columbia. Although all of the 200 largest charities were included, nonprofit organizations from each state were selected through a stratified random sampling technique. A random starting point was selected and every 20th organization was sampled for each state. This allowed for the representation of nonprofit organizations from different sizes as well as from different geographic locations. The email address for the main communications officer at each organization was recorded from their website. If an organization did not have a communications officer listed on its website, the senior executive's email address or the organization's general email address was recorded.

A survey instrument with close-ended questions was created that asked respondents about the duration and frequency of their social media engagement for their organizations on Facebook, Twitter, YouTube, Google+, Tumblr, and LinkedIn, which are all among the most popular and widely used social media platforms and websites in the U.S. (Alexa.com, 2012). In addition, questions about organizational social media policies and guidelines were asked as well as questions about their development and implementation. Respondents were also given the opportunity to provide additional insights about their social media policies and engagement in an open-ended question.

The survey was carried out between December 5, 2012 and January 17, 2013. The organizations in the sample were contacted four times via email during the time period. In addition, the link to the survey was posted on relevant pages and groups for nonprofit organizations on Facebook and LinkedIn and was posted on Twitter with relevant hashtags for the nonprofit community. The use of this technique resulted in 395 completed surveys.

The final sample included responses from organizations in 44 states and the District of Columbia. No responses were recorded from Hawaii, Kentucky, Montana, North and South Dakota, as well as Wyoming. Of the overall respondents, 77% (n=304) were female, 93.4% (n=369) had a college degree, and 57.7% (n=228) described social media as one of their current primary job functions. The ages of the respondents were distributed evenly with 50.4% (n=199) under 40 and 49.6% (n=196) more than 40 years old. In addition, 71.9% (n=284) of the respondents described to be in a supervisory role at their organizations and 68.1% (n=269) had worked at their organizations for five or fewer years. 68.4% (n=270) of the organizations in the sample employed fewer than 50 people. The organizations came from a variety of different sectors, including 16.5% (n=65) from education, 15.2% (n=60) from health, 11.1% (n=44) from cultural, and 10.1% (n=40) from youth related areas. Plus, 35.7% (n=141) of the organizations described their geographic reach as local, 26.8% (n=106) described it as statewide, 9.6% (n=38) as regional with several states, 11.7% (n=46) as national, and 16.2% (n=64) as international.

RESULTS

Frequency of Social Media Engagement

In the national survey of nonprofit organizations in the U.S. conducted for this study, 95.4% (n=369) of respondents said that they use Facebook,

Table 6.1   Duration of Engagement by Social Media Platform

Social media platform	Fewer than 2 years	2-5 years	More than 5 years	Don't use/ Don't know
Facebook	40.3% (n=159)	46.3% (n=183)	6.8% (n=27)	6.6% (n=26)
Twitter	44.1% (n=174)	31.4% (n=124)	3.0% (n=12)	21.5% (n=85)
YouTube	33.7% (n=133)	31.6% (n=125)	7.8% (n=31)	26.8% (n=106)
Google+	21.3% (n=84)	3.0% (n=12)	0% (n=0)	75.7% (n=299)
Tumblr	10.3% (n=41)	1.5% (n=6)	0.5% (n=2)	87.6% (n=346)
LinkedIn	30.4% (n=120)	12.9% (n=51)	2.8% (n=11)	53.9% (n=213)
Average	30.0% (n=118.5)	21.1% (n=83.5)	3.5% (n=13.8)	45.4% (n=179.2)

78.5% (n=310) use Twitter, and 73.2% (n=289) use YouTube. However, the user rates for the other three platforms were lower with only 46.1% (n=182) of respondents saying that they use LinkedIn, 24.3% (n=96) use Google+, and 12.4% (n=49) use Tumblr. When asked about the duration of their use of the different social media platforms, respondents said that they were earlier adopters of Facebook, Twitter, and YouTube than they were of the other three platforms. Almost half of the respondents had used Facebook between two and five years at the time of the survey and about a third had used Twitter and YouTube. There had also been a strong increase in the adoption of Facebook, Twitter, and YouTube in the two years before the survey. On the other hand, there was hardly any use of Google+ and Tumblr two to five years ago and only very little of LinkedIn. Although LinkedIn and Google+ have seen greater adoption among nonprofit organizations during the two years before the survey, the adoption of Tumblr has been low throughout (see Table 6.1).

Table 6.2   Number of Weekly Content Postings by Social Media Platform

Social media Platform	Fewer than 1 post	1-10 posts	11-20 posts	More than 20 posts
Facebook	14.2% (n=56)	68.9% (n=272)	12.4% (n=49)	4.6% (n=18)
Twitter	31.9% (n=126)	43.3% (n=171)	13.7% (n=54)	11.1% (n=44)
YouTube	85.8% (n=339)	7.3% (n=29)	0.5% (n=2)	6.3% (n=25)
Google+	79.7% (n=315)	5.8% (n=23)	1.3% (n=5)	13.2% (n=52)
Tumblr	82% (n=324)	4.3% (n=17)	0.8% (n=3)	12.9% (n=51)
LinkedIn	81% (n=320)	9.1% (n=36)	0.3% (n=1)	9.6% (n=38)
Average	62.5% (n=246.7)	23.1% (n=91.3)	4.8% (n=19)	9.6% (n=38)

When asked about the frequency of their engagement on the six social media platforms, the majority of the respondents indicated that it only regularly engages on Facebook and Twitter. Around four-fifth of the respondents do not post any kind of content on YouTube, Google+, Tumblr, and LinkedIn on a weekly basis. On Facebook, however, 68.9% (n=272) of the respondents publish one to 10 posts every week, 12.4% (n=49) between 11 and 20 posts, and 4.6% (n=18) more than 20 posts. On Twitter, 43.3% (n=171) of the respondents post between 1 and 10 posts every week, 13.7% (n=54) between 11 and 20 posts, and 11.1% (n=44) more than 20 posts (see Table 6.2).

Development and Implementation of Ethical Guidelines

Of the nonprofit organizations questioned in the national survey, 35.9% (n=142) indicated that they have a written policy that describes ethical guidelines for the social media engagement of employees and volunteers. An additional 24.1% (n=95) of the respondents said that their organizations have verbally provided ethical guidelines. Although 21.5% (n=85) of the respondents said that their organizations have no policy or guideline for their social media engagement, 18.5% (n=73) said that they did not know whether organizational policies or guidelines were in place. 38.2% (n=151) of the respondents said that their organizations' social media engagement is mainly guided by management decisions and 28.6% (n=113) said that the staff is mainly responsible. 2.5% (n=10) of the organizations mainly rely on outside consultants to guide the social media engagement.

The respondents were also asked for which social media platforms policies and guidelines existed in their organizations. The results showed that 44.8% (n=177) have a policy or guideline specifically for Facebook, 36.2% (n=143) for Twitter, 19.5% (n=77) for YouTube, 11.1% (n=44) for LinkedIn, 4.8% (n=19) for Google+, and 4.6% (n=18) for Tumblr. The most common issue addressed in organizational policies and guidelines were ethical standards at 37.7% (n=149) of the organizations, organizational goals at 33.7% (n=133), work responsibilities at 32.7% (n=129), personal responsibilities at 27.9% (n=110), community building 27.6% (n=109), legal standards and requirements at 26.8% (n=106), transparency at 21.8% (n=86), and authenticity at 21% (n=83).

However, the respondents did not view social media in general as very likely to cause an ethical problem for their organizations. Although Facebook is considered by 44.8% (n=177) of the respondents to be the main platform that can cause ethical problems, only 6.6% (n=26) of the respondents think the same about Twitter, and 4.6% (n=18) about YouTube. Less than 1% think that Google+, Tumblr, and LinkedIn likely to cause ethical problems for them.

Impact of Engagement Duration and Frequency on Implementation of Ethical Guidelines

The survey results also show that the longer and more frequent nonprofit organizations engage on social media, the more likely they are to have

Table 6.3   Policy/Guideline Adoption Based on Duration of Facebook Engagement

Type of policy/ guideline	Facebook (fewer than 2 years)	Facebook (2-5 years)	Facebook (more than 5 years)
Written	27% (n=43)	41.5% (n=76)	51.9% (n=14)
Verbal	23.9% (n=38)	25.1% (n=46)	33.3% (n=9)
Don't know	22.6% (n=36)	13.7% (n=25)	7.4% (n=2)
None	26.4% (n=42)	19.7% (n=36)	7.4% (n=2)
Total	100% (n=159)	100% (n=183)	100% (n=27)

implemented ethical guidelines for their engagement. When analyzing the frequency and duration of the engagement on the two most used platforms Facebook and Twitter, it becomes apparent that the adoption of written and verbal ethical guidelines increases with the increase in frequency and duration. Only 27% (n=43) of the nonprofit organizations that started their Facebook engagement in the last two years have a written policy, but 51.9% (n=14) of the organizations with more than 5 years of Facebook engagement have such a policy (see Table 6.3). A similar trend can be detected for Twitter. Although 35.1% (n=61) of the nonprofit organizations that started their Twitter engagement in the last two years have a written policy, 75% (n=9) of the organizations with more than 5 years of Twitter engagement do (see Table 6.4).

When analyzing the results for the type of implemented policy based on the frequency of the engagement on Facebook and Twitter, the likelihood of an organization having a written ethical policy is also higher with a more frequent engagement. Although 21.4% (n=12) of organizations who do not post regularly every week on Facebook have a written policy, 37.5% (n=102) of organizations who post one to 10 times per week, and 46.9% (n=23) of those who post 11 to 20 times have such a policy. On the other hand, the percentage decreases for those organizations with more than 20 Facebook posts per week, but it is still higher than the one for the less engaged organizations (see Table 6.5). For Twitter, the results also

Table 6.4   Type of Policy/Guideline Based on Duration of Twitter Engagement

Type of policy/ guideline	Twitter (up to 2 years)	Twitter (2-5 years)	Twitter (more than 5 years)
Written	35.1% (n=61)	41.1% (n=51)	75% (n=9)
Verbal	24.7% (n=43)	27.4% (n=34)	25% (n=3)
Don't know	20.1% (n=35)	12.9% (n=16)	0% (n=0)
None	20.1% (n=35)	18.5% (n=23)	0% (n=0)
Total	% (n=174)	% (n=124)	% (n=12)

Table 6.5   Type of Policy/Guideline Based on Frequency of Weekly Facebook Engagement

Type of policy/ guideline	Fewer than 1 post	1-10 posts	11-20 posts	More than 20 posts
Written	21.4% (n=12)	37.5% (n=102)	46.9% (n=23)	27.8% (n=5)
Verbal	14.3% (n=8)	25% (n=68)	26.5% (n=13)	33.3% (n=6)
Don't know	26.8% (n=15)	17.3% (n=47)	16.3% (n=8)	16.7% (n=3)
None	37.5% (n=21)	20.2% (n=55)	10.2% (n=5)	22.2% (n=4)
Total	100% (n=56)	100% (n=272)	100% (n=49)	100% (n=18)

Table 6.6   Type of Policy/Guideline Based on Frequency of Weekly Twitter Engagement

Type of policy/ guideline	Fewer than 1 post	1-10 posts	11-20 posts	More than 20 posts
Written	25.4% (n=32)	40.9% (n=70)	37% (n=20)	45.5% (n=20)
Verbal	25.4% (n=32)	21.1% (n=36)	33.3% (n=18)	20.4% (n=9)
Don't know	19% (n=24)	19.9% (n=34)	14.8% (n=8)	15.9% (n=7)
None	30.2% (n=38)	18.1% (n=31)	14.8% (n=8)	18.1% (n=8)
Total	100% (n=126)	100% (n=171)	100% (n=54)	100% (n=44)

showed that engaged organizations are more likely to have a written policy. Although 25.4% (n=32) of organizations who do not post regularly every week on Twitter have a written policy, 40.9% (n=70) of organizations who post one to 10 times per week, and 37% (n=20) of those who post 11 to 20 times have such a policy. The highest adoption rate of a written policy is at 45.5% (n=20) for organizations with more than 20 weekly posts on Twitter (see Table 6.6).

DISCUSSION & CONCLUSION

This study attempted to analyze the development and implementation of ethical social media guidelines and policies at nonprofit organizations in the U.S. Results show that the development of ethical policies and guidelines increased at the organizations in the study's sample as their social media engagement matured over time and increased in frequency as measured by content postings per week. Whereas the overall social media engagement on the six platforms in the study still has room for improvement, the adoption rate for polices and guidelines has already reached 60% at these organizations. This is remarkable as the sample included many small non-profit organizations as well. It is surprising to see, however, that only very few address specific platforms in their guidelines, despite the fact that most social media engagements of nonprofit organizations focus specifically on Facebook, Twitter, and YouTube. It seems that the ethical guidelines of nonprofit organizations are more concerned with the overall social media engagement of the organization than the day-to-day operations of individual platforms. This big picture approach is also stressed by the fact that only few specific social media platforms are seen as an ethical challenge.

Ethical Implications for the Practice of Social Media

Many organizations surveyed for this study took the opportunity to provide additional insight on their social media engagement and elaborated on the ethical policies and guidelines they implemented. The respondents described the balance between personal and professional time on social media as one of the areas that needs to be addressed in organizational guidelines. One nonprofit social media manager wrote that "I'm realizing that my organization might need some policies on social media. It's a difficult decision because we do community organizing, so staff members are connected to the community via Facebook and that is important to us. At the same time, social networking really blurs professional and personal time."

Many respondents also described the rigid nature of social media policies as having a chilling effect on an effective staff engagement. "I am aware of prominent nonprofits that have very rigid social media guidelines that are more of a hindrance to their community engagement than anything else. Social media continues to be a balancing act of responsibility and productivity for many organizations," wrote one practitioner. Another one added that "Policies and guidelines should be supportive of staff use of social media as organizational ambassadors, and should be very easy to follow—or else they will either be ignored, or feel too restrictive to encourage active community building."

The theme that emerged from the responses is that it is most effective for the social media engagement an organization when management and staff make a collaborative effort to develop ethical guidelines. "We are a small enough staff that we developed guidelines together—using expert guidance we searched for online as a basis. In larger organizations, I think the danger is much greater for unethical use/bad PR and so policies are more important and require management input," wrote one respondent. Another one wrote that "Our non-profit is so small that I think we know and trust our employees to use social media wisely. The larger an organization, the more opportunity for inappropriate content to be posted, and therefore a greater need for parameters."

The results of this study show that although many nonprofit organizations already have social media policies in place, there is still much room for improvement as well. Almost every fifth respondent stated in the survey that they did not know whether their organization had some sort of guideline for an ethical social media engagement and many other were aware that they did not have one. Nonprofit organizations who have not done so should take the results of the survey as motivation to develop their own guidelines. As some responses showed, the moment ethical problems occur in the social media engagement, the implementation of rigid guidelines is likely to be the consequence. "Our policy appears to have been created as a reaction to some regrettable incident. I recognize the importance of oversight and guidelines, but the review process instituted at my organization makes it impossible to move at the speed necessary to use social media effectively. There must be a balance of clear guidance and trust in the person tasked with using these media," wrote one nonprofit social media manager. Proactive steps within an organization that bring social media managers, executives, and legal experts together in a collaborative effort to develop effective guidelines are to be the best practice to avoid ethical problems before they can turn into a crisis on Facebook, Twitter, and the other popular platforms.

Limitations and Future Research

As with all research, this study has limitations. As the study attempted to target a national sample of nonprofit organizations in the U.S., it displays combined results for social media engagements and ethical guidelines at small and large organizations. Future research should attempt to study differences between large and small organizations as they can range from an international organization campaigning for human rights, to a community health nonprofit organization. Many nonprofit organizations are also active at the international level. Although this study only analyzed responses from nonprofit organizations about their social media engagement and their ethical guidelines, future research should content analyze a sample of nonprofit social media guidelines to develop best practices for the nonprofit sector and compare the high standards of ethical guidelines with the actual day-to-day engagement on social media.

Discussion Questions

1. Which common themes as well as differences do you find when comparing the ethical social media guidelines of national or international nonprofit organizations? Which best practices for the ethical social media engagement in the nonprofit sector do the guidelines display?
2. Can the ethical guidelines for the social media engagement at national and international nonprofit organizations be applied to a local nonprofit organization in your community? Which areas in the guidelines have to be changed, erased, or added?

3. Conduct research online on ethical problems that have arisen from the social media engagement of nonprofit organizations. How could written social media policies at these organizations have prevented these problems? Or could they have not?

SUGGESTED READINGS

Kanter, B., & Fine, A. (2010). *The networked nonprofit: Connecting with social media to drive change.* Jossey-Bass: San Francisco, CA.

Lovejoy, K., Waters, R., & Saxton, G. D. (2012). Engaging stakeholders through Twitter: How nonprofit organizations are getting more out of 140 characters or less. *Public Relations Review, 38*(2), 313–318.

Messner, M., Jin, Y., Medina-Messner, V., Meganck, S., Quarforth, S., & Norton, S. (2013). 140 characters towards a better health: An exploration of the Twitter engagement of leading nonprofit organizations. In Hana Noor Al-Deen and John Allen Hendricks (Eds.). *Social Media and Strategic Communication.* Palgrave Macmillan.

Nah, S., & and Saxton, G. D. (2012). Modeling the adoption and use of social media by nonprofit organizations. *New Media & Society, 15*(2), 294–313.

Ward, S. J. A., & Wasserman, H. (2010). Towards an open ethics: Implications of new media platforms for global ethics discourse. *Journal of Mass Media Ethics, 25,* 275–292

REFERENCES

Alexa.com (2012). Top sites in United States. Retrieved from http://www.alexa.com/topsites/countries/US.

Avery, E., Lariscy, R., Amador, E., Ickowitz, T., Primm, C., & Taylor, A. (2010). Diffusion of social media among public relations practitioners in health departments across various community population sizes. *Journal of Public Relations Research, 22*(3), 336–358.

Barnes, N. G., & Mattson, E. (2009). *US charities' adoption of social media outpaces all other sectors for the third year in a row.* Retrieved from http://www1.umassd.edu/cmr/studiesresearch/charitystudy.pdf.

Bell, J. (2010). Clearing the AIR. *Communication World, 27*(1), 27–30.

Burns, K. S. (2008). The misuse of social media: Reactions to and important lessons from a blog fiasco. *Journal of New Communications Research, 3*(1), 41–54.

Craig, D. A. (2007). Wal-Mart public relations in the blogosphere. *Journal of Mass Media Ethics, 22*(2–3), 215–218.

Curtis, L., Edwards, C., Fraser, K. L., Gudelsky, S., Holmquist, J., Thornton, K., & Sweetser, K. D. (2010). Adoption of social media for public relations by nonprofit organizations. *Public Relations Review, 36*(1), 90–92.

Duggan, M., & Brenner, J. (2012). The demographics of social media users—2012. *Pew Internet & American Life Project.* Retrieved from http://www.pewinternet.org/Reports/2013/Social-media-users/The-State-of-Social-Media-Users.aspx

Greenberg, J., & MacAulay, M. (2009). NPO 2.0? Exploring the Web presence of environmental nonprofit organizations in Canada. *Global Media Journal— Canadian Edition, 2*(1), 63–88.

Greenblatt, A. (2012a). How teenagers learned to hate Joseph Kony. *National Public Radio.* Retrieved from http://www.npr.org/2012/03/09/148305533/how-teenagers-learned-to-hate-joseph-kony

Greenblatt, A. (2012b). The social media shuffle: From Kony to spooning. *National Public Radio*. Retrieved from http://www.npr.org/2012/04/19/150964208/young-people-turn-from-kony-to-spooning-record.

Hallett, J. (2013). What strategies should global organizations adopt when creating social media guidelines? *PR Week*. Retrieved from http://www.prweekus.com/what-strategies-should-global-organizations-adopt-when-creating-social-media-guidelines/article/294334/.

Hay, P. (2010). Social media—What's your policy. *PR Week*. Retrieved from http://www.prweek.com/article/1041541/digital-social-media-policy—whats-policy.

Henderson, A., & Bowley, R. (2010). Authentic dialogue? The role of "friendship" in social media recruitment campaign. *Journal of Communication Management, 14*(3), 237–257.

Kanter, B. (2013). A nonprofit's legal counsel is the social media manager's best friend. *Beth's Blog*. Retrieved from http://www.bethkanter.org/legal-counsel-friends/.

Kanter, B., & Fine, A. (2010). *The networked nonprofit: Connecting with social media to drive change.* San Francisco: Jossey-Bass.

Liu, B. F. (2012). Toward a better understanding of nonprofit communication management. *Journal of Communication Management, 16*(4), 388–404.

Lo, K. D., & Waters, R. D. (2012). New technologies, new cultural traditions: The impact of Facebook on Chinese nongovernmental organizations. *China Media Research, 8*(4), 99–110).

Lovejoy, K., & and Saxton, G. D. (2012). Information, community, and action: How nonprofit organizations use social media. *Journal of Computer-Mediated Communication, 17*, 337–353.

Lovejoy, K., Waters, R., Saxton, G. D. (2012). Engaging stakeholders through Twitter: How nonprofit organizations are getting more out of 140 characters or less. *Public Relations Review, 38*(2), 313–318.

McCorkindale, T. (2010). Can you see the writing on my wall? *Public Relations Journal, 4*(2), available at http://www.prsa.org/Intelligence/PRJournal/Documents/content_analysis_of_the_fortune_50s_facebook.pdf.

Messner, M., Jin, Y., Medina-Messner, V., Meganck, S., Quarforth, S., & Norton, S. (2013). 140 characters towards a better health: An exploration of the Twitter engagement of leading nonprofit organizations. In Hana Noor Al-Deen and John Allen Hendricks (eds.). *Social Media and Strategic Communication*. Palgrave Macmillan.

Muralidharan, S., Rasmussen, L., Patterson, D., & Shin, J. H. (2011). Hope for Haiti: An analysis of Facebook and Twitter usage during the earthquake relief efforts. *Public Relations Review, 37*(2), 175–177.

Nah, S., & Saxton, G. D. (2012). Modeling the adoption and use of social media by nonprofit organizations. *New Media & Society, 15*(2), 294–313.

Vorvoreanu, M. (2009). Perceptions of corporations on Facebook: An analysis of Facebook social norms. *Journal of New Communications Research, 4*(1), 67–86.

Ward, S. J. A., & Wasserman, H. (2010). Towards an open ethics: Implications of new media platforms for global ethics discourse. *Journal of Mass Media Ethics, 25*, 275–292.

Waters, R. D., & Lo, K. D. (2012). Exploring the impact of culture in the social media sphere: A content analysis of nonprofit organizations' use of Facebook. *Journal of Intercultural Communication, 41*(3), 297–319.

Waters, R. D., Tindall, N. T. J., & Morton, T. S. (2010). Media catching and the journalist-public relations practitioner relationship: How social media are changing the practice of media relations. *Journal of Public Relations Research, 22*(3), 241–264.

Wright, D. K., & Hinson, M. D. (2011). A three-year longitudinal analysis of social and emerging media use in public relations practice. *Public Relations Journal, 5*(3), available at http://www.prsa.org/intelligence/prjournal/documents/2011wrighthinson.pdf.

Part III

Corporate Responsibility

7 Social Media as a CSR Communication Channel

The Current State of Practice

Kati Tusinski Berg and Kim Bartel Sheehan

INTRODUCTION

According to a 2010 study on Social Media Influence by Custom Communications, firms rarely use social media to inform the public about their brands' Corporate Social Responsibility (CSR) activities. At the same time, these same firms use social media (such as Twitter, Facebook, and blogs) for other branded promotions. Social media is popular; since the Social Media Influence study was published, consumer use of social media has increased to the point that a quarter of time spent online is spent on social media. Social media is powerful; it helps individuals find others who share their interests and convictions, as well as its power to strengthen community ties. This study investigates whether brands' usage of social media reflects the increase in consumer use, specifically regarding brands' use (or avoid using) social media to communicate CSR activities. In addition, we examine whether consumers respond to CSR messages at the same rates as other types of branded messages.

This research adds to the small body of literature on CSR channels, identifying the types of CSR messages delivered in social media channels and understanding decision-making processes and motivations for placing these messages.

LITERATURE REVIEW

CSR is defined as a company, firm, or brand's "commitment to improve societal well- being through discretionary business practices and contributions of corporate resources" (Kotler and Lee, 2005). As such, CSR encompasses the "economic, legal, ethical and discretionary expectations that society has of organizations at a given point in time" (Carroll, 1979). Whereas many firms have always participated in CSR activities, the use of CSR as a marketing tool has increased over the past several decades (Becker-Olsen & Hill, 2006). Perhaps as a result of the increased use of CSR, today's consumers and other firm stakeholders expect businesses to act responsibly. Globally, we are seeing the emergence of a global business ethic; specifically, a growing sense among society that the responsibility for righting social wrongs belongs to all organizations. At the same time, there is a growing business need for increased attention to business ethics in order to reduce operating uncertainties and to be able to manage their reputations in both calm and stormy seas.

Firms participating in CSR activities can reap several benefits. First, CSR activities can enhance a brand's corporate reputation (Fombrun & Shanley, 1990; Menon & Kahn, 2003) and consumers often see these brands as caring about society (Sen & Bhattacharya, 2001). Boston College's Reputation Institute assessed consumer perceptions regarding CSR activities of firms and found that companies like Johnson & Johnson, Walt Disney Company and Kraft Foods have a high level of CSR activities that correlate with their positive reputations. Companies with poor perceptions among consumers tended to be in industries with major reputation challenges such as automotive and financial services (Boston College Reputation Institute, 2010). These findings support other research that shows that stakeholders such as consumers, employees, and investors take actions to reward good corporate citizens, and to punish bad ones (Du, Bhattacharya & Sen, 2007).

Companies with strong CSR reputations also benefit because consumers often chose to buy products from companies with strong CSR reputations, employees want to work for those companies, and investors chose to invest in those companies. As a result, brands with strong CSR reputations have an opportunity to turn these different stakeholders into brand ambassadors, stimulating positive word of mouth (Du et al, 2007).

CSR Communication

A small but growing body of literature has investigated strategic and tactical approaches to CSR communication. Building on the idea of legitimacy strategy, researchers have identified two types of strategic approaches to CSR communication: reactive and proactive (Wagner, Lutz & Weitz, 2009).

With a reactive strategy, the firm communicates CSR information in reaction to some event or crisis facing the industry and/or the firm (van Staden and Hooks, 2007), increasing legitimacy through the quality of the response. With a proactive strategy, a company's CSR communication is designed to prevent any legitimacy concerns that may arise. Interestingly, though, regardless of which type of strategy a brand or firm chooses, overall awareness of the firms' CSR activities is generally low among both internal stakeholders (employees) and external stakeholders (consumers) (Du, Bhattacharya, & Sen, 2010). Communications strategies then often may not resonate well with some stakeholders. Perhaps the positive ratings seen by companies such as Johnson & Johnson are less the result of a strong CSR campaign but instead are based on an individual's past involvement with the firm and its brands or with the individual's own information search.

For some brands, consumers are aware of CSR messages yet are skeptical of such messages (Bronn & Vrioni, 2001). Consumer skepticism increases as messages become more aggressive (Pirsch, Gupta, & Grau, 2007). Consumers seem to want to determine whether a firm's CSR activities are extrinsically or intrinsically motivated: that is, whether a company uses such messages merely to increase profits (an extrinsic motivation) or if the company seems to want to truly do something positive for society (an intrinsic benefit) (Schiefelbein, 2012). One key challenge for CSR messaging, then, is to minimize stakeholder skepticism and convey intrinsic motives for CSR activities. In fact, stakeholders are tolerant of extrinsic motives as long as CSR initiatives are attributed to intrinsic motives as well (Sen, Bhattacharya & Korschun, 2006).

Of particular interest to this study is CSR media channel selection, as limited research in this area exists. Media selection can affect a consumer's perceptions on a firm's motivations. For example, Philip Morris's CSR television campaign promoted its Kraft brand's food donations to refugees in Kosovo. The actual donation though, was much less than the millions of dollars spent on the TV campaign, and consumers responded negatively (Sheehan, 2004). Promoting this message through a less-expensive channel might have made all the difference in consumers' perceptions of the firm. More recently, BP's television and print campaigns airing after the Gulf oil spill received similar criticisms.

When selecting media channels, one important factor is the degree of control the channel allows. Some channels have a high level of control, giving the firm complete or near complete control of the message. Such channels include official CSR reports and press releases, brand-based websites, television commercials, and product packaging. Other channels offer less control as consumers and other communicators interact with, adapt, or respond to the message. Such channels include word of mouth, consumer forums and rating sites, and social media such as Facebook, Twitter, and blogs.

Whereas many firms prefer a high degree of control, reduced control has benefits. Messages delivered from low control channels tend to be more credible than messages from high control channels, as individuals are more likely to trust these messages (Du, Bhattacharya & Sen, 2010). Given this focus on community engagement, it would seem CSR messages would be a clear fit with social brands. Where such messages might reside and have a high degree of impact is not clear, since social media offers a variety of "outposts" where CSR messages would live, (such as Facebook, Twitter, YouTube, branded communities, and geo-location platforms). Brands use these different outposts for different reasons, and discovering which outpost, (or channel), is most utilized helps to learn how CSR messages might evolve for social brands.

Social media sites such as Facebook offer a moderate level of control as brands can post messages, videos, images, and the like at a social network site and allow consumers and other stakeholders to participate in a dialogue with the brand. Stakeholders become a key element in the firm's external environment that can affect the organization (Murray & Vogel, 1997). Social media makes CSR information accessible to more people more of the time. Additionally, social media can encourage "citizen philanthropy," a movement where consumers connect with all types of organizations through meaningful social networking. One successful example is Lance Armstrong's Livestrong initiative, which raised awareness and funds for cancer research through a variety of community-building activities.

Given the power of social media, it is surprising that Custom Communications reports only 22.5% of 287 companies have social media communications dedicated to CSR issues such as sustainability. In an April 2011 white paper, Greenstein and Watson suggested that companies were avoiding using social media for CSR until there was greater adoption by consumers. Given the huge growth in social media usage since Greenstein and Watson's white paper, we propose that current usage of social media for CSR should be investigated with the following research questions:

RQ1:   Do brands use social media for CSR activities?
RQ2:   What types of CSR activities do companies discuss via social media?
RQ3:   Do consumers respond to CSR messages in social media as they respond to other types of messages?

RESEARCH PLANS

To answer these questions, we conducted two studies. First, a study of the types of messages on popular Facebook sites identified CSR activity and consumer responses to the different types of messages posted at such sites to see the level of frequency and engagement. Next, a content analysis of top brand social networking sites was conducted to confirm the findings from the SMI study and to identify the types of CSR activities being discussed on such sites. The content analysis also determined the level of consumer interaction on the site via a social media audit.

Together, these studies will map the landscape of CSR communication channels and will provide guidance for a range of firms to better create and target CSR messages.

Study 1: CSR at Popular Facebook Sites

The top ten most popular branded Facebook sites were identified, and eight of these sites were examined during the month of August 2011. Facebook was selected to be examined because it is the most popular social outpost with more than 500 million users worldwide. At the end of 2011, Facebook was used by one in every 13 people on earth, with over 250 million people (over 50%) logging in every day (Digital Buzz, 2011). The eight sites selected had the highest number of people who "liked" the page, and included Coke (33.4 million fans), Converse (20 million fans), Disney (28 million fans), MTV (27 million fans), Oreo Cookies (23 million fans), Redbull (22.1 million fans), Skittles (19.2 million fans), and Starbucks (24.6 million fans). These eight brands all have CSR activity: Coke promotes energy and resource conservation, Converse is affiliated with project Red, Disney is involved with sustainability and children's causes, MTV campaigns against cyber bullying, Oreo is part of Kraft Food's CSR promotions to support sustainability and family causes, RedBull supports volunteering, Skittles is part of Wrigley's CSR promotions to support environmental issues, and Starbucks promotes several causes, including Fair Trade issues. Two other branded pages rounded out the top ten, but were both focused on Facebook itself and thus were not included.

A total of 274 posts were made by brands on these eight sites during the month of August. Of these 274 posts, only one was a CSR message: Disney posted about donations made to children's hospitals, a proactive post. Therefore, it is clear that the most popular brands rarely use CSR messages on their social brand Facebook pages.

These brands' posts all generated significant commentary from fans. Commentary, such as "liking" a post or adding a comment to a post, is a good measurement of engagement among the community (Smith, 2011). The mean number of "likes" to the average comment made during the time period examined was 8,334 (.035% response); Disney's CSR post generated 27,738 "likes" (.099% response). The mean number of comments made by fans to the average comment during the time period examined was 901 (.006% response); Disney's CSR post generated 870 (.003% response). Disney's CSR post generated a higher percent of "likes" among the site's fans than the average post on a top-eight site, although the CSR post generated fewer comments than a top-eight site.

Study 2: CSR at the World's Most Sustainable Companies

A content analysis of top brand social networking sites was conducted to confirm the findings from the SMI Social Media Sustainability Index study and to identify the types of CSR activities being discussed on such sites. The content analysis also determined the level of consumer interaction on the site via a social media audit.

The SMI report lists 15 companies that are using social media for smart sustainability communications. Because the report specifically highlighted these companies, they were used as the sample for the content analysis. The following companies were analyzed: AMD (Advanced Micro Devices, Inc.), Allianz, Dell, Microsoft, PG&E, Fed Ex, Ford, General Electric, Intel, IBM, PepsiCo, Starbucks, BBVA, Philips and Nokia. Only Starbucks appears on both the top-eight and the SMI lists.

Data was collected during September 2011 and includes all Facebook activities, (wall posts, note posts, event posts, photos, video posts, and linked documents), from official company accounts. All the materials were collected in a week, (during the first week of October 2011), and saved as Word documents for the next stage of content analysis.

Data was then coded for types of CSR activities being discussed and level of consumer interaction on the site. The SMI report describes the wide definition of sustainability as communicating about environmental issues, climate and clean energy issues, social and community causes, charitable giving, and employee well-being and development. These apriori categories were then used for the content analysis of CSR messages to determine topic area and message valence in order to detect patterns of activities and whether they vary by channel.

These 15 companies made a total of 477 posts during the month of September 2011. Of these 477 posts, 15.7% (75 posts) were CSR messages. Although these companies made significantly more CSR-related posts than the top branded sites evaluated in our first study, it is not a primary focus of corporate branding on social media.

The majority of CSR messages (37.3% or 28 posts) were about social and community causes. For example, Dell posted the following message on its Facebook page: "Happy Social Good Day from our friends at (RED)! Dell is a proud partner and we want to know who's meeting up to discuss how social media can be used for social good?" Another example for this type of message came from FedEx: "FedEx Cares Week: Nearly 4000 FedEx volunteers worldwide will donate a combined 20,000 service hrs to local orgs." About 27% of CSR messages (20 posts) were about environmental issues, like this post from Dell: "*Hey corporate citizens! Learn how Dell makes being 'green' easier for our customers and provides underserved youth access to technology, education and training. Dell releases its FY'11 Corporate Responsibility Report. Tell us what you think in the comments below.*" Climate and clean energy issues made up 17.3% (13 posts) of the CSR posts. For example, Allianz posted the following message on its Facebook page: "Looking to invest in greenhouse gas cuts? Small scale projects like energy-saving light bulbs for Asia or solar cooking stoves in Africa offer new carbon credit opportunities, says Martin Ewald, Investment Manager at Allianz Climate Solutions." Only 12% (nine posts) of CSR messages focused on employee well-being and development. AMD made the following wall post on its Facebook page to reach out to its employees: "Serious wildfires continue in central Texas including the Greater Austin metropolitan area near Bastrop, Pflugerville and the Steiner Ranch neighborhoods forcing many, including a number of AMD employees and their families, to be evacuated from their homes. If you are in central Texas please stay informed and take great care." Lastly, 6.6% (five posts) were about charitable giving, like this post from Dell about its military charities: "*Dell is donating $100,000 to military related charities and giving away 250 PCs to soldiers. Nominate a soldier*

Table 7.1   Average Likes per Facebook Post and Average Likes per CSR Post

Company	Average Likes Per Post	Average Likes Per CSR Post
Allianz	13.4	13
AMD	145	127
BBVA	57.3	72
Dell	177.6	276
FedEx	115.9	194
Ford	158.4	38
GE	85.9	95
IBM*	N/A	N/A
Intel	3,953	5,892
Microsoft	1,952	0
Nokia	1,121.5	1,013
PepsiCo	739.5	747
PG&E	46.6	58
Philips	78	78
Starbucks	15,774.8	47,090

*IBM did not have an official company Facebook page at the time of data collection.

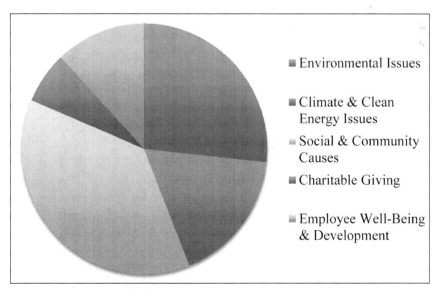

Figure 7.1   Types of CSR messages.

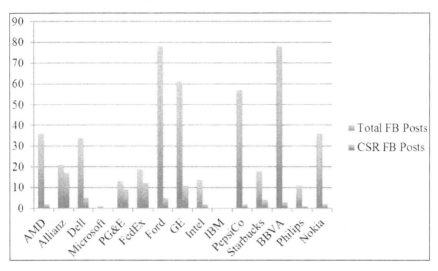

Figure 7.2   Total Facebook posts and total CRS posts.

today: http://del.ly/6039Rprf." Figure 7.1 provides a visual representation of the types of CSR messages.

Ford and BBVA had the highest number of Facebook posts with 78 each but less than 10% of those posts (6.4% for Ford and 3.8% for BBVA) were related to CSR. PepsiCo was also fairly active on Facebook during the month with 57 posts but only 2 of those posts or 3.5% were related to CSR. Likewise, GE had a total of 61 Facebook posts but only 11 were related to CSR.

Allianz had the highest percentage of CSR-related content with 17 of its 21 Facebook posts (80.9%) being focused on environmental issues, climate and clean energy issues, and social and community causes. Sixty-nine percent of PG&E's Facebook posts were related to CSR issues. FedEx had the third highest percentage with 63% of its Facebook posts focusing on CSR issues; however it should be noted that FedEx was celebrating FedEx Cares during the time of data collection so more posts were about this program. Figure 7.2 illustrates a comparison of the total Facebook posts with the number of CSR-related posts for all 15 companies.

More than half of the companies analyzed received on average the same amount or more likes per post for CSR-related content (see Figure 7.3). These companies included BBVA, Dell, FedEx, GE, Intel, PepsiCo, PG&E, and Starbucks. Only Ford and Nokia averaged more likes on its generic content. Microsoft only made one Facebook post during the month and it was not related to CSR, and at the time of data collection IBM did not have an official Facebook page. Thus, CSR-related content on average generates at least the same or often more interaction from consumers than other types of branded content.

DISCUSSION

These studies indicate that firms still do not regularly use social media to share CSR activities with external publics. Unlike previous studies, however, this study examines the types of messages that brands do post at their social outposts, which adds a new level of information to understanding the reluctance of brands to capitalize on this new medium. As this study examined activities at sites with millions of fans, the excuse that firms are waiting for people to adopt the medium falls short. We suggest several reasons why brands aren't using social media for CSR.

First, for many of these brands, a CSR message doesn't fit the "voice" of the brand at a social outpost. Social brands are creating voices that mirror the voices of the others in the community, which for many of the brands we examined is a youthful, fun, and casual voice. Shifting gears to a more serious CSR message may be at cross-purposes to the feeling of the community that the brands are trying to achieve.

Second, messages as social outposts are more "in the moment" rather than focused on long-term branding. Posts on social media often refer to something happening that very day in the world—an event that the brand is involved in, a comment on the weather that translates into a connection with the brand, a special promotion available only that day for social media followers. Similar to the first concern regarding the brand voice, interrupting this type of flow with a CSR message may not serve to support the community.

Third, social media postings are not text bound: brands often use a simple visual, which do not translate well into a CSR message. Disney, for example, often posts images from their movies to instigate discussions on what the characters and the movie mean to customers. This can develop a strong bond among fans, but may not be an effective technique for CSR.

Finally, brands create unique sites on social outposts for their CSR messages. For example, PepsiCo created a special Facebook page for the Pepsi Refresh Project, which provided information about their $20 million donations in lieu of Super Bowl ads. The public was encouraged to vote for their favorite projects. In a similar interactive community, JP Morgan used the Chase Community Giving Facebook page to allow the public to cast votes for charities to receive part of a $5millin donation. Timberland set up a special page for its Earth Keeper's program, which allows fans of the page to donate funds to plant both virtual and real trees in Haiti and China (Pannesidi, 2010).

Ethical Implications for the Practice of Social Media

This research contributes to the study of social media, ethics and the profession of public relations in several ways. It adds to the small body of literature on CSR channels, identifying the types of CSR messages delivered in social media channels. Because consumers often identify CSR dialogue as a key factor in increasing a company's image (Bruchell & Cook, 2006), it contributes to the practice of public relations by helping firms understand the importance of channel selection for CSR messages as well as the implications of channel selection for CSR messages. Public relations professionals strive to develop effective CSR strategies that engage with key stakeholders and are ethical in execution and communication so that the messages and the firm are authentic to a range of stakeholders. These studies beg the ethical question of separating branded messages with CSR messages, particularly at a time when consumers want to support companies whose values are consistent with their own values.

Limitations and Future Research

These studies investigated one social media outlet: Facebook. Future research should address if and how companies use other social media such as Twitter to disseminate both branded and CSR messages. A comparison of the two types of social networks could prove useful, particularly because the users of these types of social media might demand different messages. Another research strand could investigate how corporations brand themselves across multiple social media accounts. For example, Microsoft's official company Facebook page did not include any CSR messages during September 2011 but its Microsoft Green page, which is the official Facebook account for Microsoft's Environmental Sustainability team, made seven posts during that same time, all of which were related to CSR.

CONCLUSION

The social media space is still in an evolutionary state, with new outposts opening up regularly and with brands and consumers deciding how and why to use what mix of outposts for their own purposes. Whereas CSR messages seem to be a way that brands can connect with consumers and other stakeholders with positive results for all, the potential is clearly untapped. This study provides benchmarks that brands can use to evaluate their social media messages, including CSR messages, to help determine the optimal messaging strategy to engage stakeholders. As social media evolves, updating these benchmarks will support firms' efforts to build brands in the social media space.

Discussion Questions

1. In your opinion, is it in the best of interest of firms to separate branded messages from CSR-related messages? Why or why not?

How can the firm develop a consistent brand image with these different message strategies?

2. We suggest one of the reasons that firms do not disseminate CSR messages via branded social media sites is because the CSR messages do not fit with the voice of the brand. From an ethical perspective, shouldn't the voice of the brand be consistent across platforms? If so, is it possible to have a consistent voice with multiple communication channels?

3. If you were on the account team for a firm, what tactics would you use to disseminate CSR messages?

SUGGESTED READINGS

Du, S., Bhattacharya, C.B., & Sen, S. (2010). Maximizing business returns to corporate social responsibility (CSR): The role of CSR communication." *International Journal of Management Review, 12*(1), 8–19.

Greenstein, H., & Watson. T. (2011). Social media and CSR: Are we there yet? Retrieved from http://onphilanthropy.com/2011/social-media-and-csr-are-we-there-yet-new-white-paper/.

Panessidi, K. (2010). Using digital media for corporate social responsibility (CSR). Retrieved from http://blogs.imediaconnection.com/blog/2010/06/18/using-digital-media-for-corporate-social-responsibility-csr/

Schiefelbein, K. (2012). (2012) *Using the right CSR communication strategy: The impact on consumer attitude and behavior* (Masters thesis). Retrieved from http://essay.utwente.nl/62190/

Smith, M. (2011). How to measure your facebook engagement. Retrieved from http://www.socialmediaexaminer.com/how-to-measure-your-facebook-engagement/

REFERENCES

Becker-Olsen, K. L., & Hill, R. P. (2006). The impact of perceived corporate social responsibility on consumer behavior. *Journal of Business Research, 59*(1), 45–53.

Boston College Reputation Institute (2010). Corporate social responsibility index. Retrieved from http://www.bcccc.net/index.cfm?pageId=2202.

Bronn, P. S., & Vrioni, A. B. (2001). Corporate social responsibility and cause related marketing: An overview. *International Journal of Advertising, 20*(2), 207–222.

Bruchell, J., & Cook, J. (2006). It's good to talk? Examining attitude towards corporate social responsibility dialogue and engagement processes. *Business Ethics, 15*(2), 154–170.

Carroll, A. B. (1979). A three-dimensional conceptual model of corporate performance, *Academy of Management Review, 4*(4), 500.

Custom Communications (2010). *SMI special report: Social media sustainability index.* Retrieved from http://socialmediainfluence.com/2010/11/16/the-social-media-sustainability-index/

Digital Buzz (2011). Facebook statistics, stats & facts for 2011. Retrieved from http://www.digitalbuzzblog.com/facebook-statistics-stats-facts-2011/

Du, S., Bhattacharyab, C. B., & Sen, S. (2007). Reaping relational rewards from corporate social responsibility: The role of competitive positioning. *International Journal of Research in Marketing, 24*(3), 224–241.

Du, S., Bhattacharyab, C. B., & Sen, S. (2010). Maximizing business returns to corporate social responsibility (CSR): The role of CSR communication." *International Journal of Management Review, 12*(1), 8–19.

Fombrun, C. J., & Shanley, M. (1990). What's in a name? Reputation building and corporate strategy. *Academy of Management Journal, 33*(2), 233–258.

Greenstein, H., & Watson, T. (2011). Social media and CSR: Are we there yet? Retrieved from http://onphilanthropy.com/2011/social-media-and-csr-are-we-there-yet-new-white-paper/.

Kotler, P., & Lee, N. (2005). *Corporate social responsibility: Doing the most good for your company and your cause.* New York: Wiley.

Menon, S., & Kahn, B. E. (2003). Corporate sponsorships of philanthropic activities: When do they impact perception of sponsor brand? *Journal of Consumer Psychology, 13*(3), 316–327.

Murray, K. B., & Vogel, C. M. (1997). Using a hierarchy of effects approach to gauge the effectiveness of CSR to generate goodwill towards the firm: Financial versus non-financial impacts. *Journal of Business Research, 38*(2), 141–159.

Panessidi, K. (2010). Using digital media for corporate social responsibility (CSR). Retrieved from http://blogs.imediaconnection.com/blog/2010/06/18/using-digital-media-for-corporate-social-responsibility-csr/

Pirsch, J., Gupta, S., & Grau, S. L. (2007). A framework for understanding corporate social responsibility programs as a continuum: An exploratory study. *Journal of Business Ethics, 70,* 125–140.

Schiefelbein, K. (2012). *Using the right CSR communication strategy: The impact on consumer attitude and behavior* (Masters thesis). Retrieved from http://essay.utwente.nl/62190/

Sen, S., & Bhattacharya, C. B. (2001). Does doing good always lead to doing better? Consumer reactions to corporate social responsibility. *Journal of Marketing Research, 38*(2), 225–243.

Sen, S., Bhattacharya, C. B., & Korschun, D. (2006). The role of corporate social responsibility in strengthening multiple stakeholder relationships: A field experiment. *Journal of the Academy of Marketing Science, 34*(2), 158–166.

Sheehan, K. B. (2004). *Controversies in contemporary advertising.* Thousand Oaks, CA: Sage Publishers.

Smith, M. (201. How to measure your Facebook engagement. Retrieved from http://www.socialmediaexaminer.com/how-to-measure-your-facebook-engagement/

Van Staden, C. J., & Hooks, J. (2007). A comprehensive comparison of corporate environmental reporting and responsiveness. *British Accounting Review, 39*(3): 197–210.

Wagner, T., Lutz, R. J., & Weitz, B. A. (2009). Corporate hypocrisy: Overcoming the threat of inconsistent corporate social responsibility perceptions. *Journal of Marketing, 73,* 77–91.

8 Corporate Social Responsibility in Environmental Crisis

A Case Study of BP's Youtube Response to the Deepwater Horizon Crisis

Denise Sevick Bortree

INTRODUCTION

On April 20, 2010, an explosion on the Deepwater Horizon platform in the Gulf of Mexico started a chain of events that would lead to 11 deaths and millions of gallons of oil pouring into the Gulf waters. BP was the key actor in the crisis, and used many communication channels during and after the crisis to inform its stakeholders about its efforts to cap the well and restore the Gulf region. On May 27, 2010, BP's YouTube channel was launched with over 20 videos. During the first 18 months of the crisis, it posted over 300 videos to the channel. This study examines the ways in which BP used the videos to communicate its corporate social responsibility and to promote its restoration efforts during the environmental crisis.

LITERATURE REVIEW

Corporate Social Responsibility and Ethics

Corporate social responsibility (CSR) has been defined as addressing legal, ethical, and economic responsibilities of an organization in relationship with key stakeholders (Carroll, 1979; Carroll, 1999; Garriga & Mele, 2004; Maignan & Ferrell, 2004). It is often understood to be discretionary acts by organizations to give back to communities and societies that have supported them (Kotler & Lee, 2005). In the environmental realm, this means that organizations need to consider their impact on people, habitat and species, and the economy. Although, social responsibility by a company can have a positive impact in its bottom line (Joyner & Payne, 2002), as does environmental responsibility (Wahba, 2008), CSR actions are considered to be ethical because of their positive impact on employees, communities, the environment, and society.

CSR can take on many forms including corporate social marketing, sustainable business practices, philanthropy, and cause promotion (Kotler & Lee, 2005). CSR has been leveraged by corporations for decades and in many cases has been incorporated into accountable reporting strategies (KPMG, 2011). Today even mid-size companies are rapidly beginning to adopt CSR strategies, with a recent report indicating that as many as two thirds are currently implementing CSR programs (CSRWire, 2013).

Research has suggested companies that have effective CSR programs may be more insulated from certain types of crisis than are those without effective programs (Eisingerich et al, 2011). Recent studies suggest that this process works the other way as well. Handling a crisis well tends to protect the reputation of an organizations' CSR programs (Haigh & Brubaker, 2010; Haigh & Dardis, 2012)

Crisis and Image Restoration Strategies

Organizations that experience crisis often suffer reputational damage and must work to restore their reputation in the public eye (Coombs, 2000; Coombs & Holladay, 2008). A crisis, often defined as any event that produces negative consequences for an organization (Fearn-Banks, 2002), must be addressed by an organization. Research suggests six strategies that may be used in this process—compensation (offering payment or gifts), ingratiation (praising stakeholders), apology (taking responsibility and asking for forgiveness), denial (stating that there is no crisis), justification (minimizing perceived damage), and reminder (pointing to good works of the organization in the past) (Coombs, 2007). The effectiveness of the strategies depends on the nature of the crisis. For example, organizations that are culpable for the crisis should not engage in denial or justification. Rather, apology and compensation would be more effective strategies.

Managing crisis through social media provides the opportunity for immediate dissemination of information; however, the effectiveness of crisis management through social media channels is still in question (Liu et al 2011; Shultz et al 2011; Moody, 2011). Research suggests that some types of information are more readily accepted through traditional media or word-of-mouth rather than social media (Liu et al, 2011). The study presented here measure responses to all crisis videos in a social media channel and compares their acceptance to those that tout CSR messages. This comparison will provide insight into the relationship between content and response in a social media outlet.

Prior research on the Deepwater Horizon crisis suggests that in its press releases BP most often accepted responsibility and offered compensation to victims (Harlow, Brantley, & Harlow, 2011). The same held true for their social media channels (Muralidharan, Dillistone, & Shin, 2011). Other research found that during the crisis, 34% of BP's press releases were official updates and 23% addressed its social responsibility. What is not known is the types of image restoration strategies that BP attempted to use through its CSR videos during and after the Deepwater Horizon crisis. One could argue that CSR is a form of image restoration strategy that takes responsibility for the damage caused by the crisis. If so, CSR could be closely aligned to apology.

Framing

As an organization emerges from a crisis and begins to leverage its CSR strategies, the way in which it frames its actions have implication for acceptance by the public. Framing, defined as structures through which individuals make sense of information (Reese, 2007), help guide readers to the most important material and offer a sense of priority for topics. Hallahan (1999) suggests that framing can be a valuable tool in public relations that can help guide publics in their understanding of situations, organizational action, news, and responsibility, among others.

Much of the dialogue around the Deepwater Horizon crisis focused on environmental issues, including impact to species and habitats, impact on individuals, and impact on broader regions in the southern U.S. Environmental framing has been studied for many years, and the results suggest that media often adopt frames from information subsidies when addressing environmental topics (Reber & Berger, 2005), making the proper selection of framing particularly important. Other studies of environmental framing (Dardis, 2007; Olausson, 2009; Davis, 1995; Bortree et al, 2012) offer insights into the most effective strategies for framing these messages. They find that when people feel that they might lose something (loss frame) or they might experience an immediate impact (current generation), they are more likely to take positive action toward the environment (Davis, 1995). In the case of the Deepwater Horizon crisis, focus on immediate needs of the stakeholders and an understanding of how loss might be prevented should be more positively received than other types of frames.

Case Study: Deepwater Horizon Crisis

This chapter will examine framing and the use of CSR as an image restoration strategy by BP during the Deepwater Horizon crisis. On April 20, 2010, an explosion at a Deepwater Horizon oil rig off the Gulf of Mexico set off a chain of events that will forever be linked to the corporation BP. When the media discovered that the oil rig was leased by BP, the company found itself in the center of the crisis. Slowly, BP began to engage in social media in response to the crisis. A week after the blast (April 27), BP took to Twitter and began to tweet at the handle @BP_America (BP, n.d.). On May 2 (day 13) the company made its first post to Facebook regarding the crisis. On May 18 (day 29) the official BP YouTube channel was launched and the first video was posted on May 27, 2010. Numerous attempts to cap the well failed, and finally on July 15, 2010, 86 days after the initial explosion, the well was officially capped (Robertson & Fountain, 2010). By then BP had suffered significant reputational damage and began an active campaign to boost its image through an aggressive corporate social responsibility campaign that it documented in video and posted to its YouTube channel. The campaign included partnerships with local organizations and activist groups, significant financial contributions to boost the local economy, and prominent use of local employees to establish a sense of proximity for the company.

On October 26, 2011 (15 months after the well was capped), BP was granted permission to resume drilling in the Gulf of Mexico (Krauss, 2011). This study takes a look at the all videos during the life of the crisis and then specifically analyzes CSR videos that BP used to repair its reputation between the end of the crisis (July 15, 2010) and the day BP received a drilling permit for the Gulf (October 26, 2011). By examining the trends of BP's CSR communication on YouTube over the 15 months, the study offers insight into the way the company leveraged a digital channel to address concerns of the residents of the Gulf, government officials, and investors.

Three Phases of the Crisis

This study examines all three phases of the crisis that are defined below.

1. *Explosion/oil spill* (4/20/10—7/14/10). On April 20, 2010, the first phase began when an explosion on the Deepwater Horizon platform in the Gulf of Mexico led to the leak of thousands of gallons of oil from an underwater well.
2. *Post well cap* (7/15-10 -9/18/10). The second phase began on July 15, 2010 when after multiple attempts over a number of weeks, BP finally capped the leaking well; however, the well was not yet declared dead, meaning it still posed a potential threat.
3. *Well declared dead* (9/19/10–10/22/11). The third phase, the post-threat phase, began on September 19, 2010, when the well was declared officially dead (Fountain, 2010), and BP could turn its full attention toward a restoration in the Gulf. The end of the crisis, in this study, was set as October 22, 2011 when BP was given a license to begin drilling for oil again in the Gulf.

Three Categories of Videos

On its YouTube channel, BP organized videos related to the Deepwater Horizon crisis into three playlist. Presumably, these categories were developed to make access to information simple and to promote its responsible actions during the crisis. These were used in the analysis of this study.

1. *Reassuring health and safety*—Videos in this category showed organizations how to address safety and health issues that had arisen during the crisis. Too, the videos showcased some of the processes that BP was using to ensure health and safety.

2. *Restoring the economy*—This series of videos focused on the economic impact of the crisis on Gulf coast communities. Videos featured local businesses talking about how they were working with BP, and some videos gave information on applying for financial assistance.
3. *Restoring the environment*—The environmental videos addressed BP's actions toward environmental damage caused by the crisis. Many of these videos featured wildlife being rescued and returned to the wild or habitat being cleaned up.

Research questions

Studies of the Deepwater Horizon crisis have not looked indepth at BP's use of YouTube to disseminate its messages to key audiences. This study will explore the way BP leveraged its CSR activities during the Deepwater Horizon crisis by answering the following research questions.

RQ1:   To what degree were BP's CSR video messages rejected (or accepted) by viewers?
RQ2:   How were BP's CSR messages framed?
RQ3:   Which image restoration strategies were used in BP's CSR video messages?
RQ4:   How were images and references to people, places, and the environment used in BP's CSR video messages?
RQ5:   Are there relationships between images and the degree to which CSR video messages are rejected?

METHOD

To answer the research questions, a quantitative content analysis was conducted on the 315 YouTube videos posted on BP's channel between May 27, 2010 (the day the channel was launched), and October 22, 2011. Two trained coders pulled information about each video from the YouTube site and then viewed the video and conducted additional coding on the content. Intercoder reliability was conducted using 10% of the videos, and results were calculated using Cronbach's alpha. Overall results were high ($\alpha = .97$), and the reliability for each category is reported below with the category descriptions.

Coding Scheme

Videos were coded for their date posted ($\alpha = 1$), length ($\alpha = 1$), number of views ($\alpha = 1$), number of comments ($\alpha = 1$), number of likes ($\alpha = 1$), and number of dislikes ($\alpha = 1$) as reported on the YouTube website. Then, each video was viewed to determine whether it included CSR content. Videos that were considered CSR were subjected to additional content coding as reported below.

YouTube permits viewers to select a "like" or "dislike" response to videos. The dislike percentages for the videos in this study were calculated by comparing the number of dislikes to the number of views. For example, if a video was viewed 100 times and disliked 10 times, it had a 10% dislike score. The author reasoned that those who indicated dislike had strong negative feelings toward the video.

Frames. Building on prior PR literature (Hallahan, 1999; Bortree et al, 2007), the study looked at ways that the videos framed the issue, including emotional vs. rational, restoration and hope, attitudes of Gulf residents (positive, neutral, or negative), and partnerships with others (nonprofit, for-profit, government, and individual/celebrity). Each potential frame was coded as present or absent in a video ($\alpha = .96$).

Image restoration strategies. Six image restoration strategies were coded in this study: compensation, ingratiation, apology, denial, justification, and reminder (Coombs, 2007). Each strategy was coded as present or absent in a video ($\alpha = .97$).

References. This study was interested in the people, locations, and other items referenced in the videos. To measure this, videos were coded as referenced (or not referenced) in images or in words for the following: Gulf residents, BP employees, government officials, specific communities (towns, cities, neighborhoods, etc.), states, species, plant life, water, beaches, or food ($\alpha = .94$).

Images. Separately, the videos were coded for the images that appeared in them. Coded images included: BP employees, employees helping others, Gulf residents, residents helping others, government officials, animals/fish, beaches, water, cities or communities, underwater images, BP-owned sites, people laughing/enjoying self, people angry/frustrated, women, men, Caucasians, or minorities ($\alpha = .95$).

FINDINGS

BP posted 315 videos to its YouTube channel between April 20, 2010 and October 22, 2011. The degree to which these videos were accepted by the public were likely influenced by time and by the number of views, as the publics' anger began to subside as the crisis moved into a post-crisis phase. Too, videos that received more views likely were more disliked, as the publics' anger about the crisis would lead it to view and share videos. A graphical representation of the relationship between time and the number of dislikes can be found in Figure 8.1, and a representation of the relationship between views and dislikes can be found in Figure 8.2. The videos were categorized into the three timeframes and an ANCOVA was run to compare degree to which the videos were disliked during each period.

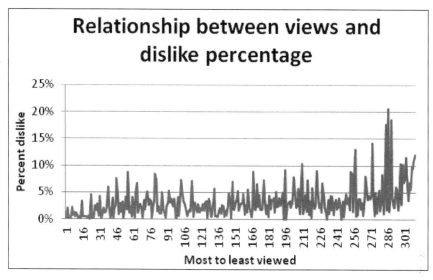

Figure 8.1   Relationship between time and dislike percentage across all BP videos.

Even controlling for time and views, there was still a significant difference between the dislike percentage for the three phases (p = .048) with phase 1 being most disliked and phase 3 being least disliked.

To answer research question one about the degree to which BP's CSR video messages were rejected by viewers, an ANCOVA analysis was run

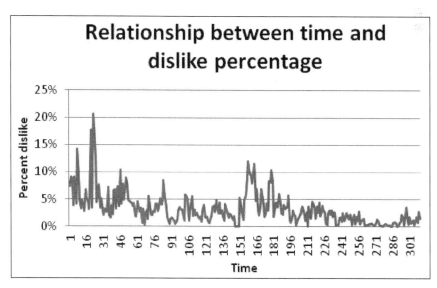

Figure 8.2   Relationship between views and dislike percentage across all BP videos.

that controlled for time and views. The analysis suggested that the three types of CSR videos—health and safety, economy, and environment—were significantly more disliked (F (1,306) =6.33, p = .01) than the other videos posted by BP during the 18-month period. Among the three types of CSR videos, health and safety was most disliked followed by environment, and videos on the economy were least disliked (F (1, 51) = 19.71, p < .001).

The second research question asked about framing of CSR messages in BP's videos. A frequency analysis of the CSR videos found a greater use of rational frames than emotional frames. This was seen most distinctly in the environmental videos (Table 8.1). At the same time, the frame of restoration and hope was most often seen in the environmental videos. BP frequently referenced Gulf residents in its videos, and one of the frames that it used was the attitude of the residents toward the spill and toward BP. Interestingly, the attitude expressed by residents in the environmental videos was always positive (100%), while attitudes in the economic videos were mostly positive (83%), and the health and safety videos were rarely positive (14%). Rather, residents in the health and safety videos expressed more neutral (43%) and negative (43%) attitudes.

Another frame used in the videos was partnership. BP often pointed to partnerships with nonprofits, for-profits, and government. This happened most often in the environmental videos.

The third research question asked about image restoration strategies in BP's CSR videos. The content analysis found that the most frequently used strategy, of the ones coded, was compensation that appeared in 35% of the health and safety videos and 46% of the economic videos. It did not appear in the environmental videos. Rather, ingratiation was the most common strategy in the environmental videos.

The fourth research question asked about images and reference in BP's CSR videos. Gulf residents were referenced in 92% of economic videos and 85% of health and safety videos. BP employees were referenced in 95% of the health and safety videos but only around 50% of the economic and environmental videos. Not surprising, 95% of the environmental videos included a reference to species and 78% included water (Table 8.1). Significant differences emerged in references to BP employees (p < .05), states (p < .05), species (p < .001), water (p < .001), beaches (p < .05), and food (p < .01).

While similar, the images used in the videos had some notable differences. For example, 85% of health and safety videos referenced Gulf employees but only 40% included their images. All economic videos showed images from local cities or communities and only 54% showed images of BP employees. The most common images in environmental videos were water (82%) and animals and fish (78%). Interestingly, women showed up in 91% of environmental videos, and 85% of economic videos but only 50% of health and safety videos. Significant differences appeared in images of BP employees (p > .01), Gulf residents (p < .01), residents helping others

Table 8.1   Analysis of BP's CSR Video Messages During Deepwater Horizon Crisis

Variable	Health and Safety Videos	Economy Videos	Environment Videos
Emotional	35.0%	30.8%	8.7%
Rational	65.0%	69.2%	91.3%
Restoration/hope	5.0%	0.0%	21.7%
Attitudes of Gulf residents	35.0%	46.2%	26.1%
Positive*	14.3%	83.3%	100.0%
Neutral*	42.9%	16.7%	0.0%
Negative*	42.9%	0.0%	0.0%
Partnerships			
Nonprofit	15.0%	23.1%	26.1%
For-profit	5.0%	7.7%	21.2%
Government	20.0%	7.7%	34.8%
Individual/celebrity	10.0%	0.0%	4.3%
Image Restoration Strategies			
Compensation**	35.0%	46.2%	0.0%
Ingratiation	25.0%	7.7%	26.1%
Apology	20.0%	0.0%	8.7%
Denial	0.0%	7.7%	0.0%
Justification	5.0%	7.7%	4.3%
Reminder	5.0%	0.0%	0.0%
References			
Gulf residents	85.0%	92.3%	69.6%
BP employees**	95.0%	53.8%	56.5%
Government officials	15.0%	7.7%	34.8%
Specific communities	70.0%	84.6%	56.5%
States*	40.0%	84.6%	56.5%
Species***	10.0%	38.5%	95.7%
Plant life	30.0%	53.8%	65.2%
Water***	33.3%	30.8%	78.3%
Beaches*	10.0%	53.8%	47.8%
Food**	15.0%	46.2%	4.3%
Images			
BP employees**	95.0%	53.8%	56.5%
Employees helping others	25.0%	23.1%	30.4%

(continued)

120   *Denise Sevick Bortree*

Table 8.1 (continued)

Variable	Health and Safety Videos	Economy Videos	Environment Videos
Gulf residents**	40.0%	92.3%	69.6%
Residents helping others**	10.0%	7.7%	52.2%
Government officials	5.0%	15.4%	26.1%
Animals/fish***	5.0%	38.5%	78.3%
Beaches*	10.0%	53.8%	47.8%
Water*	33.3%	22.2%	81.8%
City/community***	35.0%	100.0%	21.7%
Underwater images	0.0%	0.0%	4.3%
BP-owned sites***	80.0%	38.5%	26.1%
People laughing/enjoying self	25.0%	61.5%	30.4%
People angry/frustrated	10.0%	7.7%	0.0%
Women**	50.0%	84.6%	91.3%
Men	85.0%	100.0%	82.6%
Caucasian	95.0%	100.0%	100.0%
Minorities	35.0%	46.2%	43.5%

Note: *p<.05, **p<.01, ***p<.001

Table 8.2 Images that Significantly Increase or Decrease Dislikes of BP's CSR Video Messages

Image type	Degree to which video is disliked when image is PRESENT	Degree to which video is disliked when image is ABSENT	x
Gulf residents	3.13%	6.21%	p < .001
Gulf residents helping others	2.37%	4.91%	p < .05
Cities/communities	3.17%	5.08%	p < .001
BP-owned sites	5.96%	2.62%	p < .05
People laughing/ enjoying self	2.76%	5.05%	p < .01
Women	3.26%	7.15%	p < .001
Minorities	3.58%	4.68%	p < .01

Note: Percentages represent the degree to which a video is disliked; a larger percentage indicates that more viewers disliked the video.

(p < .01), animals/fish (p < .01), beaches (p < .05), water (p < .05), city/community (p < .001), BP-owned sites (p < .001), and women (p < .01).

The final research question asked about the relationship between images and the rejection of CSR videos. To answer this question an ANCOVA analysis was run. Results suggested that seven images influenced the degree to which videos were disliked by viewers (Table 8.2). These results were controlled for time, views, and CSR type. One of the images created a greater—degree of dislike—BP-owned sites. For the other six images, videos were disliked less when the images were present—Gulf residents, Gulf residents helping others, local cities/communities, people laughing/enjoying themselves, women, and minorities. Videos that included these images appeared to be more accepted by the public or at least created less anger among viewers.

DISCUSSION

Looking at the 315 videos that BP created and disseminated between April 20, 2010, and October 22, 2011, it is apparent that BP considered YouTube to be an important channel of communication during the crisis. Many of the videos appeared to be quickly created and uploaded to keep audiences up to date on developments in the restoration. The analysis in this study suggests that videos with CSR messages were more disliked than other types of videos. To get a better sense of the characteristics of the CSR videos, below is a summary of the findings for each.

Reassuring Health and Safety

Videos in the reassuring health and safety playlist employed image restoration strategies of compensation, ingratiation, and apology. The videos relied heavily on images of BP employees and frequently referenced Gulf Coast residents, though their images were not used as often. Most of the videos in this category featured male Caucasians, and only half featured females. BP-owned sites were frequently included in these videos, and the attitudes of Gulf residents were reflected as neutral or negative. The videos rarely featured partnerships with other entities, but when they did, the partners were often government entities.

Restoring the Economy

Videos on restoring the economy used the compensation image restoration strategy. Gulf residents were often featured in the videos, as were specific communities and states in the Gulf region. The attitude of Gulf residents were portrayed as mostly positive, with frequent use of people laughing and enjoying themselves. All videos showed male Caucasians, and many featured women as well. Some minorities appeared in the videos.

Restoring the Environment

Videos on the environmental restoration used the ingratiation image restoration strategy. Gulf residents were often featured and were more likely
to be helping others than were those featured in the other types of CSR
videos. BP employees were also portrayed as helping others. Gulf residents'
attitudes were portrayed as entirely positive toward BP, and the videos portrayed messages of hope and restoration more than any other CSR type.
Images in the video were often environmental, including animals, fish,
water, and plant life. Women appeared more in this type of video than any
other. The videos also were more likely to feature partnerships with other
entities than were other types of videos.

The most common image restoration strategy identified in this study was
compensation that appeared in 46% of the economy videos and 35% of the
health and safety videos. During the restoration period, compensation was
a popular topic in the media, so the presence of that strategy here is reason-
able. Ingratiation appeared in 26% of the environmental videos, and 25%
of the health and safety videos. Most often, these videos were praising local
residents or employees for their efforts in the cleanup. And finally, apology
appeared in 20% of the health and safety videos, 9% of the environmental
videos, and none of the economic videos suggesting that BP made a great
effort to apologize and accept responsibility in the health and safety areas
but much less so in the environmental and economic areas.

More broadly, this study found that videos were more disliked (CSR
or non-CSR videos) when a BP-owned site appeared in them. By contrast,
images of Gulf residents, Gulf residents helping others, local cities/communi-
ties, people laughing/enjoying themselves, women, and minorities seemed to
mitigate some of the negative feelings toward the videos. Research suggests
that focusing on how to avoid loss and focusing on the current time will
motivate more action (Davis, 1995). The results reported here suggest that
viewers want to see information about the local community and its residents.

Ethical Implications for the Practice of Public Relations

Environmental crises can be difficult to navigate for corporations. The purpose of this study was to explore one case in which an organization used
YouTube to promote its CSR efforts during a crisis. Results of the study
suggest that promoting CSR efforts by the organization during and immediately after a crisis may be dangerous territory. In this study, CSR videos
were less liked than other kinds of videos. That may not be the case in all
crises, but considering the magnitude of this crisis, this held true for BP.
The findings in this study raise ethical concerns about the purpose of CSR
as an image restoration strategy. If organizations are focusing on their own
facilities and their own action, this does not meet the needs of the public
that is enduring the crisis. Rather, publics wish to learn more about the

people and communities affected by the crisis. BP's videos on the economy were less disliked than health and safety and environmental videos, possibly because BP was perceived as making good on its promise to compensate businesses that suffered during the crisis.

CONCLUSION

This study found that BP actively used its YouTube channel to engage with publics during and after the Deepwater Horizon crisis. However, its strategy to use CSR for image restoration does not appear to be successful. The data in this study were collected for one organization using a census. This method of collection presents some limitations. First, the findings cannot be generalized beyond this one case study, and second, it is possible that some videos were missed in the collection process and/or some were removed by BP before they were captured for the study. Any missed videos may have influenced the results in this study. Future research should test the effectiveness of CSR strategies for image restoration. It is possible that the acceptance of CSR strategies may be dependent on the company reputation, the industry, and the nature of the crisis.

Discussion Questions

1. What strategies have you observed organizations using during a crisis? In your opinion, are these strategies a form of corporate social responsibility? What types of corporate social responsibility might be acceptable as an image restoration strategy?
2. How can an organization use YouTube to promote its CSR strategies?
3. What should the priorities be for organization encountering an environmental crisis?

SUGGESTED READINGS

Coombs, W. T. (2007). *Crisis management and communications.* Retrieved from http://www.instituteforpr.org/topics/crisis-management-and-communications/.

Haigh, M. M., & Brubaker, P. (2010). Examining how image restoration strategy impacts perceptions of corporate social responsibility, organization-public relationships, and source credibility. *Corporate Communications: An International Journal, 15*(4), 453–468.

Hallahan, K. (1999). Seven models of framing: Implications for public relations. *Journal of Public Relations Research, 11*(3), 205–242.

Kotler, P., & Lee, N. (2005). *Corporate social responsibility: Doing the most good for your company and your cause.* Hoboken, NJ: Wiley.

Liu, B. F., Austin, L., & Jin, Y. (2011). How publics respond to crisis communication strategies: The interplay of information form and source. *Public Relations Review, 37,* 345–353.

124   *Denise Sevick Bortree*

REFERENCE

Bortree, D.S., Ahern, L., Dou, X. Smith, A.N. (2012). Framing the environmental movement: A study of advocacy messages. *International Journal of Nonprofit and Voluntary Sector Quarterly, 17*(2), 77–99.

BP (nd). BP's Twitter account. Retrieved from https://twitter.com/BP_America.

Carroll, A. B. (1979). A three-dimensional conceptual model of corporate performance. *Academy of Management Review, 4*(4), 497–505.

Carroll, A. B. (1999). Corporate social responsibility evolution of a definitional construct. *Business & Society, 38*(3), 268–295.

Coombs, W. T. (2000). Crisis management Advantages of a relational perspective. In J. Ledingham & S. D. Bruning (Eds.), *Public relations as relationship management: A relational approach to the study and practice of public relations.* Mahwah, NJ: Lawrence Erlbaum Associates.

Coombs, W. T. (2007). Crisis management and communications. Retrieved from http://www.instituteforpr.org/topics/crisis-management-and-communications/.

Coombs, W. T., & Holladay, S. J. (2008). Comparing apology to equivalent crisis response strategies: Clarifying apology's role and value in crisis communication. *Public Relations Review, 34*, 252–257.

CSRWire (2013). *New research report reveals corporate social responsibility trends in mid-sized companies.* Retrieved from http://www.csrwire.com/press_releases/35439-New-Research-Report-Reveals-Corporate-Social-Responsibility-Trends-in-Mid-sized-Companies

Dahlsrud, A. (2008). How corporate social responsibility is defined: an analysis of 37 definitions. *Corporate Social Responsibility and Environmental Management, 15*(1), 1–13.

Dardis, F. E. (2007). The role of issue-framing functions in affecting beliefs and opinions about a sociopolitical issue. *Communication Quarterly, 55*(2), 247–265.

Davis, J. J. (1995). The effects of message framing on response to environmental communications. *Journalism and Mass Communication Quarterly, 72*(2), 285–299.

DesJardins, J. (1998). Corporate environmental responsibility. *Journal of Business Ethics, 17*(8), 825–838.

Eisingerich, A. B., Rubera, G., Seifert, M., & Bhardwaj, G. (2011). Doing good and doing better despite negative information? The role of corporate social responsibility in consumer resistance to negative information. *Journal of Service Research, 14*(1), 60–75.

Fearn-Banks, K. (2002). *Crisis communications: A casebook approach.* Mahwah, NJ: Lawrence Erlbaum.

Fountain, H. (2010, September 20). U.S. says BP well is finally 'Dead.' *New York Times.* Retrieved from http://newyorktimes.com/2010/9/20/us/20well.html?ref=gulfofmexico2010.

Garriga, E., & Melé, D. (2004). Corporate social responsibility theories: mapping the territory. *Journal of Business Ethics, 53*(1–2), 51–71.

Godemann, J., & Michelsen, G. (2011). Sustainability communication–An introduction. In *Sustainability Communication* (pp. 3–11). Springer Netherlands.

Haigh, M. M., & Brubaker, P. (2010). Examining how image restoration strategy impacts perceptions of corporate social responsibility, organization-public relationships, and source credibility. *Corporate Communications: An International Journal, 15*(4), 453–468.

Haigh, M. M., & Dardis, F. (2012). The impact of apology on organization–public relationships and perceptions of corporate social responsibility. *Public Relations Journal, 6*(1), 1–16.

Hallahan, K. (1999). Seven models of framing: Implications for public relations. *Journal of Public Relations Research, 11*(3), 205–242.

Harlow, W. F., Brantley, B. C., & Harlow, R. M. (2011). BP initial image repair strategies after the Deepwater Horizon spill. *Public Relations Review, 37*(1), 80–83.

Joyner, B. E., & Payne, D. (2002). Evolution and implementation: a study of values, business ethics and corporate social responsibility. *Journal of Business Ethics, 41*(4), 297–311.

KPMG (2011). *KPMG International corporate responsibility reporting survey 2011.* Retrieved from http://www.kpmg.com/global/en/issuesandinsights/arti-clespublications/corporate-responsibility/pages/default.aspx

Kotler, P., & Lee, N. (2005). *Corporate social responsibility: doing the most good for your company and your cause.* Hoboken, NJ: Wiley.

Krauss, C. (2011, October 26). BP to drill again in the Gulf of Mexico. *New York Times* Green Blog. Retrieved from: http://green.blogs.nytimes.com/2011/10/26/bp-to-drill-again-in-the-gulf-of-mexico/.

Liu, B. F., Austin, L., & Jin, Y. (2011). How publics respond to crisis communication strategies: The interplay of information form and source. *Public Relations Review, 37,* 345–353.

Maignan, I., & Ferrell, O. C. (2004). Corporate social responsibility and marketing: an integrative framework. *Journal of the Academy of Marketing science, 32*(1), 3–19.

Moody, M. (2011). Jon and Kate Plus 8: A case study of social media and image repair tactics. *Public Relations Review, 37,* 405–414.

Muralidharan, S., Dillistone, K., & Shin, J. H. (2011). The Gulf Coast oil spill: Extending the theory of image restoration discourse to the realm of social media and beyond petroleum. *Public Relations Review, 37*(3), 226–232.

Olausson, U. (2009). Global warming-global responsibility? Media frames of collective action and scientific certainty. *Public Understanding of Science, 18*(4), 421–436.

Reber, B. H., & Berger, B. K. (2005). Framing analysis of activist rhetoric: How the Sierra Club succeeds or fails at creating salient messages. *Public Relations Review, 31*(2), 185–195.

Reese, S. D. (2007). The framing project: A bridging model for media research revisited. *Journal of Communication, 57*(1), 148–154.

Robertson, C. & Fountain, H. (2010, July 16). BP says oil flow has stopped as cap is tested. *New York Times.* Retrieved from http://www.newyorktimes.com/2010/07/16/us/16spill.html?ref=gulfofmexico2010.

Schultz, F., Utz, S., Goritz, A. (2011). Is the medium the message? Perceptions of and reactions to crisis communication via twitter, blogs and traditional media. *Public Relations Review, 37,* 20–27.

Stiller, Y., & Daub, C. H. (2007). Paving the way for sustainability communication: evidence from a Swiss study. *Business Strategy and the Environment, 16*(7), 474–486.

Wahba, H. (2008). Does the market value corporate environmental responsibility? An empirical examination. *Corporate Social Responsibility and Environmental Management, 15*(2), 89–99.

9 Nestlé and Greenpeace
The Battle in Social Media for Ethical Palm Oil Sourcing

W. Timothy Coombs

INTRODUCTION

In 2009, Nestlé and Greenpeace engaged in a social media battle over palm oil sourcing. Palm oil is used in a wide range of products. Greenpeace argued that Nestlé was irresponsibly sourcing palm oil and contributing to the destruction of orangutan habitat by using a supplier that eliminated rain forests to build palm oil plantations. Greenpeace defined Nestlé's purchasing palm oil from the Sinar Mas Group, a company linked to rain forest destruction, as a problem. What began with an online PDF file and YouTube video quickly escalated into a battle fought largely in social media. Media critics proclaimed Greenpeace the winner and lamented Nestlé's inept handling of the situation (Warner & Yeomans, 2012).

The Nestlé-Greenpeace palm oil sourcing battle represents a case of failed social media use. This chapter is a case study that uses a variety of theories and principles to explain why critics deemed Nestlé's effort in its social media battle in a failure. Moreover, the ethical implications from the Nestlé-Greenpeace battle are explored. The chapter starts by explaining the concept of the challenge crisis and how it serves as a frame for the case analysis. This is followed by the case analysis and the ethical implications for utilizing social media.

LITERATURE REVIEW

The Challenge Crisis

A crisis can be defined as, "an unpredictable event that threatens important expectancies of stakeholders and can seriously impair the organization's performance and generate negative outcomes" (Coombs, 2012, p. 2). A challenge crisis is an event driven by violations of stakeholder perceptions that can threaten an organization's reputation. A challenge crisis emerges when stakeholders claim that a corporation is behaving in an unethical, immoral, or irresponsible manner (Lerbinger, 1997). The challenge is premised on perceptions of organizational behavior, not legal or regulatory concerns. Stakeholder expectations drive the challenge crisis because they perceive that current organizational behaviors and practices do not meet their expectations.

The challenge crises can actually have three variations: organic, expose, and villain (Coombs, 2010). The different challenge variants have implications for crisis communication and the potential effects on the organizational reputation. The organic challenge arises from the values and beliefs of the stakeholders. Overtime, stakeholder values and beliefs can change whereas organizational behaviors may not. The new values and beliefs lead stakeholders to expect different behavior from the organization. This is a natural process where organizational behavior can lag behind stakeholder expectations.

The expose challenge occurs when stakeholders demonstrate an organization's words are not matching its actions. Charges of "washing" appear when managers overstate their commitment to some social or environmental concerns or talk about social and environmental concerns with little to no corresponding action. Expose challenges create the impression of malice by managers. It is implied that there is a purposeful attempt to confuse stakeholders about the organization's social performance—to pretend to meet stakeholder expectations.

The villain challenge is simply one act in a larger play between particular stakeholders and an organization or industry. The villain challenge typically involves a professional activist group trying to force change on a specific company or industry. The villain challenge is one in a serious of actions designed to paint the organization or industry as a villain that must reform its wicked ways (Coombs, 2010).

It does matter if stakeholders view the violation as naturally occurring rather than intentional, unethical behaviors by management. Drawing from Attribution Theory, an expose challenge is a much greater risk to the corporate reputation because of its intentional nature. In general, organizations suffer increased reputational damage from a crisis as stakeholder attributions of crisis responsibility strengthen (Coombs, 2010).

Stakeholder Salience and Assessing Challenges

Managers must determine if the challenges are a true threat to its reputation or something they can ignore. Crisis threats are typically evaluated by assessing the likelihood (the chance a threat will become a crisis) and impact (the potential effect of the crisis on the organization and its stakeholders) (Barton, 2001). For challenge threats, which are reputation-based, we can refine likelihood and impact using stakeholder salience.

Mitchell, Agle, and Wood (1997) developed a widely used system for assessing stakeholder salience—how important a stakeholder is to an organization—based on three factors: power, legitimacy, and urgency. Power is the ability of the stakeholders to make the organization do something it would not otherwise do and is the most important of the factors. Legitimacy indicates that a stakeholder concern is considered appropriate or proper according to some standards. Willingness is the stakeholder's desire to pursue its goals and can be intensified by the need to meet a deadline. Stakeholders are more salient when they have power, their concern is legitimate, and they are willing to advocate for their concerns (Mitchell et al., 1997).

Power is the most fluid of the salience factors. Stakeholders can build power by increasing the number of people who support their concern. Internet Contagion Theory (ICT) argues that communication is one means of building power by creating awareness and recruiting supporters. By using a mix of communication channels, especially those found on the Internet, stakeholders have the potential of increasing their power by using additional communication channels increasing the number of people reached (centrality in network terminology) as well as increasing the repetition of a message (Coombs & Holladay, 2007; 2012). But the message is important too and legitimacy is a critical contributor to this point. If other stakeholders are unlikely to view a concern as legitimate, they will not support the concern. Part of the challenge communication effort must be to establish the legitimacy of the challenge. Finally, if the stakeholders and their supporters are unwilling to press the concern, there is less motivation for managers to address the concern. Willingness is enhanced when the challengers are skilled at communicating their messages (Coombs & Holladay, 2012).

Managers can utilize power, legitimacy, and willingness to assess the potential threat posed by a challenge. In terms of reputation-based threats, likelihood can be defined as legitimacy combined with willingness whereas impact can be defined as power combined with legitimacy. A challenge is more likely to become a crisis when the core concern is legitimate and the challengers are committed to the concern. A challenge will have greater impact when the challengers have more power and a legitimate concern (Coombs, 2012). The greater the threat, the more attention the challenge should receive from management. Power, legitimacy, and willingness are dynamic concepts because challengers can utilize Internet-based communication to enhance any of the three salience factors.

Crisis Response

Challenge crises mirror the concepts of agitation and control. Agitation is an effort by those outside of the decision-making process to advocate for change in the face of resistance to those efforts. Control represents the reactions by those in power to agitation (Bowers, Ochs & Jensen, 1993). If we take a challenge as agitation, the response by managers is a form of control. Drawing from the rhetoric of control, I have identified four broad strategic responses managers can use to address a challenge: (1) refutation, (2) repression, (3) reform, and (4) repentance. Refutation seeks to demonstrate the challenge is invalid. Managers are denying a problem exists and must supply evidence to support claims that there is no violation and provide evidence of how the organization is meeting important stakeholder expectations. The situation may simply be a result of a lack of awareness or a misinterpretation of actual organizational behaviors. Another variation of refutation is to debate the merits of the expectations. The organizational managers argue that the expectations are invalid—that most of their stakeholders do not hold that violated expectations. Hence, no change is necessary because the violated expectation is limited to small group of stakeholders that lack salience. Part of the dispute response includes efforts to marginalize the challenging stakeholders.

Repression involves efforts to stop the challenge from spreading. Managers take actions to prevent challengers from communicating about the concern. Lawsuits are a typical strategy organizations used to silence critics (Coombs & Holladay, 2010). People fear the costs of lawsuits, hence the mere threat of a lawsuit may silence challengers. Repression, however, can be a pyrrhic victory. Repression precludes the free flow of ideas, a foundational element of free speech and democracy. Repression tactics can create a backlash as other stakeholders express their displeasure over such a harsh response.

The responses to challenges can be connected to the type of challenge. Reform is associated with organic challenges. Managers use reform to note there is a problem and they are working with stakeholders to overcome the expectation violation. The violation is legitimized and the organization takes action to change behaviors. By partnering with the stakeholders who identified the violation, other stakeholders can have increased confidence that the solution will indeed correct the expectation violation.

Repentance is associated with the expose violation. Managers recognize the error of misrepresenting their efforts and work to address the expectation violation. Again, partnerships can be used to enhance the credibility of the repair efforts. But the critical feature is acknowledging the wrongdoing. The admission of wrongdoing serves as the foundation for repairing the expectation violation. This is a dangerous strategy because admitting wrongdoing can lead to additional stakeholders becoming angry with the organization (Kim, Ferrin, Cooper, & Dirks, 2004). However, repentance is a long term investment, actions are needed to validate the claim of repentance (Smith, 2008).

Challenge assessment and crisis responses can be combined to develop a set of recommendations for managers facing challenge crises. Illegitimate challenges fit well with refutation. Managers can argue very easily that the challenge should be dismissed and does not require action. Refutation is more difficult with a legitimate issue but can work when stakeholder power is low. Managers can resist a change when they know the stakeholders lack the resources to force them to make the change. Refutation can even work when the stakeholder is powerful but lacks willingness. If stakeholders are unlikely to press for the change, there is little risk of them exercising their power and forcing a change. Repression is a risky strategy because it can create a negative reaction among stakeholders. As with refutation, the repression strategy is best suited for illegitimate concerns because stakeholders can recognize the need to prevent the spread of untrue information.

Reform can be used with organic challenges. Reform fits well when a challenge is legitimate, the stakeholders have power, and willingness is strong. But with reform comes an additional set of concerns: cost and consistency. If the cost of a change is prohibitive, refutation is preferred to reform. Managers need to explain why they cannot meet the demands. If the change is inconsistent with organizational objectives, refutation is preferred, and managers explain why the proposed change does not work for the organization. If the costs are low and the actions are consistent, reform is a viable option. Managers describe how they have been given a new view of the situation and are acting on that new perspective.

Repentance is a difficult response to use effectively because it is used with an expose challenge. Expose challenges are the most damaging because they compromise stakeholder trust in the organization. Why should stakeholders believe an organization has repented when it has lied in the past about similar behaviors? It is critical that managers prove they have made changes (Smith, 2008). Verification from a trusted third-party source is one option for attempting to build trust in changes. Whatever strategy is used, managers must assess the stakeholder reactions to the communicative effort and adjust accordingly. Ideally stakeholders become quiescent after the challenge response because their concerns have been addressed or they realize the organization will not take action on the concern. If stakeholders continue to agitate for change, another assessment must be conducted to determine if the strategy requires revision.

Ethic of Care

The ethic of care is an ethical theory rooted in relationships. Actors (people, organizations, and even the environment) are interdependent with one another. That interdependence raises special considerations for those with the most power in the interdependent relationships. The powerful actors (those who are less vulnerable) need to give extra consideration to the needs of the less powerful actors (those that are vulnerable). Powerful actors have a responsibility to take care of the less powerful actors bound together by a web of interdependence. Powerful actors should not impose their will on others (Vanacker & Breslin, 2006). Crisis researchers have even argued that the ethic of care should be the moral compass in a crisis (e.g., Simola, 2003; 2005). The ethic of care can be used to illustrate how the interests of the less powerful are treated in a challenge crisis.

The ethic of care is associated with Carol Gilligan (1982). She developed the ethic of care as part of a gender bias critique of Lawrence Kohlberg's theory of moral development. Care should reflect a concern for maintaining and improving relationships. People need to understand and respond to the needs and feelings of others (Simola, 2005). Organizations and stakeholders find themselves linked together through a web on interconnected relationships. By their definition, crises threaten those relationships. Crisis managers employ the ethic of care when their actions reflect a concern for others and value for the relationship (Simola, 2003).

Research Questions

The various principles identified in this section will be utilized to answer the following research questions:

RQ1:   How can we explain Nestlé's failed in its response to the palm oil sourcing crisis triggered by Greenpeace?

RQ2:   What insight does the ethic of care offer into the Nestlé palm oil sourcing crisis?

METHOD

Case studies are a common, qualitative research technique in public relations and other disciplines. This section provides a short explanation of the case study method along with an overview to the Nestlé-Greenpeace case.

The Case Study Method

The case study method analyzes actual events to understand what was executed properly and/or improperly in the case. Case studies are not simply a statement of opinion by the researcher. The key to the case study method is to have one or more analytic tools. The analytic tools are the theories or principles that help to explain why a particular action was effective or ineffective. The analytic tools are used to supply evidence for the researcher's conclusions about the effectiveness or ineffectiveness of actions taken in the case (Garvin, 2003).

Summary of Nestlé-Greenpeace Battle

In March of 2009, Greenpeace initiated a campaign called "Ask Nestlé to give Rainforests a Break." Typical for Greenpeace actions, a website was created to supply detailed information about the campaign. The central concern for the campaign was to stop the destruction of rain forest orangutan habit caused by irresponsible palm oil sourcing. Nestlé is one of the largest users of palm oil that was still using the Sinar Mas Group, a company strongly linked to rainforest destruction to create palm oil plantations, and had not yet agreed to responsible palm oil practices. However,

Nestlé had pledged to move toward sustainable palm oil sourcing by 2015. A focal point of the Greenpeace campaign website was a PDF that documented Nestlé's connection to rain forest destruction. In addition to a website devoted to the campaign, Greenpeace created a video for YouTube that as a parody of a Nestlé commercial, intended to expose the destruction of orangutan habitat. Nestlé responded by trying to have the video removed from YouTube. The effort to remove the video from the Internet spawned social media discussions about censorship.

The battlefield then shifted to Facebook. Greenpeace and others began posting to Nestlé' Facebook page questioning why Nestlé would take six years to source palm oil responsibly. Some people posted comments using a "Killer version" of the Nestlé Kit Kat candy bar logo as their picture. People often use images instead of their own pictures on Facebook when trying to make a point about an issue. Nestlé announced anyone using this altered logo would have their messages deleted. This resulted in additional charges of censorship by Nestlé. Nestlé responded to the censorship charges with a sarcastic response that increased negative reactions toward the company. Eventually Nestlé apologized for the posts and agreed to immediate actions to comply with responsible palm oil sourcing. Greenpeace won the battle in part due to Nestlé's ineptitude in social media.

Analytic Tools

Four conceptually-related analytic tools were selected for this case analysis: the challenge crisis, stakeholder salience, crisis response, and ethic of care. The Nestlé and Greenpeace case can be considered a challenge crisis. Challenges are crises because they threat to damage organizational reputations. Analyzing a challenge crisis requires detailing what constitutes a challenge, how organizations assess a challenge, communicative options in a challenge crisis, and the role of ethics of care in a challenge. Stakeholder salience is helpful in understanding the reason Greenpeace's action represent a threat to Nestlé. The crisis response explores the options and factors affecting Nestlé's reaction to the Greenpeace effort. The ethic of care provides a mechanism for examining the ethical dimension of the case.

RESULTS

Case Study

In March of 2010, Nestlé found itself in a challenge crisis with Greenpeace. Greenpeace felt Nestlé was moving too slowly in efforts to sustainably source palm oil. Greenpeace's organic challenge noted how Nestlé was still buying palm oil from suppliers, such as the Sinar Mas Group, known to be destroying the rain forests and orangutan habitats. Greenpeace launched a social media-based, organic challenge based on saving orangutans. The challenge was organic because Greenpeace was highlighting how Nestlé was out of step with current stakeholder expectations about palm oil sourcing. Greenpeace launched a website to serve as the base for their communicative efforts. The website provides a centralized, digital location for Greenpeace's effort to change Nestlé's palm oil sourcing. The initial message outside of the website was a YouTube video that parodied a Nestlé commercial for its Kit Kat candy bar. Nestlé responded by trying to force the removal of the video from YouTube. In the video a man begins to eat a Kit Kat bar. Blood drips from the candy bar and we see that it is really the digits of an orangutan. The video ends with orangutans clinging to a lone tree as we here chain saws cutting. An appeal is made to make Nestlé stop destroying orangutan habitat by switching to sustainable palm oil sourcing. Greenpeace claimed Nestlé was trying to censor their message and interest in the video and challenge increased.

Soon the venue migrated to Nestlé's Facebook page. Greenpeace activists began posting messages to the Nestlé wall detailing why Nestlé was acting irresponsibility and asking them to end the practices that were killing orangutans by contributing to rainforest destruction (their habitat). The first response from Nestlé was stating it would be sustainable in palm oil sourcing by 2015 and proved a link for more information. The negative postings began to increase in number with many people using the image of the "Killer" version of the Kit Kat logo as their photograph. The "Killer" logo was the white circle of the Kit Kat logo that replaced Kit Kat with Killer. Nestlé responded by telling people not to post messages with altered Nestlé logos. This action was labeled censorship to which a Nestlé represented responded: "Oh please. ...it's like we're censoring everything to allow only positive comments" (Riding, 2010). This comment triggered additional comments and charges of being callous. The negative reactions to the Nestlé request increased interest from the traditional media as well. For over two days the activists controlled what was posted to Facebook. Nestlé had been hijacked in the social media. Shortly after the Facebook hijacking, Nestlé changed its palm oil sourcing to reflect the demands of Greenpeace. Once the changes were made, the challenge ended and Greenpeace accepted the change as legitimate. Nestlé was pillared in the social media for not understanding social media and mismanaging the situation (e.g., Warner & Yeomans, 2012).

Case Analysis

Two research questions drove this case analysis. RQ1 involves finding an explanation for why Nestlé' failed in its efforts to manage the palm oil sourcing crisis. Popular opinion said Nestlé' failed but how do we justify that conclusion? The framework of a challenge crisis combined with IRT is used to justify Nestlé as a failure in the palm oil sourcing case.

ICT and stakeholder salience can be used to explain why Greenpeace could not be ignored by Nestlé and had to offer some public response. Nestlé could not ignore the palm oil sourcing challenge because Greenpeace effectively leveraged the Internet, including social media, to increase its salience for Nestlé in terms of palm oil sourcing. Responsible palm oil sourcing is a legitimate concern because of its environmental impact. Nestlé never challenged to legitimacy of responsible palm oil sourcing. From the perspective of the ethic of care, corporations, (powerful actors), should give extra consideration to the environment, (a powerless actor), when selecting palm oil suppliers. Nestlé was guilty of not providing the proper level of care in its palm oil sourcing decisions. Hence, Nestlé's' palm oil sourcing could be considered unethical and irresponsible thereby establishing it was a legitimate concern.

Greenpeace generated power by using multiple Internet channels to spread the challenge message. The website for the campaign served as the hub, but links to that hub were provided on YouTube, Facebook, and blogs. According to Internet Contagion Theory (ICT), such a hub and spoke design is an effective means of building power because it can intensify attention on a cause. Using multiple channels in one way to increase power and that power is amplified by strategically linking the channels together (Coombs & Holladay, 2012). The messages built legitimacy by documenting the link between irresponsible palm oil sourcing and rainforest destruction, a link that went unchallenged. Greenpeace showed a willingness to stay with the concern backed with communicative skill. Taken together, these stakeholder salience factors create strong likelihood and impact ratings for the Greenpeace challenge threat.

The challenge was *organic* because Nestlé was accused of being slow to respond to new stakeholder expectations about responsible palm oil sourcing. Nestlé's initial response to the YouTube video and posts on its Facebook page reflect a *repression response*. Nestlé was trying to limit how challengers expressed their view on the palm oil sourcing concern and that can be taken as an effort to stop the spread of the challenge. The response was ineffective and served only to intensify interest in the YouTube video and further spread the challenge. Social media users value the free expression of ideas and any hint of censorship will trigger a backlash. Nestlé learned this lesson the hard way.

After creating a backlash, Nestlé then acknowledged the need to meet these new stakeholder expectations and how they would make the change—a reform response. The reform was an immediate change to responsible palm oil sourcing rather than using 2015 as the target date. The second response was effective because Greenpeace and others supporting the challenge accepted Nestlé's changes as a victory. The reform response was the best fit to the situation. Nestlé had already noted the value of responsible palm oil sourcing and now has committed to stop using any problem suppliers within a year. The change reflects an ethic of care as Nestlé' was providing additional care for the environment. Moreover, the reform was a step toward repairing relationships damaged by Nestlé's initial repressive response. The problem was Nestlé's original misstep in employing a repressive response erode the benefits it could derive from the reform response.

The second research question added an ethical component by exploring what the ethic of care can add to the analysis. It can be argued that the palm oil sourcing challenge was a result of a failure of the ethic of care. Nestlé' was not showing care by sourcing palm oil in a manner that allowed continued harm to a less powerful stakeholder. Using the ethic of care as a standard for behavior, there was a legitimate reason to challenge Nestlé on its palm oil sourcing. Moreover, Nestlé's repression efforts violate an ethic of care. Nestlé's was continuing its failure to show special care for a vulnerable actor and was damaging additional relationships by offending other stakeholders committed to the free expression of ideas on the Internet. The initial challenge response by Nestlé's reflected the antithesis of care. The second response by Nestlé, (reform), finally honored the idea of care and ended the crisis. The ethic of care illustrated how behavior deemed as unethical can trigger a crisis and why a repression response can be viewed as unethical and serve to escalate a crisis.

DISCUSSION AND CONCLUSIONS

Implications for Public Relations Practice

As noted in the introduction, Nestlé had become an example of ineffective social media use in its battle with Greenpeace. The challenge crisis provided an overall lens for understanding why Nestlé failed that was expanded with insights from ICT. Nestlé was faced with a challenge crisis. Because Greenpeace had arrayed Internet communication channels to build power, establish legitimacy for the challenge, and demonstrate its willingness to push the challenge, Nestlé had to respond. ICT can be used to determine the salience of a challenge. Practitioners must assess a challenge to determine if a response is necessary and what response might be most appropriate for the challenge. Nestlé's action demonstrated the danger of an inappropriate response using social media in a challenge crisis. Communicating during any crisis can make the situation worse when the communication strategy is a poor fit with the demands of the crisis. Nestlé then moved to a reform response to the challenge crisis but only after intensifying the damage created by the crisis.

Ethical Implications for the Practice of Social Media

From an ethical standpoint, Nestlé choose an inappropriate initial response. By trying to repress the challenge, Nestlé increased awareness of and support for the challenge. A repression response to a challenge risks backlash when the organization cannot justify stopping a message. The backlash is intensified in social media because of the specter of censorship. Any hint of censorship in social media will raise ethical alarms and rebukes. Nestlé was charged with censorship and unethical behavior. From an ethic of care perspective, the repression further illustrated Nestlé's failure to protect the powerless groups it affected and a willingness to damage relationships with other stakeholders. Organizations must be cognizant of how the power relationship in a challenge can influence ethical evaluations of their actions. This case provides insights into how to select both and effective and ethical response by illustrating an ineffective and ethically questionable response.

Discussion Questions

1. How ethical was Greenpeace in its utilization of social media in this case? What is the rationale behind your evaluation?
2. Besides the ethic of care, what other ethical framework(s) could to explain Nestlé's actions as unethical?
3. Was Nestlé's failure more a matter of ethics or skill? Explain your decision.

SUGGESTED READINGS

Caught red-handed: How Nestlé's use of palm is having a devastating impact on rainforests, the climate and orang-utans. (2010). Retrieved from: http://www.greenpeace.org/international/en/publications/reports/caught-red-handed-how-nestle/

Coombs W. T., & Holladay, S. J. (2012). Internet contagion theory 2.0: How internet communication channels empower stakeholder. In S. Duhé (Ed.) *New Media and public relations* (2nd ed.), (pp. 21–30). New York: Peter Lang.

Simola, S. (2005). Concepts of care in organizational crisis prevention. *Journal of Business Ethics, 62,* 341–353.

Warner, B. & Yeomans, M. (2012). *#FAIL: The 50 greatest social media screw-ups and how to avoid being the next one.* Raleigh, NC: Lulu.

REFERENCES

Barton, L. (2001). *Crisis in organizations II* (2nd ed.). Cincinnati, OH: College Divisions South-Western.

Bowers, J. W., Ochs, D. J., & Jensen, R. J. (1993). *The rhetoric of agitation and control* (2nd ed.). Prospect Heights, IL: Waveland Press, Inc.

Carol G. (1982). *In a different voice, psychological theory and women's development.* Cambridge, MA: Harvard University Press.

Caught red-handed: How Nestlé's use of palm is having a devastating impact on rainforests, the climate and orang-utans. (2010). Retrieved from: http://www.greenpeace.org/international/en/publications/reports/caught-red-handed-how-nestle/

Coombs, W. T. (2010). Crisis communication: A developing field. In R. L. Heath (Ed.) *Handbook of public relations* (2nd) (pp. 477–488). Thousand Oaks, CA: Sage.

Coombs, W. T. (2012). *Ongoing crisis communication: Planning, managing, and responding* (3rd ed.). Thousand Oaks, CA: Sage.

Coombs, W. T., & Holladay, S. J. (2007). Consumer empowerment through the web: How Internet contagions can increase stakeholder power. In S. C. Duhe (Ed.) *New media and public relations* (pp. 175–188). New York: Peter Lang Publishing.

Coombs, W. T., & Holladay, S. J. (2010). *PR strategy and application: Managing influence.* Malden, MA: Wiley-Blackwell.

Coombs W. T., & Holladay, S. J. (2012). Internet contagion theory 2.0: How internet communication channels empower stakeholder. In S. Duhe' (Ed.) *New media and public relations* (2nd ed.), (pp. 21–30). New York: Peter Lang.

Garvin, D. (2003, Sept–Oct). Making the case: Professional education for the world of practice. *Harvard Magazine, 106*(1), 56–65, 107.

Gilligan, C. (1980). *In a different voice.* Cambridge: Harvard University Press.

Kim, P. H., Ferrin, D. L., Cooper, C.D., & Dirks, K. T. (2004). Removing the showdown of suspicion: The effects of apology versus denial for repairing competence-versus integrity-based trust violations. *Journal of Applied Psychology, 89*(1), 104–118.

Lerbinger, O. (1997). *The crisis manager: Facing risk and responsibility.* Mahwah, NJ: Lawrence Erlbaum.

Mitchell, R. K., Agle, R. A., & Wood, D. J. (1997). Toward a theory of stakeholder identification and salience: Defining the principle of who and what really counts. *Academy of Management Review, 22*(4), 853–886.

Ridings, M (2010). Take a look at what Nestle thinks a brand manager does. Retrieved from http://techguerilla.com/nestle-facebook-greenpeace-timeline-in-process/.

Simola, S. (2003). Ethics of justice and care in corporate crisis management. *Journal of Business Ethics, 46,* 351–361.

Simola, S. (2005). Concepts of care in organizational crisis prevention. *Journal of Business Ethics, 62,* 341–353.

Smith, N. (2008). *I was wrong.* New York: Cambridge University Press.

Vanacker, B., & Breslin, J. (2006). Ethics of care: More than just another tool to bah the media? *Journal of Mass Media Ethics, 21*(2–3), 196–214.

Warner, B., & Yeomans, M. (2012). *#FAIL: The 50 greatest social media screwups and How to avoid being the next one.* Raleigh, NC: Lulu.

10 Coca-Cola, Community, Diversity, and Cosmopolitanism

How Public Relations Builds Global Trust and Brand Relevance with Social Media

Nneka Logan and Natalie T. J. Tindall

INTRODUCTION

Global corporations—especially those that have been the subject of anti-corporate activism and charges of discrimination—face two major communicative challenges: maintaining trust with their diverse, multicultural publics, and sustaining brand relevance in a highly competitive environment. These two interrelated challenges help to explain why Coca-Cola would send three diverse young people on a year-long, 275,000-mile global adventure as part of the largest social media campaign in company history.

Coca-Cola's Expedition 206 campaign unites in-person, face-to-face human interaction with social media in a comprehensive communication strategy based on the idea of happiness. The concept of happiness functions as a vehicle to build brand awareness, cultivate community locally and globally, create positive sentiments about Coke, and spread happiness within a fragmented, multicultural world where multinational corporations such as Coca-Cola are often the subject of social skepticism.

Tony Martin, a 29-year-old kindergarten teacher from Washington, D.C.; 23-year-old Kelly Ferris, a university student from Brussels; and Antonio Santiago, a 24-year-old student from Mexico City, were selected as Coca-Cola "happiness ambassadors." Their mission was to find out what makes people happy in the 206 countries and territories where Coca-Cola operates, document their experiences, and share stories of happiness with the world in 365 days or less (Coca-Cola, press release, 2009). To accomplish these goals, the trio received laptops, digital cameras, smartphones, and everything necessary to bring the campaign to life on Facebook, Twitter, YouTube, Flickr, and social media sites.

Expedition 206 officially launched with a celebration in Madrid on January 1, 2010, and ended on December 30, 2010, in Atlanta at the World of Coca-Cola Museum with a live celebration and webcast. During the journey, happiness ambassadors visited countries from Aruba to Zimbabwe. They made stops in large cities and small towns. They spent time visiting with everyday people as well as attending marquee global events such as the Olympic Winter Games in Vancouver, British Columbia, the FIFA World

Cup in South Africa, and the World Expo in Shanghai, China in 2010 (Coca-Cola Expedition 206).

Despite Expedition 206's innovative, comprehensive marketing, and public relations strategy, the campaign also raised questions and issues of significant concern. For example, what were the logistical, cultural, and business risks associated with sending three young people on a worldwide adventure with little substantive supervision? How could Coca-Cola be sure that the trio could handle the rigor and responsibilities of the journey? How could Coca-Cola communicate multiculturalism and diversity in the campaign? Were there any ethical considerations involved that could adversely impact the campaign's chances for success?

Complicating matters, members of the public could perceive it inappropriate for corporations to equate human attributes such as happiness with consumerism. An additional cause for concern was the perception that authentic community cannot be achieved by corporate campaigns. In light of these circumstances, what could the company do to manage the concept of happiness so that the campaign resonated as sincere with its various publics around the world? The Expedition 206 communication strategy had to address all of these challenges and anticipate others in order to avoid disaster.

LITERATURE REVIEW

Public Relations and Community Building

Kruckeberg and Starck (1988) have argued that the primary aim of public relations practice is community building. According to Kruckeberg and Starck (1988),

> Those who take public relations seriously, professionals as well as scholars, should not view public relations as a means of "us"—communication specialists—simply doing something to "them"—targeted publics. Instead, those responsible for public relations should approach communication as a complex multi flow processes having the potential to help create a sense of community. (p. xii)

A multi flow process is advantageous because it is flexible enough to accommodate innovative communication technologies that foster socializing and community building in new ways. In 2004, Kruckeberg and Starck expanded their theory of the community building capacity of public relations to include consumer communities. Consumer communities are a group of enthusiasts who believe in the superiority of a product or service and who publicly identify with it. In contrast to naturally occurring human communities based on geographic or cultural similarities, consumer communities can be created by corporations that provide the product or service.

They are sustained through members' loyalty to the brand and their belief in the merits of the product or service.

Community building efforts and the concept of requisite variety. Kruckeberg and Starck (1988) also advised that public relations practitioners should be responsible for the development and maintenance of communities formed around a corporation's products and services. This idea ties to the Excellence theory's concept of diversity. In the context of the Excellence theory, the concept of requisite variety is essential to the promise and need for diversity in public relations. As L. A. Grunig, J. E. Grunig, and Dozier (2002) explained, requisite variety is the notion that an organization should have as much difference and variety internally as exists in its external environment and among its stakeholders. In an earlier discussion of the subject, Dozier, L. A. Grunig, and J. E. Grunig (1995) wrote, "The variety within provides a basis for building mutually beneficial relationships with diverse people and groups outside the organization. Without such requisite variety, misunderstandings occur" (p. 4).

Other scholars have argued that the ability to create community through the public relations function can be achieved through the practitioners' knowledge, understanding, and application of multicultural communication skills. Echoing Rakow (1989), Sha and Ford (2007) argued that all practitioners who work in the area of strategic communication "must learn to consider multiple diversities as constituting integral and integrated aspects. ...rather than as 'Others'" (p. 383). In multiple articles on intersectionality, identity, and publics, Vardeman-Winter and Tindall (2010) have argued that practitioners must cross cultural boundaries without bias and place the audiences' standpoint and perspective at the forefront in campaign development.

Intersection of Identity, Care, and Cosmopolitanism in Communities

Beyond the tenets just mentioned, the communitarianism theory outlined by Kruckeberg and Starck (1988) has not developed to include the concepts of belonging and the intersections between identity and place relating to where and how communities are defined. This section outlines theories explored in other disciplines that add value to how we in public relations conceptualize community and implement community building.

Community

Communities are built around social classifications and identities. Social classifications are the demographic categories that we sort people into, defined by "the prototypical characteristics abstracted from the members" (Ashforth & Mael, 1989, p. 20). Social classification serves to order the environment, define others, and allow individuals to define themselves and construct social identities. The concept of social identity radiates from the belief of a connectedness or a "oneness with or belonging to human aggregate" (Ashforth & Mael, 1989, p. 21). According to Owens (2003), social identity stems from the "categories to which individuals are socially recognized as belonging. It is one of their labels. The world encounters the individual—and the individual the world—in varying categorical terms" (p. 224).

Yuval-Davis (2011) considered social identity as the narratives we tell ourselves and others about who we are, writing that these identities

> can shift and change, be contested and multiple. These identity narratives can relate to the past, to a myth of origin; they can be aimed to explain the present, and probably; above all, they function as a projection of future trajectory. (p. 14)

This aligns with what Owens (2003) and Sha (1995) articulated, people can define who they are, accepting or rejecting the social labels that groups or society places on them. They can choose to avow certain identities and to shun ascribed identities. Ascribed identities are those socially constructed identities attached to an individual upon birth (Jenkins, 1996); Khakimova, Briones, Madden, and Campbell (2011) conceptualized ascribed identities as those "given to a person by an assigned reference group and may not necessarily align with that person's avowed identity" (p. 3). Avowed identities are accumulated over one's lifetime, emerge from things such as career choices and organizational affiliations, and "are generally—although not necessarily—the outcome of a degree of self-direction" (Owens, 2003, p. 142). Sha (1995) considered these identities as the ones that people used to "claim and assert . . . themselves, through identifying with a particular cultural group" (Khakimova et al., 2011, p. 3). Public relations practitioners must be aware of the complex constellation of factors influencing identity and self-perception so they can craft messaging in ways that will be most receptive to the audience, and most conducive to the objectives of community building.

Ethic of Care

Gilligan (1982) first articulated the concept of care as an alternative to masculine, hegemonic approaches to ethics. Rather than devaluing care as a woman-only skill or strength, Gilligan elevated it to a noble aptitude that should be activated and expected across gendered lines. The adoption of this ethical approach is "reflected in concern about how to fulfill conflicting responsibilities to different people, as opposed to questions of how to resolve claims of conflicting rights among them" (Simola, 2003, p. 354). The scholarly conversations around the ethic of care have been centered in organization studies (Lawrence & Maitlis, 2012), geography (Popke,

2006), business ethics (Jordan, Diermeier, & Galinsky, 2012), nursing science (Green, 2012), feminist studies, and philosophy. Public relations scholarship is a latent field regarding the integration of the ethic of care into the scholarship and into our tactical approaches, especially when organizations consider themselves as part of a global community and as global citizens.

In her vision of ethics of care, Tronto (1993) situated care (along with other emotions) within citizenship and argued that care should "become an integral part of practices of democratic citizenship" (Yuval-Davis, 2011, p. 184). One important aspect of both citizenship and community are relationships. At the core of those relationships are care, regardless of whether it is defined as "a species activity that includes everything we do to maintain, continue, and repair our world" (Tronto, 1993, p. 103), "warmth" (Jordan et al., 2012), "connectedness to others" (Lloyd, 2004, p. 247), "mutual obligations and relations of trust" (McDowell, 2004, p. 157), "cooperation rather than competition" (Smith & Easterlow, 2004, p. 115), and "interdependence over individualization" (Smith, 2005, p. 11). To distill this slippery concept into something concrete, Popke (2006) summed it up best by stating care is a relationally focused way of life that has "a normative concern for inclusion" (p. 506). The ethic of care undergirds the public relations concept of community and communitarianism as explicated by Kruckeberg and Starck (1988). Those authors detailed how public relations functioned as community building, and they advanced the idea of community building because communication technologies have contributed to the loss of social community and to the subsequent feelings of individual alienation and isolation (Habermas, 1991). Public relations is concerned with gathering and inclusiveness—the main principles guiding the ethics of care, and new communication technologies do not necessarily have to be an obstacle to community building. Public relations practitioners could counteract these conditions with a "fight fire with fire" strategy that employs communication technologies to restore that which they fractured—the sense of human, social community.

Cosmopolitanism

Appiah's (2006) theory of cosmopolitanism is a philosophical worldview that embraces ideas of community, individuality, commonality, and difference. Central to its focus is the concept of globalization. Cosmopolitanism is a process of intelligence, curiosity, and engagement about the world and its inhabitants. Cosmopolitanism encourages people to become citizens of the world by:

- Recognizing that all human beings have obligations to one another.
- Advocating equal respect for local cultures and global society.
- Embracing both commonality and difference.

- Encouraging people to learn more about the diverse cultures that inhabit the planet that all human beings share. (Appiah, 2006, pp. xi–xi)

The ideal cosmopolitan citizen of the world would be the polyglot person, experiencing many different cultures, who would feel just as comfortable in the boardroom as on an urban street corner.

Appiah (2006) asks an important question: "A citizen of the world: how far can we take that idea?" (p. xv). Coca-Cola's Expedition 206 campaign lays the foundation for a new form of cosmopolitanism to be considered— corporate cosmopolitanism. For the purposes of this case study, corporate cosmopolitanism should be understood as the philosophical orientation of global corporations that:

- Recognize that corporations have social obligations to human actors.
- Demonstrate respect for individual and cultural differences and commonalities.
- Demonstrate a commitment to learning about the diversity of the world's cultures.
- Dedicate themselves to building community by amplifying positive values with wide public support.

RESEARCH QUESTIONS

Based on the literature reviewed in the previous sections, the researchers proposed the following research questions:

RQ1: How did Expedition 206 and Coca-Cola manage the idea of happiness?

RQ2: How did Expedition 206 and Coca-Cola demonstrate respect for individual and cultural differences and commonalities to build community?

RQ3: How did Expedition 206 and Coca-Cola use the concepts of cosmopolitanism to build community?

METHOD

This case study employs a qualitative content analysis. According to Bromley (1990), a case study is the "systematic inquiry into an event or a set of related events which aims to describe and explain the phenomenon of interest" (p. 302). The case study can be seen as both an approach to understanding public relations praxis and as a scholarly methodology. A theoretically-enriched case study bridges the all-too-frequent gap between scholarship and professional practice, and theoretical analysis draws attention to the reciprocal nature of the relationship between theory and practice. Whereas theory illuminates the implications of practice, practice functions as a barometer for the accuracy of theory and its utility in the real world.

The researchers deployed qualitative content analysis to understand and interpret the data in this study. The unit of analysis for this single-case, descriptive study is the Coca-Cola Company's Expedition 206 campaign. Most simply put, "researchers use content analysis to identify, enumerate, and analyze occurrences of specific messages and message characteristics embedded in texts" (Frey, Botan, & Kreps, 2000). This case study is based on dozens of documents and content available on The Coca-Cola Company website including press releases about Expedition 206, social media posts from the ambassadors, descriptions of the company's history and values, and mainstream media coverage about the company and the Expedition 206 campaign. We explore how these texts build community, create the concept of happiness, address multicultural audiences, and embrace a sense of cosmopolitanism to inspire positive sentiments toward the brand. The authors also used critical analysis (Lindlof & Taylor, 2002) to interpret the texts and qualitative content analysis to systematically extract thematic threads from textual data. According to Elo and Kyngäs (2008), the aim of qualitative content analysis "is to attain a condensed and broad description of the phenomenon, and the outcome of the analysis is concepts or categories describing the phenomenon" (p. 108).

Case Background: The Coca-Cola Company

Today, the Atlanta-based Coca-Cola Company dominates the global market. It is number one in sales of sparkling beverages, juices, drinks, and ready-to-serve coffee and teas; number two in sports drinks sales; and number three in bottled water sales. With more than 3,300 beverage products, 92,800 employees, operations in 206 countries and nearly 1.6 billion servings daily, Coca-Cola is the world's largest beverage company, and its name is one of the most recognized brands in the world. The company's corporate mission, vision, and values statement include commitments to inspiring optimism and happiness, being a responsible citizen that makes a difference in communities, celebrating diversity, and focusing on profitability by maximizing long-term return on investment in responsible ways (The Coca-Cola Company, Vision, Mission & Values, 2009).

A Brief History of the Coca-Cola Company

In many ways, ideas of happiness, social unity, and joy were foundational to Coca-Cola's creation and early marketing strategies. Its flagship soft drink was invented in Atlanta just after the Civil War as a "feel good product intended for every, race, creed, and color" (The Coca-Cola Company, The Heritage Timeline). During the company's first year of operation in 1886, sales were slow. By 1915, Coke was available to anyone in the U.S. who could afford to spare a nickel (The Coca-Cola Company, The Heritage Timeline). When its 100-year anniversary came in 1986, The Coca-Cola Company was a multinational corporation and global brand. The company continued its domination of the competitive ready-to-serve beverage industry through the 1990s and 2000s, even during the toughest economic times, delivering 49 consecutive years of increased dividend payments (The Coca-Cola Company, A Letter From Our Chairman and Chief Executive Officer, 2010). In 2010, during the midst of a global economic recession, the company generated more than $9.5 billion in cash, an increase of 16% above 2009 (The Coca-Cola Company, A Letter From Our Chairman and Chief Executive Officer, 2010). Yet, all has not always been well at Coca-Cola.

Dark Days at Coca-Cola

Over the years, Coca-Cola has been involved in several high-profile controversies. For example, in November 2000, Coca-Cola agreed to pay $192.5 million to settle a racial discrimination lawsuit brought by African-American employees who claimed that they were not being promoted and paid at rates comparable to their white counterparts. It was the largest racial discrimination lawsuit settlement to date at that time (Parker, 2006).

In 2001 and 2006, lawsuits alleging that The Coca-Cola Company was involved in the execution of pro-labor activists in Latin America were filed. In response to these allegations, activists launched The Killer Coke Campaign to raise global public awareness of Coca-Cola's labor issues ("Campaign to stop killer Coke", 2004). The Killercoke.org website has received more than 1.6 million views since October 2004. This well-known, anti-corporate campaign compromised the brand's image within the youth market and led to the widespread boycott of Coca-Cola products on several U.S. college campuses. High-profile student demonstrations occurred at New York University and the University of Michigan, where students succeeded in banning Coke from their campuses.

In 2004, internal strife about legal and reputational issues led to a shake-up in executive management, which resulted in the early departure of Deval L. Patrick, former Coca-Cola executive vice president, general counsel, and corporate secretary. Patrick, the current governor of Massachusetts, publicly expressed his concerns over the company's management of its legal issues. In 2010, India's Kerala state cabinet recommended that Coca-Cola be held responsible for causing pollution and water depletion in the town of Plachimada (India Resource Center, 2010). To complicate matters, the Coca-Cola corporation's high profile consistently attracts the attention of anti-corporate activists around the world who target well-known brands to bring notoriety to their causes.

This brief overview of Coca-Cola's history reveals the image of a very successful corporation that has experienced significant challenges, especially in the areas of diversity, developing markets, and community relations. While these issues were not raised in the Expedition 206 campaign, they provide important insights about Coca-Cola's relationship to its publics and the social context in which the Coca-Cola brand operates. These circumstances suggest the need for complex communication strategies that do more than merely advocate the corporate position or attempt to favorably shape public opinion. Strategies that regain and retain public trust, build brand relevance, demonstrate a genuine commitment to community, and show respect for all peoples of the world, while reminding consumers of the egalitarian origins of the brand are needed. Although this is not an easy task, Expedition 206 is an interesting example of how a communication strategy designed to accomplish these goals might unfold.

Inside the Expedition 206 Campaign

"We wanted to bring the idea of happiness to life and have as many people participate as possible."
—Adam Brown, Director, Office of Digital
Communications and Social Media

Clyde Tuggle, Coca-Cola's senior vice president of global affairs and communications, developed the idea of Expedition 206. This meant the project commenced with top-level, executive buy-in and could avoid the often arduous task of gaining such support (Zmuda, 2009). Expedition 206 also included a close collaboration with marketing. While the communications department led the overall effort and spearheaded the digital media campaign, both departments participated in preparing local markets for ambassador arrival, and the marketing department also used the happiness ambassadors for promotional events (Zmuda, 2009). This collaborative effort allowed Coca-Cola to maximize its internal creative resources for the campaign.

Social Media Strategy

"The challenge we put to the communications team was to think about the social and digital media space as a new venue for driving good public relations for the company."
—Clyde Tuggle, senior vice president, Global
Public Affairs and Communications

One simple premise guided the social media strategy for this first-time public relations experiment: Fish where the fish are. According to Michael Donnelly, Coca-Cola's group director of worldwide interactive marketing,

Social media is where our consumers are at the moment. Our strategy is to be everywhere our consumers are, but as a member of the community. Within the social media marketing realm, our approach is to be a strong member of the community and that's enabling consumers to celebrate manifestations of the brand. (Zmuda, 2009)

Social media is the ideal vehicle for consumers to celebrate manifestations of the brand. Unlike traditional media that is based on a one-way view of communication from organizations to consumers, social media transforms consumers into participants in the brand by empowering them with voice and engaging them in conversations about the corporation's products and services. This interactive, more democratic process of communication and information sharing allows corporations to involve the public as partners in creating a sense of community around their products and services.

Moreover, the image and video sharing capacities of social media bring campaigns to life through the process of visualization. Images and videos are powerful tools in a social media strategy because they allow corporations to transmit meaning multiculturally, across a variety of different languages. For example, still or moving images of smiles, hugs, and laughter communicate happiness almost anywhere in the world. For global businesses such as Coca-Cola, the "fish" are everywhere, and social media provides a very effective, efficient mechanism to connect with geographically dispersed and culturally diverse publics.

Culture, Community, Cosmopolitanism, and Expedition 206: Research Questions in Context

RQ1:   How did Expedition 206 and Coca-Cola manage the idea of happiness?

The success (or failure) of Expedition 206 hinged upon Coca-Cola's ability to convincingly associate itself with the concept of happiness. To its advantage, the company has had a long and close affiliation with the concept of happiness, beginning with its founding after the Civil War. In 2007, the company opened the Happiness Institute to study the concept of happiness. Although Coca-Cola might consider itself an expert on the subject, the corporate appropriation of any human emotion such as happiness remains a challenging prospect for two main reasons. First, it can create the perception that the corporation is disingenuously trying to manipulate the emotions of its publics to sell more products. Second, the entire campaign can come across as the elaborate attempt to distract the public from the negative and more serious circumstances a company has faced or is currently facing.

These issues manifested in October 2010, just before the official start of Expedition 206, when Coca-Cola sponsored its first Happiness Congress. At the conference, Jigme Thinley, the prime minister of Bhutan, delivered a speech about happiness and claimed that authentic human happiness is not found in financial and material gain—a seemingly appropriate message for the audience and occasion. However, someone asked Mr. Thinley if it was not somehow unethical to promote the egalitarian ideals of happiness at an event sponsored by a consumer goods conglomerate? (Mallet, 2010). The question illuminated the difficulty many have in equating corporate actors with altruistic, positive human values. The implication was that Coca-Cola could never be legitimately associated with happiness because it was a corporation dedicated to its own financial gain.

To address or possibly overcome these challenges, Coca-Cola's communication strategy could not simply and straightforwardly attempt to associate the brand's name with the concept happiness. To be truly efficacious, it had to also create the tangible experience of happiness, contribute to global knowledge about happiness, and share happiness in ways that would be received as sincere and legitimate.

RQ2:   How did Expedition 206 and Coca-Cola demonstrate respect for individual and cultural differences and commonalities to build community?

If a survey were to ask the public to describe what type of global citizen Coca-Cola is, the results would likely be mixed. The Coca-Cola mission, vision, values statement, and press coverage about Expedition 206 indicate that the company views itself as a good global citizen. Its strong record of corporate social responsibility is evident. In 2008, for example, Coca-Cola gave a total of $82 million in charitable donations to community, educational, environmental and other groups around the world. However, ongoing negative media coverage continued to shape public perception of the corporation. The challenge, then, for the public relations team was to use Expedition 206 as a mechanism to more definitively establish Coca-Cola as a positive, respected—and respectable—member of the global community. This goal was likely furthered by the ambassadors who accomplished their goal of learning the secret to happiness. The team worked to collect local responses about happiness throughout their travels. As ambassador Kelly Ferris explained, "People of all countries and cultures told us family and friends are what make them happy most, and they often mentioned good music, good food, and sports. The general rule is that people make people happy. When they mention food or music or sports, they talk about sharing those experiences with other people as the true source of happiness" (Coca-Cola, press release 2010).

RQ3:   How did Expedition 206 and Coca-Cola use the concepts of cosmopolitanism to build community?

While it would have been more cost-efficient to send the ambassadors to only a few major markets and rely on social media to carry the rest of the campaign across the globe, Expedition 206 aimed to demonstrate a respect for the diversity of Coke's consumer base by sending ambassadors to industrialized and developing countries alike. Moreover, the local communities visited by the ambassadors were not merely passive recipients of Coca-Cola's ideas of happiness. Their input in describing and defining happiness in their cultures made them active participants in a global conversation about the concept. Collectively, these circumstances could reinvigorate Coca-Cola's image as a good global citizen making a sincere attempt to live out the founding values of its brand and help Coke to embody the concept of corporate cosmopolitanism.

Ethical Implications for the Practice of Social Media

Expedition 206 relied on a combination of social media and face-to-face, physical, interpersonal interactions to achieve its key goals: to stimulate excitement about the Coke brand and to use the brand as a vehicle to create happiness in several of Coke's markets around the world. Ethics were arguably a critical component of the campaign's success. Expedition 206 was the largest social media campaign in Coca-Cola company history and it involved one of the corporation's most important assets—its flagship Coke brand—as well as three young people from various backgrounds and cultures. Given the magnitude and scope of the campaign, naturally, there were ethical issues to consider. Some of these ethical include the selection of the ambassadors and transparency in social media campaigns.

The selection of the Happiness Ambassadors presented an ethical issue because the three people selected functioned as the embodiment of the Coke brand. They represented the brand's identity. In an age where diversity, multiculturalism, discrimination, and exclusion are all a part of the milieu, the selection of the ambassadors was a sensitive issue with ethical implications. How should a public relations team endeavoring to position their company as a cosmopolitan corporate citizen proceed? In Expedition 206, Coke allowed fans used social media to help elect happiness ambassadors, with the company vetting finalists. This approach that included both the public and the company in the selection process seemed an ideal way to select ambassadors. Yet critics pointed out that no one from the Arab region was selected (Hamadeh, 2009). This suggests that global corporations communicating with diverse publics around the world may still experience challenges when their approaches use social media to facilitate democratic decision making, because some members of their various publics may still feel underrepresented or excluded. It is challenging to create a fully inclusive campaign, but proceeding with an ethic of care and/or an ethic of justice can help public relations practitioners operate fairly, mindfully and with an appropriate level of sensitivity as well as anticipate potential scrutiny.

Another important ethical issue in Expedition 206 concerns transparency in social media. Once the Happiness Ambassadors were selected, how should communication between the ambassadors and the public proceed? Should the corporate communications team manage all communications between the ambassadors and the public? Should the ambassadors be allowed to "post at will" or should the public relations team manage and edit the ambassadors' communications with the public? While one bad ambassador tweet or post could do significant harm to the brand (and perhaps even to the public), corporate editing or ghost writing the ambassadors' messages could compromise the authenticity of the campaign and position Coke as an insincere company, not as a transparent, cosmopolitan one and certainly not as an ethical organization. As DiStaso & Bortree (2012) wrote, "With the decline of public trust in corporate America, organizations must consider ways to improve their relationships with key publics. One of the best strategies to build trust is through engaging and transparent communication" (p. 511) and social media is a primary mechanism corporations can leverage to increase transparency and reap the accompanying rewards of organizational transparency.

Given the complexity, duration, novelty, and global nature of Coca-Cola's Expedition 206 campaign, there were many opportunities for ethical breakdowns resulting in the kinds of scandals that have affected the company in the past. The success of the campaign is, in many ways, a result of strong corporate communications planning, sophisticated public relations practice, and especially the ethical use of social media—ethical here meaning transparent and truthful. By being transparent and truthful in their Expedition 206 social media messaging, Coke's public relation's team demonstrated an ethic of care that exemplified "the creation or strengthening of relationships among people" (Simola, 2003, p. 324) around the Coke brand. This resulted in the kind of progressive consumer communities (Kruckeberg & Starck, 2004) described.

Ethical Implications for Public Relations Practice

The Expedition 206 campaign expands the conventional practice of public relations by demonstrating that social media is a critical tool for building ethical, productive relationships between organizations and publics. In addition, this study of Expedition 206 has implications for the practice of social media. It supports the assertion that social media campaigns can be enhanced by in-person interactions, and that adding the physical, in-person interaction component to a social media campaign can make a meaningful difference.

In sum, this case study provides a compelling way to understand both the theoretical and practical implications of the Expedition 206 campaign. Beyond the example of Coca-Cola, the study highlights theoretical and practical tools for all public relations professionals to consider when they develop and execute their own communication strategies. Consistent with the work of Kruckeberg and Starck (1988) and Appiah (2006), this case study suggests that in today's complex world, not just any public relations practitioner will do. The best public relations practitioners will have multicultural understanding, an international perspective of the world and the ability to communicate ethically with diverse peoples and cultures. The global strategy combined with the attention to local markets that the Expedition 206 campaign employed succeeded in generating goodwill and happy feelings about the company. No communication strategy will prevent allegations from surfacing or guarantee positive media coverage, but when public relations professionals position their organizations as cosmopolitan corporations committed to creating positive communities, they help the corporation to remain a trusted, influential participant in the global conversations about its brands, and about its actions.

Discussion Questions

1. What role does or should transparency play in helping public relations practitioners and organizations manage socially media campaigns ethically?
2. Did Coca-Cola's Expedition 206 social media campaign demonstrate ethical communications and interactions with the public? If so, please explain how? If not, please explain why not?
3. Are there any ethical challenges or risks unique to large, global corporations that can arise from international social media campaigns such as Expedition 206? If so, how can such challenges or risks be appropriately managed to avoid or ameliorate potential issues?
4. Did Coca-Cola's Expedition 206 social media campaign demonstrate either an ethic of care or an ethic of justice or both? If so, how did these ethics shape the campaign and its outcomes?

SUGGESTED READINGS

Best social media campaigns. (2011). *Advertising Age, 82*(44), 18.

Breakenridge, D. K. (2012). *Social media and public relations: Eight new practices for the PR professional.* Upper Saddle River, New Jersey: FT Press.

DiStaso, M., & Bortree, D. S. (2012). Multi-method analysis of transparency in social media practices: Survey, interviews and content analysis. *Public Relations Review, 38*(3), 511–514.

Gilpin, D. (2010). Organizational image construction in a fragmented online media environment. *Journal of Public Relations Research 22*(3): 265–287.

How PR pros are using social media for real results. (2010, 16 March). *Mashable. com.* Retrieved from http://mashable.com/2010/03/16/public-relations-social-media-results

REFERENCES

Appiah, K. (2006). *Cosmopolitanism: Ethics in a world of strangers.* New York: W. W. Norton & Company.

Ashforth, B. E., & Mael, F. (1989). Social identity theory and the organization. *Academy of Management Review, 14,* 20–39.

Bromley. (1990). Academic contributions to psychological counseling: I.A. philosophy of science for the study of individual cases. *Counseling Psychology Quarterly 3*(3), 299–307.

Campaign to stop killer Coke. (2004). Retrieved from http://www.killercoke.org/

Coca-Cola. (2009, November 16). The votes are in! Fans choose three young people to represent Coca-Cola on unprecedented, 275-mile journey around the world [Press release]. Retrieved from http://www.thecoca-colacompany.com/presscenter/presskit_expedition_206_press_release2.html

Coca-Cola. (2010). A letter from our chairman and chief executive officer. Retrieved from http://assets.cocacolacompany.com/fe/63/bebfb66b42809dc-870cfb545fc8a/TCCC_2010_Annual_Review_Chairman_Letter.pdf

Coca-Cola. (n.d.) Expedition 206. Retrieved from http://www.worldofcoca-cola.com/expedition206.htm.

Coca-Cola. (n.d.). Mission, vision, & values. Retrieved from http://www.thecoca-colacompany.com/ourcompany/mission_vision_values.html

Coca-Cola. (n.d). Heritage timeline. Retrieved from http://heritage.coca-cola.com/

DiStaso, M. W. & Bortree, D. S. (2012). Multi-method analysis of transparency in social media practices: Survey, interviews and content analysis. *Public Relations Review, 38,* 511–514.

Dozier, D. M., Grunig, L. A., & Grunig, J. E. (1995). The manager's guide to excellence in public relations and communication management. Mahwah, NJ: Lawrence Erlbaum Associates.

Elo, S. & Kyngäs, H. (2008). The qualitative content analysis process. *Journal of Advanced Nursing, (62)*1, 107–115.

Frey, L., Botan, C, H. & Kreps, G. (2000), *Investigation communication: An introduction to research methods.* Boston: Allyn and Bacon.

Gilligan, C. (1982). *In a different voice: Psychological theory and women's development.* Cambridge, MA: Harvard University Press.

Green, B. (2012) Applying Feminist Ethics of Care to Nursing Practice. *Journal of Nursing Care, 1,* 111.

Grunig, L. A., Grunig, J. E., & Dozier. (2002) Models of public relations. *Excellent public relations and effective organizations: A study of communication management in three countries* (pp. 306–383). Mahwah, NJ: Lawrence Erlbaum Associates.

Habermas, J. (1991). The structural transformation of the public sphere: An inquiry into a category of bourgeois society. Trans. Burger, T. with Lawrence, F. Cambridge, MA: The MIT Press.

Hamadeh, D. (2009, October 27). No Arab blogger in Coca-Cola's open happiness contest. Retrieved from http://www.emirates247.com/eb247/companies-markets/media/no-arab-blogger-in-coca-cola-s-open-happiness-contest-2009-10-27-1.19002

India Resource Center. (2010, July 2). Government moves to claim $48 million compensation from Coca-Cola: Will set up claims tribunal to process claims from affected parties. Retrieved from http://www.indiaresource.org/news/2010/1037.html

Jenkins, R. (1996). *Social identity.* New York: Routledge.

Jordan, J., Diermeier, D. A., & Galinsky, A. D. (2012). The strategic Samaritan: How effectiveness and proximity affect corporate responses to external crises. *Business Ethics Quarterly, 22,* 621–648.

Khakimova, L., Briones, R. L., Madden, S., & Campbell, T. (2011). The letting girls Glow! communication campaign: Methodological and conceptual lessons for segmenting teen publics. *PRism, 8*(2). Retrieved from http://www.prismjournal.org/

Kruckeberg, D., & Starck, K. (1988). *Public relations and community: A reconstructed theory*. New York: Praeger.

Kruckeberg, D., & Starck, K. (2004). The role and ethics of community building for consumer products and services. *Journal of Promotion and Management*, 10(1–2), 133–146.

Lawrence, T. B., & Maitlis, S. (2012). Care and possibility: Enacting an ethic of care through narrative practice. *Academy of Management Review, 37*, 641–663.

Lindlof, T. R. & Taylor, B.C. (2002). *Qualitative communication research methods. Second Edition*. Thousand Oaks, CA: Sage Publications.

Lloyd, L. (2004). Morality and mortality: ageing and the ethics of care. *Ageing and Society, 24*, 235–256.

Mallet, V. (2010, October 22). Bhutan and Coke join hands for happiness. *Financial Times*. Retrieved from http://www.ft.com/

McDowell, L. (2004). Work, workfare, work/life balance and an ethic of care. *Progress in Human Geography, 28*, 145–163.

Owens, T. J. (2003). Self and identity. In J. Delamater (Ed.), *Handbook of social psychology* (pp. 205–232). New York: Kluwer.

Parker, P. (2006). Keeping it real: Race, difference, and corporate ethics at Coca-Cola. In S. K. May (Ed.), *Cases in organizational communication: Ethical perspectives and practices* (pp.169–184). Thousand Oaks, CA: Sage.

Popke, J. (2006). Geography and ethics: Everyday mediations through care and consumption. *Progress in Human Geography, 30*(4), 504–512.

Rakow, L. F. (1989). Information and power: Toward a critical theory of information campaigns. In C. T. Salmon (Ed.) *Information campaigns: Balancing social values and social change* (pp. 164–184). Newbury Park, CA: Sage Publications.

Sha, B-L. (1995). *Intercultural public relations: Exploring cultural identity as a means of segmenting publics* [Unpublished master's thesis.]. University of Maryland, College Park.

Sha, B-L., & Ford, R. (2007). Redefining "requisite variety": The challenge of multiple diversities for the future of public relations excellence. In E. L. Toth (Ed.) *The future of excellence in public relations and communication management: challenges for the next generation* (pp. 381–398). Mahwah, NJ: Lawrence Erlbaum Associates.

Simola, S. K. (2003). Ethics of justice and care in corporate crisis management. *Journal of Business Ethics, 46*, 351–361.

Smith, S. (2005). States, markets and an ethic of care. *Political Geography, 24*, 1–20.

Smith, S. & Easterlow, D. (2004) The problem with welfare. In R. Lee and D. Smith (Eds.) *Geographies and moralities: international perspectives on development, justice and place* (pp. 100–119). Malden, MA: Blackwell.

Starck, K., & Kruckeberg, D. (2001). Public relations and community: A reconstructed theory revised. In R.L. Heath (Ed.) and G. Vasquez (Contributing Ed.) *Handbook of public relations* (pp. 51–59). Thousand Oaks, CA: Sage.

Tronto, J. (1993). *Moral boundaries: A political argument for the ethics of care*. New York: Routledge.

Vardeman-Winter, J., & Tindall, N. T. J. (2010). "If it's a woman's issue, I pay attention to it": Gendered and intersectional complications in The Heart Truth media campaign. *PRism, 7*(4). Retrieved from http://www.prismjournal.org/

Yuval-Davis, N. (2011). *The politics of belonging: Intersectional connections*. Thousand Oaks, CA: Sage.

Zmuda, N. (2009, 17 November). Behind Coca-Cola's biggest social-media push yet: How Expedition 206's global search for happiness came together. *Ad Age*. Retrieved from http://adage.com/

Part IV

Ethical Frameworks for Communication

11 The Dialogic Potential of Social Media

Assessing the Ethical Reasoning of Companies' Public Relations on Facebook and Twitter

Angela M. Lee, Homero Gil de Zuñiga, Renita Coleman, and Thomas J. Johnson

INTRODUCTION

With the emergence of interactive communication that more easily allows consumers to contact public relations offices, researchers are increasingly investigating the dialogic potential of online communication for maintaining relations with the general public (Bortree & Seltzer, 2009; Kent & Taylor, 1998, 2002; Kent, Taylor, & White, 2003; Rybalko & Seltzer, 2010). Kent and Taylor (1998) defined dialogic communication as "any negotiated exchange of ideas and opinions" (p. 325) with the purpose of engaging in honest, open, and ethical give-and-take with the public. The authors urged public relations organizations to facilitate dialogue by establishing channels and procedures for fostering dialogue, including social network sites (i.e., Facebook and Twitter). Specifically, public relations professionals argue social network sites and Twitter facilitate two-way communication by opening up new direct avenues of communication between organizations and their public, providing more transparency by creating additional information channels and making it difficult for those who practice public relations to help companies manage, regulate, and influence information. That is, the extent to which companies may systematically control the mode of company-to-public (and public-to-company) communicative interaction and information flow. This study puts these assertions to an empirical test by analyzing comments on the Facebook and Twitter accounts of 25 randomly selected *Fortune 500* companies according to which of the four Excellence Theory models they best describe, and how well they achieve each of the five objectives—truthfulness, authenticity, respectfulness, equitability, and social responsibility—of the TARES test. By analyzing the ethicality of public relations practitioner's comments on Facebook and Tweets, this study adds the dimension of behavior to the broader studies of the ethical reasoning of public relations practitioners; what they *actually do* is addressed in this research, and can be considered in context of other studies that show what they are capable of.

LITERATURE REVIEW

Public relations agencies are increasingly seeing the advantage of using social media to communicate with a variety of stakeholders including journalists, employees, and customers (McCorkindale, 2010), acknowledging social media to have enhanced public relations practice by providing a low-cost mechanism for public relationships to interact with members of various strategic publics (Wright & Hinson, 2012).

Research suggests new media technology that is highly interactive allows organizations to establish more dialogues with online publics than static websites (Sweetser & Metzgar, 2007). Social media sites like Facebook and Twitter have an additional advantage in creating dialogic discussions with stakeholders because they are inherently social and communicative, and thus, have the potential to humanize an organization by allowing SNS users to become "friends" with and "like" the organization, which allows organizations to build relationships at a more personal level (Men & Tsai, 2012).

Studies indicate that public relations companies are doing a better job of taking advantage of dialogic opportunities on Twitter than on social network sites, but communication professionals in public relations may not entirely be taking advantage of either medium very well. For instance, Rybalko and Seltzer (2010) found that for Twitter, corporations used the dialogic loop more than any other feature with the three most common dialogic features found in Tweet posts being an organizational response to a specific user's post (60.2%), posting of newsworthy information about the company (58.1%), and attempting to stimulate dialogue by posting a question (30.1%). On the other hand, Bortree and Seltzer (2009) found that although organizational profiles provided the opportunity for dialogue such as allowing for wall posts and sending messages, they did not build on those opportunities by having anyone available to answer the posts. Other studies also have found that although organizations have the potential to use Facebook to interact with employees and customers, they rarely do (McCorkindale, 2010; Nordstrom, 2012; Waters, Burnett, Lamm, & Lucas, 2009). More recent studies however, do suggest that public relations are using both Twitter and social network sites like Facebook (Brightman, 2012) to establish a dialogue with its constituents. One reason why organizations may not effectively use Twitter and social media to foster dialogue is that they see the major role of these technologies as linked with providing information rather than building community (Gil de Zúñiga & Rojas, 2009; Lovejoy & Saxton, 2012).

Although a host of studies have examined the ethics of companies harvesting information from people's social network sites (Baase, 2008; Debatin, Lovejoy, Horn, & Hughes, 2009), no studies could be found that have explored the ethics of companies editing comments on their Facebook pages or editing Tweets. However, studies have found evidence that companies do indeed edit comments on their Facebook group and fan pages. McCorkindale (2010) found that, on average, 4 of the 40 comments she coded on each site were negative and that most negative posts were recent ones, suggesting that the companies simply had not gotten around to deleting the negative posts.

Excellence Theory

The theory that most closely helps us answer the questions in this study is Grunig and Hunt's Excellence Theory (1984). This theory describes four models of different ways to perform public relations—as press agentry, public information, in a one-way asymmetrical fashion, or a two-way symmetrical fashion. The two-way symmetrical model is considered to be ethically superior to the others because it incorporates reciprocity and mutual understanding through communication exchange (Cutlip, Center, & Broom, 2006). This model sees public relations as a forum for discussion in which a variety of individuals, opinions, and values come together (Fitzpatrick & Gauthier, 2001). The main difference between the two models is that one-way asymmetric communication is focused on understanding audience attitudes and behaviors in order to better persuade them to accept an organization's point of view, whereas two-way symmetric is focused more on listening to the concerns of significant publics and considering possible accommodations to address those concerns (Grunig & Hunt, 1984).

Although the two-way symmetrical model is considered superior, the other models are not considered to be unethical; the one-way asymmetrical model is considered next best, with some critics saying it is more practical because the two-way symmetrical model is an ideal that cannot be achieved because public relations is partisan and undemocratic by necessity.

TARES Test

A second theory useful for understanding ethics in public relations is Baker and Martinson's (2001) TARES test, which evaluates public relations' messages on five philosophically-based criteria: the truthfulness of the message, authenticity of the persuader, respect for the one being persuaded, equity of the appeal, and social responsibility. Public relations practitioners have been evaluated for their level of ethical reasoning and placed seventh among the 20-some-odd professions that have been studied (Coleman & Wilkins, 2009). The mean score on a widely used test of ethical development was 46.2 for public relations professionals compared with 31.64 for advertising professionals and 48.68 for journalists; average adults score about 40. Public relations practitioners were listed in the top tier with practicing physicians (49.2) and nurses (46.3). Public relations practitioners may rank in the top half of professions in terms of ethical development, but more than 85% of public relations practitioners believe the industry has a credibility problem and that more than half of PR officials say their company provides no ethics training (Lee & Cheng, 2012).

Public relations practitioners believe that social media have made public relations firms more transparent and have improved the ethical perceptions of PR because the public perceives that social media create a truthful, transparent, and ethical culture (Wright & Hinson, 2012). Similarly, open conversations with the public through social network sites and Twitter can make a public relations organization appear more transparent and ethical (Coombs & Holladay, 2010; Nordstrom, 2012).

This study analyzed the ethicality of public relations practitioner's edited comments on Facebook and Tweets to add the dimension of behavior to the broader studies of the ethical reasoning of public relations practitioners; what they *actually do* will be determined in this research, and can be considered in context of other studies that show what they are capable of.

RESEARCH QUESTIONS

To better understand whether and how *Fortune 500* companies are (or are not) using social media sites like Facebook and Twitter in an *ethical* fashion, the following research questions are proposed:

Excellence Theory

RQ1a: How often do the *Fortune 500* companies use social media to achieve symmetrical communication?

RQ1b: Do such practices differ between Facebook and Twitter?

TARES test

RQ2a: How truthful, authentic, respectful, equitable, and socially responsible are the *Fortune 500* companies' social media content?

RQ2b: Do such practices differ between Facebook and Twitter?

Baker's Trustworthiness

RQ3a: How trustworthy are the *Fortune 500* companies on their social media sites?

RQ3b: Do such practices differ between Facebook and Twitter?

METHOD

This study used one constructed week from a six-month period to content analyze Facebook and Twitter accounts of 25 randomly selected *Fortune 500* companies.

Sampling

Constructed sampling is a stratified sampling method that effectively yields a representative sample for media content by minimizing possible skew due to cyclic variations (Riffe, Lacy, & Fico, 2005; Lacy, Riffe, Stoddard, Martin, & Chang, 2001). Constructed sampling has been found to produce sufficient, if not better, generalizable media content than simple random sampling or consecutive day sampling both offline (Stempel, 1952; Riffe, Aust & Lacy, 1993) and online (Hester & Dougall, 2007). Because large corporations' communication habits with the general public are unlikely to vary dramatically on a daily basis for practical purposes (e.g., to maintain a coherent online presence and follow centralized customer service protocol) as proposed by (Culnan, McHugh, & Zubillaga, 2010; Scott, 2011), this study adopted this recommendation and created one constructed week.

The constructed week was drawn between September 2011 and February 2012 (N = 182 days).

Sample

This study analyzed 25 *Fortune 500* companies. The companies were randomly selected by using a random number generator. Only companies with working Facebook (e.g., ones that enable wall activities) and Twitter accounts were used for analysis. The following 25 *Fortune 500* companies, with respective *Fortune 500* ranks in parentheses, were used in the study: General Electric (6), AT&T (12), Pfizer (31), Target (33), Lockheed Martin (52), Cisco Systems (62), Morgan Stanley (63), Amazon (78), Allstate (89), Macy's (107), Kimberly-Clark (130), Nike (135), Progressive (164), Qualcomm (222), Visa (297), Henry Schein (317), Charter (333), Mattel (392), Clorox (411), Pitney Bowes (421), Ryder System (437), Avaya (445), Con-way (454), Rockwell Collins (478), and Dick's Sporting Goods (464).

Unit of Analysis

Each company's Facebook and Twitter pages were examined. The unit of analysis was the individual tweet or Facebook post. For Facebook, everything that had been posted during the constructed week was coded; on Twitter only original tweets were coded (e.g., no retweets).

Data

All of the data were collected over a 24-hour period by one of the authors and two graduate students from a large research university in the Southwestern U.S. Training sessions were held for all personnel involved in data collection. All of the posts and original tweets on the 25 companies' Facebook and Twitter accounts were collected.

Codebook

Grounded in the Excellence Theory and the TARES test, and adopting measures created in previous studies (Baker & Martinson, 2001; Lieber, 2005; Grunig, 2008; Grunig & Grunig, 2010; Martinson, 1995; McCoy & Black, 2002; Lee & Cheng, 2010; Hon & Grunig, 1999; Cobat, 2005), this study created 25 variables to measure symmetrical communication in the Excellence Theory (e.g., "Does the site ask what their consumers need or want?"), truthfulness (e.g., "Are the responses from the company to consumer's questions reasonably informative?"), authenticity (e.g., "Are more than half of the photos used candid photos?"), respect (e.g., "Are the company's responses to audiences respectful?"), equity (e.g., "Has information on the page been presented in an unnecessarily convoluted fashion?"), and social responsibility (e.g., "Is the information presented clearly and easily understandable?") in the TARES test, and trustworthiness (e.g., Does the company answer questions on the page, if asked?") as a measure of moral authority and ethical practices in public relations (Baker, 2002).

Inter-Coder Reliability

Two graduate students from a large research university in the Southwestern U.S. were trained as coders for this study. They were both fluent English speakers and experienced Internet users familiar with Facebook and Twitter. Additionally, authors met with both coders to discuss observed disparities. The group worked as needed taking both coders' accounts and suggestions into consideration to generate a final codebook as objectively reliable as possible.

For example, one of the variables for truthfulness of the message from the TARES test asks whether the company asks questions and also offers answer in the same spot (e.g., Want to have better hair? Try our new shampoo). Coders had a different interpretation on the issue so it was discussed a common understanding. Several similar issues as this one were addressed and discrepancies resolved.

Coders went through extensive training and expressed confidence in understanding the codebook. The authors generated content randomization of about 30% of the total collected data used to calculate inter-coder reliability at the beginning of the coding process. Scott's Pi for individual variables are: Does the site ask what their consumers need or want? 1.0; Does the company interact with consumers on the site? .72; Does the company engage in dialogue with consumers? .88; Are the responses from the company to consumer's questions reasonably informative? .79; PR language: Does the company ask questions and also offer answer in the same post? 1.0; Visual: Do more than half of the photos used look manipulated? .68; Is the information presented on the page useful or beneficial to audiences? .74; Are the company's responses to audiences respectful? .89; Has information on the page been presented in an unnecessarily convoluted fashion? .50; Does the information take advantage of human weaknesses such as anxieties, fears, low self-esteem, etc.? .50; Is the information presented clearly and easily understandable? .96; Is the information presented by the company harmful to individuals or society? .94; Does the company offer reward if someone does something for society? .83; Does the company encourage audiences to give back to society in ways other than offering personal reward? 1.0; Does the company answer questions on the page, if asked? .81; Does the page enable troubleshooting? .74; Is gratitude (e.g., "thanks" or "thank you") from consumers found on the page? .69; Is the page professional (e.g., use formal or distant language, no "lol," "nm," or slang, etc.) .96; Does the page allow Q&A? .53; Does the page have emails listed for contact? .53; Phone numbers listed for contact? .63; Private messaging function? .95; Does the page provide private policy info? .63.

The way Scott's Pi is calculated makes it conducive to skewed values for variables that do not have a lot of variation. For example, even although two variables have a .50 Scott's Pi, both variables actually have 99% coder-agreement. To ensure that all the variables are reliable, the primary coder analyzed all the pretest data in detail to systematically document variation in variables, and the variables are deemed acceptable despite the apparently low Scott's Pi because they have extraordinarily high coder-agreement (above 97%), and are only suffering low Scott's Pi due to the nature of this particular reliability test. After accounting for these special cases, Scott's Pi for all variables analyzed in this study range between .72 and 1.0, which is deemed acceptable by conventional standards.

Operationalization

All of the indices used in this study are not uni-dimensional repetition factors. For example, "Does the company use 2 or more adjectives in one sentence?" and "Are more than half of the photos used candid photos?" make up the "authenticity" index, there is no inherent reason to believe that verbal and visual authenticity need or should coexist on a company's social media site (e.g., a company may communicate in a authentic fashion verbally but not visually). For this reason, reliability tests are not computed for these multi-dimension indices.

Sum of the following three variables made up the "excellence theory: symmetrical communication" index: Does the site ask what their consumers need or want? Does the company interact with consumers on the site? Does the company engage in dialogue with consumers?

Sum of the following three variables made up the "truthfulness" index: Are the responses from the company to consumer's questions reasonably informative? Does the company ask questions and also offer answer in the same post? Do more than half of the photos used look photoshopped?

Sum of the following two variables made up the "authenticity" index: Does the company use 2 or more adjectives in one sentence? Are more than half of the photos used candid photos?

Sum of the following two variables made up the "respect" index: Is the information presented on the page useful or beneficial to audiences? Are the company's responses to audiences respectful?

Sum of the following two variables made up the "equity" index: Has information on the page been presented in an unnecessarily convoluted fashion? Does the information take advantage of human weaknesses such as anxieties, fears, low self-esteem, etc.?

Sum of the following four variables made up the "social responsibility" index: Is the information presented clearly and easily understandable? Is the information presented by the company harmful to individuals or society? Does the company offer reward if someone does something for society? Does the company encourage audiences to give back to society in ways other than offering personal reward?

Sum of the following nine variables made up the "trustworthiness" index: Does the company answer questions on the page, if asked? Does the page enable troubleshooting? Is gratitude from consumers found on the page? Is the page professional? Does the page allow Q&A? Does the page have emails listed for contact? Phone numbers listed for contact? Private message functions? Does the page provide privacy policy info?

RESULTS

As Table 11.1 indicates, *Fortune 500* Companies differ in their management of ethical communication on Facebook and Twitter. Specifically, *Fortune 500* Companies did the most poorly in achieving equitable communication, with over 90% of all the posts examined in the data on both Facebook and Twitter *not* achieving equitable communication. On the other hand, *Fortune 500* Companies successfully achieved trustworthy communication on both Facebook and Twitter.

RQ1a asks how often *Fortune 500* companies use social media to achieve symmetrical communication (range = 0 to 3). The data suggest that these companies do, in an overall trend, use social media to achieve symmetrical communication to a certain degree ($M = .75$, $SD = 1.06$).

RQ1b asks whether *Fortune 500* companies use Facebook and Twitter differently to achieve symmetrical communication. Tables 11.2 and 11.3 provide the comparison. The data suggest that overall Twitter ($M = .94$, $SD = 1.10$) was used more efficiently than Facebook ($M = .57$, $SD = .99$) to achieve symmetrical communication, and the difference is statistically significant; $t(26) = 3.07$, $p < .01$.

Table 11.1 Summary of the Extent to Which *Fortune 500* Companies Failed to Communicate Ethically on Facebook and Twitter

	% Scoring 0 in each index	
	Facebook	Twitter
Symmetrical Communication	70.3	53.7
Truthfulness	22.9	2.0
Authenticity	81.1	95.4
Respect	2.9	0
Equity	91.2	93.1
Social responsibility	17.4	18.2
Trustworthy	0	0

RQ2a explores the extent to which *Fortune 500* companies' social media content is truthful (0 to 3), authentic (0 to 2), respectful (0 to 2), equitable (0 to 2), and socially responsible (0 to 4). Because these five indices are based on different scales, the following comparisons were done after each mean was divided by its own range. The data suggest that their content is most respectful ($M = .87$, $SD = .23$), followed by truthful ($M = .36$, $SD = .19$), social responsible ($M = .25$, $SD = .15$), authentic ($M = .06$, $SD = .17$), and equitable ($M = .04$, $SD = .14$). Of these differences, Paired-Sample T tests revealed that respectful is significantly different from truthful; $t(73)= 17.35$, $p<.001$; social responsibility; $t(98)= 22.03$, $p<.001$, authenticity; $t(103)= 27.34$, $p<.001$ and equity; $t(100)= 27.33$, $p<.001$. Truthful is significantly different from authenticity; $t(97)= 7.04$, $p<.001$ or equity; $t(97)= 9.49$, $p<.001$. Social responsibility is significantly different from authenticity; $t(251)= 12.21$, $p<.001$ or equity; $t(252)= 18.19$, $p<.001$ (Also see Table 11.4).

The data suggest these companies' content on Twitter is more truthful ($M=1.20$, $SD=.45$ compared to $M=.96$, $SD=.65$); $t(17)= 1.65$, *n.s.*, respectful ($M=1.76$, $SD=.43$ compared to $M=1.69$, $SD=.53$); $t(18)= .89$, *n.s.*, and socially responsible ($M=1.00$, $SD=.62$ compared to $M=.96$, $SD=.58$) than on Facebook; $t(23)= 2.25$, $p<.001.$, whereas their content on Facebook is more authentic ($M=.19$, $SD=.41$ compared to $M=.05$, $SD=.21$); $t(26)= .42$, *n.s.* , and equitable ($M=.09$, $SD=.31$ compared to $M=.07$, $SD=.25$) than on Twitter; $t(26)= 1.88$, $p<.001$ (Also see Table 7.4).

RQ3a asks how trustworthy *Fortune 500* companies are on their social media sites. The data suggest that they on average score below the median on trustworthiness (range 0 to 9, $M=3.96$, $SD=1.44$).

RQ3b explores difference in trustworthiness between *Fortune 500* companies' use of Facebook and Twitter. The data suggest that *Fortune 500* companies are more trustworthy on Twitter ($M=4.70$, $SD=1.15$) than on Facebook ($M=3.26$, $SD=1.33$); $t(15)=1.46$, *n.s.*

Table 11.2   Ethical Practices of Fortune 500 Companies on Facebook: Mean (SD)

Company	Excellence Theory		TARES Test				Baker
	Symmetrical Communication	Truthfulness	Authenticity	Respect	Equity	Social Responsibility	Trust-worthiness
GE	2.29 (1.11)	1.33 (.52)	.57 (.53)	1.67 (.52)	0 (0)	1.00 (0)	3.17 (.98)
AT&T	1.00 (1.29)	1.00 (.71)	.43 (.53)	1.67 (.58)	.29 (.49)	1.29 (.76)	4.00 (1.00)
Pfizer	0 (0)	0 (0)	.14 (.38)	0 (0)	0 (0)	.60 (.55)	2.0 (0)
Target	.14 (.38)	.33 (.58)	0 (0)	0 (0)	.29 (.49)	1.33 (.52)	1.67 (1.15)
Lockheed Martin	0 (0)	0 (0)	0 (0)	0 (0)	0 (0)	.50 (.58)	1.00 (0)
Cisco Systems	.57 (1.13)	0 (0)	0 (0)	2.00 (0)	0 (0)	.83 (.41)	0 (0)
Morgan Stanley	0 (0)	0(0)	0(0)	0(0)	0(0)	0(0)	0 (0)
Amazon	.57 (.53)	.50 (.58)	.29 (.49)	0 (0)	.43 (.53)	1.50 (.55)	2.20 (.84)
Allstate	1.57 (1.51)	1.25 (.50)	.14 (.38)	1.75 (.50)	0 (0)	.83 (.41)	4.33 (.58)
Macy's	.71 (.76)	1.40 (.55)	.71 (.49)	0 (0)	.57 (.53)	1.86 (.69)	3.00 (.71)
Kimberly- Clark	.14 (.38)	0 (0)	0 (0)	2.00 (0)	0 (0)	.50 (.71)	4.40 (.55)

Nike	.29 (.76)	.50 (.71)	.43 (.53)	0 (0)	.14 (.38)	1.00 (.82)	1.00 (0)
Progressive	0 (0)	2.00 (0)	0 (0)	1.50 (.71)	0 (0)	.67 (0)	0 (0)
Qualcomm	.43 (.53)	0 (0)	0 (0)	0 (0)	0 (0)	.80 (.45)	0 (0)
Visa	.43 (1.13)	0 (0)	.29 (.49)	1.00 (0)	0 (0)	.75 (.50)	0 (0)
Henry Schein	0 (0)	1.00 (0)	.14 (.38)	2.00 (0)	0 (0)	.60 (.55)	2.00 (0)
Charter	1.43 (1.40)	1.00 (.71)	.14 (.38)	1.50 (.58)	.43 (.79)	1.17 (.41)	4.80 (.84)
Mattel	0 (0)	0 (0)	0 (0)	2.00 (0)	0 (0)	0 (0)	0 (0)
Clorox	1.00 (1.15)	1.33 (.58)	.14 (.38)	1.50 (.71)	.14 (.38)	1.00 (0)	3.67 (1.15)
Pitney Bowes	.43 (1.13)	1.00 (0)	.29 (.49)	2.00 (0)	0 (0)	1.00 (.71)	4.00 (0)
Ryder System	0 (0)	0 (0)	0 (0)	0 (0)	0 (0)	.75 (.50)	0 (0)
Avaya	.43 (.79)	0 (0)	0 (0)	2.00 (0)	0 (0)	.75 (.50)	0 (0)
Con-way	1.00 (1.00)	.67 (.58)	.43 (.79)	2.00 (.00)	0 (0)	1.00 (.63)	4.00 (1.00)
Rockwell Collins	.14 (.38)	0 (0)	.29 (.49)	0 (0)	0 (0)	1.00 (0)	0 (0)
Dick's Sporting Goods	1.57 (1.13)	.67 (.58)	.43 (.53)	2.00 (0)	0 (0)	1.00 (0)	4.00 (1.00)

Table 11.3   Ethical Practices of Fortune 500 Companies on Twitter: Mean (SD)

Company	Excellence Theory		TARES Test				Baker
	Symmetrical Communication	Truthfulness	Authenticity	Respect	Equity	Social Responsibility	Trust-worthiness
GE	2.71 (.49)	1.25 (.50)	0 (0)	1.86 (.38)	0 (0)	1.00 (0)	3.75 (.50)
AT&T	1.43 (1.40)	.75 (.50)	0 (0)	1.50 (.58)	.14 (.38)	1.60 (.55)	4.00 (0)
Pfizer	.29 (.76)	1.00 (0)	0 (0)	2.00 (0)	0 (0)	.83 (.41)	5.00 (4.24)
Target	2.00 (0)	1.29 (.49)	0 (0)	2.00 (0)	.14 (.38)	1.29 (.49)	5.00 (0)
Lockheed Martin	1.43 (1.13)	1.00 (0)	.43 (.53)	2.00 (0)	0 (0)	.83 (.41)	3.50 (.71)
Cisco Systems	1.58 (1.51)	1.00 (0)	0 (0)	1.75 (.50)	0 (0)	.83 (.41)	4.75 (1.26)
Morgan Stanley	0 (0)	0 (0)	0 (0)	0 (0)	0 (0)	0 (0)	0 (0)
Amazon	0(0)	0 (0)	0 (0)	0 (0)	0(0)	.67 (1.15)	0 (0)
Allstate	1.57 (1.51)	1.25 (.50)	.14 (.38)	1.75 (.50)	0 (0)	.83 (.41)	4.33 (.58)
Macy's	1.86 (.90)	1.50 (.55)	.43 (.53)	1.83 (.41)	.43 (.53)	1.83 (.41)	4.40 (.55)

Kimberly- Clark	0 (0)	0 (0)	0 (0)	0 (0)	0 (0)	.50 (.71)	0 (0)
Nike	1.86 (.90)	1.00 (0)	0 (0)	2.00 (0)	0 (0)	1.57 (.53)	5.00 (.63)
Progressive	1.71 (.95)	1.40 (.55)	0 (0)	1.40 (.55)	0 (0)	.86 (.38)	6.75 (.50)
Qualcomm	1.00 (1.00)	1.00 (0)	.14 (.38)	1.00 (0)	0 (0)	1.00 (.63)	4.00 (0)
Visa	.14 (.38)	0 (0)	0 (0)	0 (0)	0 (0)	.60 (.55)	0 (0)
Henry Schein	.86 (.90)	0 (0)	0 (0)	1.33 (.58)	0 (0)	1.00 (.63)	0 (0)
Charter	.57 (.79)	0 (0)	0 (0)	0 (0)	.29 (.49)	.80 (.45)	0 (0)
Mattel	0 (0)	0 (0)	0 (0)	0 (0)	0 (0)	0 (0)	0 (0)
Clorox	1.00 (1.00)	1.50 (.71)	0 (0)	1.50 (.58)	.43 (.53)	1.33 (.52)	4.50 (.71)
Pitney Bowes	.86 (1.21)	2.00 (0)	0 (0)	2.00 (0)	0 (0)	.80 (.84)	4.00 (0)
Ryder System	0 (0)	0 (0)	0 (0)	0 (0)	0 (0)	0(0)	0 (0)
Avaya	.29 (.49)	0 (0)	0 (0)	0 (0)	.14 (.38)	1.00 (.63)	0 (0)
Con-way	.57 (.98)	0 (0)	0 (0)	2.00 (.00)	0 (0)	.83 (.41)	0 (0)
Rockwell Collins	.43 (1.13)	0 (0)	.17 (.41)	1.50 (.71)	0 (0)	1.00 (0)	0 (0)
Dick's Sporting Goods	1.57 (1.13)	1.00 (0)	0 (0)	2.00 (0)	.14 (.38)	1.29 (.95)	4.00 (0)

Table 11.4   Key Differences Between *Fortune 500* Companies' Twitter and Facebook Uses

	Twitter		Facebook		
	M	SD	M	SD	T-Test
Symmetrical Communication	.94	1.10	.57	.99	t(26)= 3.07***
Truthfulness	1.20	.45	.96	.65	t(17)= 1.65
Authenticity	.05	.21	.19	.41	t(26)= .42
Respect	1.76	.43	1.69	.53	t(18)=.89
Equity	.07	.25	.09	.31	t(26)= 1.88***
Social responsibility	1.00	.62	.96	.58	t(23)= 2.25***
Trustworthy	4.70	1.15	3.26	1.33	t(15)= 1.46

Note: *p<.05; **p<.01; ***p<.001.

DISCUSSION

Scholars have long argued that a two-way symmetrical model is considered to be ethically superior to other models because it incorporates reciprocity and mutual understanding through communication exchange (Cutlip, Center, & Broom, 2006; Grunig & Hunt, 2004). Therefore, organizations are increasingly using social network sites such as Facebook and Twitter to increase dialogue with important stakeholders because they facilitate two-way communication by opening up new direct avenues of communication between organizations and their publics.

This study analyzed Facebook and Twitter accounts of 25 randomly selected *Fortune 500* companies to shed light over the degree to which these companies practice the two-way symmetry model and explores how ethically public relations practitioners engage in Facebook and Twitter by exploring how well they achieve symmetrical communication (Excellence Theory) and each of the five objectives of the TARES test.

Ethical Implications for the Practice of Social Media

Social media are more interactive than most earlier Internet components (Gil de Zúñiga, 2002; 2006), and can create a more human face for a company by allowing social network site users to become "friends" with and "like" the organization (Men & Tsai, 2012), several scholars question the degree to which organizations are taking advantage of Facebook (McCorkindale, 2010; Nordstrom, 2012; Waters et al., 2009) and Twitter (Rybalko & Seltzer, 2010). Recent studies suggest companies are doing a better job of employing social network sites and Twitter to build dialogue with various stakeholders (Brightman, 2012), but that was not apparent in this study. Companies were gauged on three measures of symmetrical communication, whether they asked consumers what they want, whether they interact with consumers and whether they engaged in dialogue and the 25 companies totaled a .75, suggesting that most companies did not engage in symmetrical communication on any of the three measures. Companies did particularly poorly engaging in dialogue on Facebook, as only 29% engaged in dialogue by replying to comments and asking for feedback and only 27% attempted to engage in dialogue. Only one company, General Electric, scored above a 2 for both Twitter and Facebook. Five companies recorded a zero on this measure for Twitter and seven for Facebook. One might expect that Facebook might produce more symmetrical communication than Twitter because of the ease of responding to those posting to a Facebook page and because to engage in a dialogue with Twitter users, companies must first follow them then engage the Tweeter. However, companies actually engaged in more dialogic communication on Twitter than Facebook, perhaps because although the 140-character limit on Twitter might make it more difficult to post long messages to followers, it makes it easier for the companies to respond. Still, companies respond to customers less than half of the time, engaging in dialogue about 38% of the time and interacting in general 40%.

Public relations practitioners overwhelmingly say that credibility is a problem in their industry and most say they do not receive ethics training on the job (Lee & Cheng, 2012). This study found that trustworthiness is indeed a problem with public relations organizations. Nearly all Facebook pages allowed questions and answers from customers, but only 60% of Facebook groups did. Fewer than 10% posted information on their profile such as email and phone numbers for contacts and allowed private message function, although 20% of companies did allow direct messaging to their companies. The 25 companies averaged fewer than four points on the nine-point scale. Only two companies, Charter and Allstate, scored above a 4 out of 9 on the Facebook trustworthiness measures. On the other hand, 8 companies scored above a 4 on the Twitter trustworthiness measures, including Progressive, which scored a 6.75. Past studies suggest that engaging in more dialogic communication can build trust in an organization (Men & Tsai, 2012). Although companies on Twitter were more likely to engender trust by engaging in troubleshooting, spell out a privacy policy, and be more professional in their posts, they also put more trust in their users by allowing anonymous comments, questions, and answers and having a private messaging function.

Lee and Chen (2012) discovered that 80% of PR practitioners perceived that the rise social media posed an ethical problem. Indeed, the increased use of social media and Twitter has not led to an increase in ethical behaviors as measured by the TARES test. The *Fortune 500* companies only scored highly on one of the ethical areas, respect, as the overwhelming percentage of companies did present information that was beneficial and treated their users on the social media sites with respect during their responses. But this is a measure of tone and style of messages, rather than interactivity. Companies were almost always respectful to their consumers and almost never wrote in convoluted sentences. However, scores for usefulness were much lower (52.4% on Facebook, 63.7% on Twitter). Means scores for truthfulness, authenticity, equity, and social responsibility were all low. For instance, for social responsibility, companies averaged less than one on a five-point scale, and for equity scores were .08 on the three-point scale. Fewer than 5% of the posts on both Facebook and Twitter offered rewards for doing something for society and even fewer encouraged consumers to give back to society. Furthermore, 18 companies scored 0 on the three-point equity scores on Facebook and numbers of companies that scored 0 on truthfulness, authenticity, and respect were in double digits. Only five of 20 companies did not receive 0 for authenticity on Twitter. Although Twitter allows people to post pictures, fewer than 3% put up candid shots that might humanize the company. Part of the reason why scores were so low is that the companies did not regularly update their Twitter feed and Facebook page, leaving their social media sites like cyber ghost towns. Another reason scores were so low is that companies often failed to use their social media to inform or engage their users, using them instead to put up strictly public relations items of little interest to their readers (such as what their CEO was doing) or use them to promote sales.

Differences were found on the TARES ethics scores between Twitter and Facebook. Facebook scored higher on authenticity of the persuader and Twitter on being truthful and socially responsible. Differences may be because of the nature of the two social media. People are more likely to friend people they already know offline and perceive Facebook as an online community (Ellison, Steinfield, & Lampe, 2007), whereas on Twitter people may follow public figures like politicians and celebrities whom they do not know (Bekafigo & McBride, 2012). Not surprising, then, people might see company speakers as more authentic on Facebook. On the other hand, because Facebook is seen as a more social outlet, companies may be more likely to employ Twitter to send more news and thus Twitter messages are more likely to be truthful and socially responsible.

Limitations

There are some caveats to this study that should be taken into consideration to improve forthcoming studies, as such we propose this limitations as challenging suggestions for future research. First, this study examined a random sample of *Fortune 500* companies, but only 25 were studied, which represents 5% of the total companies encompassing the list. It is possible that a larger sample may have yielded somewhat different responses. The TARES test has been most commonly used to study advertising messages, particularly public service messages such as anti-smoking (Lee & Chen, 2010). In this study, we have drawn our measures based on this test, which may not be the most appropriate for social media. Nevertheless, we are confident this test translates well when it comes to explaining social media messages albeit only scores of studies will prove this feasibility as empirical evidence continues to accumulate. These are all, of course, suggestions for future research to enhance our understanding on the dialogic potential of social media.

Discussion Questions

1. How often do the *Fortune 500* companies use social media to achieve symmetrical communication? Do such practices differ between Facebook and Twitter?
2. How truthful, authentic, respectful, equitable, and socially responsible are the *Fortune 500* companies' social media content? Do such practices differ between Facebook and Twitter?
3. How trustworthy are the *Fortune 500* companies on their social media sites? Do such practices differ between Facebook and Twitter?

SUGGESTED READINGS

Coombs, W. T. & Holladay, S. J. (2010). *PR strategy and application: Managing influence*. West Sussex: Wiley- Blackwell.

McCorkindale, T. (2010) Can you see the writing on my wall? A content analysis of the Fortune 50s' Facebook social network sites. *Public Relations Journal*, 4(3), 1–13.

Men, L. R., & Tsai, W-H S. (2012). How companies cultivate relationships with publics on social network sites: Evidence from China and the United States. *Public Relations Review*, 38, 723–730.

REFERENCES

Baase, S. (2008). *A gift of fire: Social, legal, and ethical issues for computing and the Internet*, 3rd ed. Upper Saddle River, NJ: Prentice-Hall.

Baker, S. (2002). The theoretical ground for public relations practice and ethics: A Koehnian analysis. *Journal of Business Ethics*, 35, 191–205.

Baker, S., & Martinson, D. L. (2001). The TARES test: Five principles for ethical persuasion. *Journal of Mass Media Ethics*, 16(2–3), 148–175.

Bekafigo, M. A., & McBride, A. (2012, Sept.). *Who Tweets about politics?: Political participation of Twitter users during the 2011 Gubernatorial elections*. Paper presented to the annual meeting of the American Political Science Association, New Orleans, LA.

Bortree, D. S., & Seltzer, T. (2009). Dialogic strategies and outcomes: An analysis of environmental advocacy groups' Facebook profiles. *Public Relations Review*, 35(3), 317–319.

Brightman, J. M. (2012). *Strategizing relationships 2.0: An analysis of international companies' use of social media*. Unpublished dissertation, University of South Florida.

Cobat, M. (2005). Moral development and PR ethics. *Journal of Mass Media Ethics, 20*(4), 321–332.

Coleman, R., & Wilkins, L (2009). Moral development: A psychological approach to understanding ethical judgment. In L. Wilkins & C. G. Christians (Eds.), *The handbook of mass media ethics* (pp. 40–54). New York: Routledge.

Coombs, W. T., & Holladay, S. J. (2010). *PR strategy and application: Managing influence.* West Sussex: Wiley- Blackwell.

Culnan, M. J., McHugh, P. J., & Zubillaga, J. I. (2010). How large US companies can use Twitter and other social media to gain business value. *MIS Quarterly Executive, 9*(4), 243–259.

Cutlip, S. M., Center, A. H., & Broom, G. M. (2006). *Effective public relations* (9th edn). Upper Saddle River, NJ: Prentice Hall.

Debatin, B., Lovejoy, J. P., Horn, A. K., & Hughes, B. N. (2009). Facebook and online privacy: Attitudes, behaviors, and unintended consequences. *Journal of Computer-Mediated Communication, 15*(1), 83–108.

Ellison, N. B., Steinfield, C., & Lampe, C. (2007). The benefits of Facebook "friends:" Social capital and college students' use of online social network sites. *Journal of Computer-Mediated Communication, 12*(1). Retrieved from http://jcmc.indiana.edu/vol12/issue4/ellison.html

Fitzpatrick, K., & Gauthier, C. (2001). Toward a professional responsibility theory of public relations ethics. *Journal of Mass Media Ethics, 16*(2), 193–212

Gil de Zúñiga, H. (2002). Internet inherentemente personal: Cómo su uso influencia nuestras vidas. *Binaria, 3,* 1–45.

Gil de Zúñiga, H. (2006). Reshaping the digital inequality in the European Union: How psychological variables affect Internet adoption rates. *Webology.* 3(4) retrieved from http://www.webology.org/2006/v3n4/a32.html

Gil de Zúñiga, H., & Rojas, H. (2009). Análisis de los efectos de los blogs en la sociedad de la información. *Comunicación y Ciudadanía, 2*(3), 60–71.

Grunig, J. E (2008). Excellence theory in public relations. In *The International Encyclopedia of Communication,* vol. 4, (pp. 1620–1622). Oxford: Wiley-Blackwell.

Grunig, J. E., & Grunig, L. A. (2010, October). The third annual Grunig lecture series. Lecture presented at the PRSA international Conference, Washington, DC.

Grunig, J. E., & Hunt, T. (1984). *Managing public relations.* Fort Worth, TX: Holt.

Hester, J. B., & Dougall, E. (2007). The efficiency of constructed week sampling for content analysis of online news. *Journalism & Mass Communication Quarterly, 84*(4), 811–824.

Hon L. C., & Grunig, J. E. (1999). Guidelines for measuring relationships in public relations. *Golden Standard paper of the Commission on Public Relations Measurement & Evaluation.* Institute of Public Relations.

Kent, M. L. & Taylor, M. (1998) Building dialogic relationships through the World Wide Web. *Public Relations Review.* 24, 321–334.

Kent, M. L., & Taylor, M. (2002). Toward a dialogic theory of public relations. *Public Relations Review, 28,* 21–37.

Kent, M. L., Taylor, M., & White, W. J. (2003). The relationship between Web site design and organizational responsiveness to stakeholders. *Public Relations Review, 29*(1) 63–77.

Lacy, S., Riffe, D., Stoddard, S., Martin, H., & Chang, K. (2001). Sample size for newspaper content analysis in multi-year studies. *Journalism and Mass Communication Quarterly, 78*(4), 836–845.

Lee, S. T., & Cheng I. (2010). Assessing the TARES as an ethical model for anti-smoking ads. *Journal of Health Communication, 15,* 55–75.

Lee, S. T., & Cheng, I-H. (2012). Ethics management in public relations: Practitioners conceptualizations of ethical leadership, knowledge, training and compliance. *Journal of Mass Media Ethics, 27*, 80–96.

Lieber, P. S. (2005). Ethical considerations of public relations practitioners: An empirical analysis of the TARES test. *Journal of Mass Media Ethics, 20*(4), 288–304.

Lovejoy, K., & Saxton, G. D. (2012). Information, community, and action: How nonprofit organizations use social media. *Journal of Computer-Mediated Communication, 17*, 337–353.

Martinson, D. L. (1995). Ethical public relations practitioners must not ignore "public interest." *Journal of Mass Media Ethics, 10*(4), 210–222.

McCorkindale, T. (2010) Can you see the writing on my wall? A content analysis of the *Fortune* 50s' Facebook social network sites. *Public Relations Journal, 4*(3), 1–13.

McCoy, L., & Black, L. D. (2002). *The role of communications departments in managing reputation: empirical evidence from Australia.* Paper presented at the 6th International Conference on Corporate Reputation, Identity, and Competitiveness, Boston, MA

Men, L. R., & Tsai, W-H S. (2012). How companies cultivate relationships with publics on social network sites: Evidence from China and the United States. *Public Relations Review, 38*, 723–730.

Nordstrom, T. (2012). Two-way communication potential of social media in public relations: Application by environmental NGOs. Unpublished dissertation

Riffe, D., Aust, C. F., & Lacy, S. R. (1993). The effectiveness of random, consecutive day and constructed week sampling in newspaper analysis. *Journalism Quarterly, 70*(1), 133–139.

Riffe, D., Lacy, S., & Fico, F. G. (2005). *Analyzing media messages: Using quantitative content analysis in research* (2nd edn.). Mahwah, NJ: Lawrence Erlbaum

Rybalko, S. & Seltzer, T. (2010) Dialogic communication in 140 characters or less: How *Fortune 500* companies engage stakeholder using Twitter. *Public Relation Review, 36*, 336–341.

Scott, D. M. (2011). *The new rules of marketing & PR: How to use social media, online video, mobile applications, blogs, news releases, and viral marketing to reach buyers directly.* Hoboken, NJ: Wiley.

Stempel, G. H. (1952). Sample size for classifying subject matter in Dailies. *Journalism Quarterly, 29*, 333–334.

Sweetser, K. D., & Metzgar, E. (2007). Communicating during crisis: Use of blogs as a relationship management tool. *Public Relations Review, 33*(3), 340–342.

Taylor, M., Kent, M. L., & White, W. J. (2001). How activist organizations are using the internet to build relationships. *Public Relations Review, 27*, 263–284.

Waters, R. D., Burnett, E., Lamm, A., & Lucas, J. (2009). Engaging stakeholders through social networking: How nonprofit organizations are using Facebook. *Public Relations Review, 35*, 102–106.

Wright, D. K., & Hinson, M. D. (2012, July), *Examining how social and emerging media have been used in public relations between 2006 and 2012: A longitudinal analysis* Paper presented at the annual BledCom conference, Bled, Slovinia.

12 Journalists and Corporate Blogs
Identifying Markers of Credibility

Kirsten A. Johnson and Tamara L. Gillis

INTRODUCTION

A growing number of companies are choosing to use corporate blogs as a way to communicate information to mainstream media outlets. At the same time, journalists are increasingly relying on social media as sources for news and information (Oriella PR Network, 2011). These two factors highlight the need for public relations professionals to develop corporate blogs that are perceived as credible by mainstream media.

Public-facing corporate blogs experienced a boom year in 2006: General Motors was on the scene with a corporate blog written by executive Robert Lutz (Welch, 2005). Sun Microsystems and Google were among the companies to establish official corporate blogs that year (Klosek, 2006). But alas, later in 2006–07 corporate blogging would make the news again for unethical practices. When Wal-Mart launched its blog, Wal-Marting across America, in 2006 the public was charmed by bloggers Laura and Jim, a couple traveling across the United States in an RV and camping in Wal-Mart parking lots (Gogoi, 2006). Later it was disclosed that Laura and Jim were receiving compensation for their efforts and that the blog was a public relations stunt set up by Wal-Mart's PR firm. In 2007 bad behavior on the part of Whole Foods CEO John Mackey was brought to light during the Federal Trade Commission investigations of a merger between the company and Wild Oats, another organic foods retailer. Among the allegations, Mackey was accused of making anonymous posts of negative information regarding Wild Oats on financial message boards (Grossman, 2007).

In 2009 Dell, Microsoft, and Petrobras were among the corporations in the spotlight for corporate blogging (Carr, 2006; Smith, 2009). Dell arrived on the scene to ridicule from the blog community. Popular Microsoft blogger Robert Scoble upstaged Bill Gates' retirement announcement when Scoble announced his own departure from Microsoft. Brazilian oil giant Petrobras' CEO Jose Sergio Gabrielli initiated a corporate blog as a means to communicate the company's position and strike back at Brazilian newspapers that he felt were misrepresenting the company's position in news reports. The corporate blog was met with mixed reviews from supporters in favor of the aggressive strategy and people who felt the blog was detrimental to the image of the company and its employees. These incidents of bad behavior call into question ethical decision making associated with corporate use of social media.

Barnes reports that since 2008 there has been a slow but steady increase in the number of companies using corporate blogs. By 2010, only 23% of *Fortune 500* companies had a public-facing corporate blog (Barnes, 2010a). Today, public relations staffers continue to develop corporate blogs as part of corporate communication strategy. Tanya Irwin (2011), writing for *Media Post News*, reported that Charles Schwab launched its corporate blog, Schwab Talk, to give a behind-the-scenes looks at the firm and the people that run it and to provide information typically not found in a company news release. Announcing company news is a typical function of corporate blogs. For example, in 2011 Motorola used its corporate blog to announce its merger with Google and Google used its public-facing blog to announce its acquisition of Zagat.

With the growing use of social media tools by corporations, it is not surprising that journalists are taking note of these outlets as sources for developing news stories. Middleberg and McClure (2011) found that journalists are increasing their use of new media tools for developing news leads and stories. Yet the credibility of these sources still leaves journalists relying on traditional newsgathering sources. What can public relations officers do to increase the credibility of corporate public-facing blogs as potential news sources?

The findings from this project provide a model for corporate communicators to use when developing and testing corporate social media applications as future media relations strategies.

LITERATURE REVIEW

Social Media as a Public Relations Strategy

At the 2011 International Association of Business Communicators (IABC) Annual Conference, corporate technology consultant and author Shel Holtz stated: "Social media are the online tools and practices people use to engage in conversation and collaboration." Charlene Li, author of *Groundswell* (2011), contends that today all media are social media, even traditional mass media. In today's business environment, public relations strategists are using all media at their disposal to reach external audiences, ultimately to influence public opinions and behaviors. Use of social media strategies and specifically corporate blogs are on the rise (Barnes, 2010b; Barnes & Mattson, 2008, 2009; McKinsey and Company, 2008).

Businesses large and small are increasingly using social media strategies to reach internal and external publics (Constant Contact, 2011; SmartBrief and Summus Limited., 2010). Steve Rubel, senior vice president of Edelman Digital (2010), suggests that blogs and other social media tools are more important to organizations due to the number of people who use these tools on a daily basis for news and information gathering. According to the 2011 Edelman Trust Barometer Executive Summary, "Search engines rank No. 1 as the place people go first for information about a company, followed by online news sources, print, and broadcast media" (2011a, p. 6). Company websites ranked number 5 in a field of 7 choices of trusted information sources.

Whalen (2005) defined blogs as "individual diaries, discussion groups or bulletin boards on the web that feature the latest news in a particular area of interest" (p. 21). Expanding on that definition, for this study a corporate blog is an organization's use of the blog format on its public-facing website to share information regarding the state and reputation of the organization with all external publics. According to Heires (2005) blogs are an effective and inexpensive way to "influence the public 'conversation' about your company . . . enhance brand visibility and credibility . . . [and] achieve customer intimacy" (p. 3). Corporate blogs allow for a two-way conversation with external publics. Five common types of corporate blogs include: sales or promotional blogs; newsletter blogs; executive blogs (written by corporate leaders); employee blogs (personal accounts written by employees of the company); and collaborative blogs. Collaborative blogs are written by more than one person in the organization and usually adhere to a set of guidelines developed by the writers or the organization (Doraiswamy, 2008). Li (2010) acknowledges that increasingly corporations are using corporate blogs to build "a desirable organizational image" (p. 2).

It is anticipated that organizations can develop greater trust from corporate stakeholders, both internal and external, if ethical public relations practices are used when developing social media. It can be argued that the ultimate goal of public relations—also labeled as corporate communications—is the cultivation and maintenance of mutually beneficial relationships between the organizational entity and its stakeholders (internal and external to the organization). Inherent in this understanding is the concept of organizational trust. Shockley-Zalabak and Morreale (2011) assert that organizational trust is a fundamental leadership responsibility of corporate communicators. Trust is: The organization's willingness, based upon its culture and communication behaviors in relationships and transactions, to be appropriately vulnerable based on the belief that another individual, group, or organization is competent, open and honest, concerned, reliable, and identified with common goals, norms, and values. (Shockley-Zalabak, Ellis, & Cesaria, 2000, p. 4)

Organizational trust is often synonymous with credibility and should include measures of benevolence, integrity, and goodwill. "Trust is an essential line of business" (Edelman, 2011b, p. 3), but there is no such thing as a perfect company (Kimmel, 2010).

Elia (2009) contends that as corporations adopt any new media tactics, they have a duty to stakeholders to foster transparency and create a mutually beneficial exchange. "Respect for transparency rights is not simply value added to a corporation's line of goods and services, but a condition of a corporation's justifiable claim to create value rather than harm, wrong, or injustice in its dealings" (p. 145).

Journalists' Use of Corporate Blogs

The success of public relations rests on maintaining relationships between the organization and its stakeholders. One key stakeholder group for organizations is mainstream media. Reporters and producers serve as gatekeepers for the general public. News (reported by journalists) influences the public's perception of an organization, from consumer behavior to investor decision making to employee recruitment. Journalists' perceptions of, and use of, corporate social media as a source for developing news stories cannot be overlooked. Journalists are increasingly relying on social media in the newsgathering process when researching news stories. "While the traditional resource of corporate websites (96%) is used by the vast majority of journalists when researching a story online, almost nine out of ten reported using blogs for their online research (89%)" (George Washington University and Cision, 2009, p. 11). Additionally, 65% turn to social networking sites and 52% of journalists use microblogging services to follow story leads. Journalists are increasingly relying on social media for their sources (Oriella PR Network, 2011).

> When it comes to sourcing new story angles, almost half (47%) of respondents said they used Twitter, and a third (35%) used Facebook. Blogs were also highlighted as a key element of the sourcing process, with 30% saying they used blogs they were already familiar with. More interesting still, 42% of respondents drew on posts from blogs they had not visited before. (Oriella PR Network, 2011, p. 3)

In the third annual study of trends and changes to journalism practices, Middleberg and McClure (2011) found that the top five social media tools journalists reported using included company websites, Facebook, blogs, Twitter, and online video. Of the journalists surveyed, 68% said that journalists' reliance on social media is increasing significantly. But only 10% of respondents indicated that social media is a reliable tool for sourcing stories. Middleberg and McClure (2011) report that journalists still prefer traditional communications and relationship-building strategies, such as email, telephone, and in-person meetings.

These findings regarding journalists' use of social media tools suggest that improving the perceived credibility of corporate blogs may increase journalists' use of blogs as sources for relationship building and news-gathering.

Credibility of Traditional and Social Media

Across a broad range of studies common markers or characteristics of traditional and social media credibility align. These common themes include:

professional appearance (Fogg, 2002; Fritch & Cromwell, 2001, 2002; Kang, 2010; Martin & Johnson, 2010; Sundar, 2008; Walthen & Burkell, 2002); documented expertise of the writer(s)/blogger(s) (Fogg, 2002; Fritch & Cromwell, 2001, 2002; Kang, 2010; Martin & Johnson, 2010; Metzger, 2007; Metzger, Flanagin, & Medders, 2010; Walthen & Burkell, 2002); factual accuracy and reliable information (Fogg, 2002; Fritch & Cromwell, 2001, 2002; Kang, 2010; Metzger, 2007; Metzger et al, 2010); navigability and interactivity of the site (Fogg, 2002; Kang, 2010; Sundar, 2008); meeting the expectations of the user (Fogg, 2002; Kang, 2010; Kaye & Johnson, 2011; Metzger, 2007; Metzger et al, 2010; Sundar, 2008; Walthen & Burkell, 2002); and objectivity (Fogg, 2002; Kang, 2010; Metzger, 2007; Metzger et al, 2010).

Metzger's (2007) research suggests that savvy media users filter information and thus determine credibility using the following five criteria: accuracy of the information, authority of the source (credentials of the source), objectivity in presenting information, currency (timeliness of information), and coverage or scope (depth of the information).

Fritch and Cromwell (2001, 2002) and Walthen and Burkell (2002) propose assessment focused on the quality of the information presented. Fritch and Cromwell suggest that users: verify the identity of the author of the website; consider the factual accuracy of the website as a document, including its presentation; and investigate the affiliations of the website or its authors. Fritch and Cromwell suggest using other web tools to verify the quality of information. If first impressions truly are accurate, they suggest that information users form a first impression of the author or organization simply by viewing the outward qualities of the site, such as the physical design and organization of the information. Second, users should look at the credibility of the source of the information, such as the expertise and credentials of the author or organization, as well as the accuracy and relevance of the information. The last stage in the Walthen and Burkell model includes the cognitive or mental state of the reader at the time that they are viewing the information. For example, if the reader is pressed for time or has prior knowledge of the subject matter, these factors may influence their assessment of the quality and thus credibility of the information.

Kaye and Johnson (2011) contend that users will not judge a blog as credible if it does not satisfy their needs. Thus, a user's disposition toward using blogs as information sources influences the user's rating of a blog's credibility. Their categories of users include a spectrum from users who were confident in the credibility of all blogs, to users who doubt the credibility of blogs due to organizational bias, to users who perceive blogs to be credible if generated by sources with first-hand information about the subject matter to users who do not consider any blogs as credible. Kaye and Johnson found that the most common motivations for using a blog as an information source included as a supplement to information found in traditional media, for links to additional sources, and simply because the information was interesting to the user.

Social media users also evaluate the credibility of online information sources by using social- and group-based credibility assessment strategies (Metzger, et al, 2010). Users rely on their network of colleagues to assess the credibility of information sources (social processing). Other factors relevant in the evaluation of online source credibility included reputation of the source, endorsement by other respected sources, consistency of information, expectancy violation, and persuasive intent (Metzger et al., 2010). When information or a source of information does not meet the user's expectation, then an expectancy violation reduced the source's credibility to the users. This included the appearance and functionality of the site as well as the type of information presented or requested to complete a transaction. Persuasive intent was described as the overt use of commercial content; "aggressive persuasive intent leads to negative credibility evaluations" (p. 433) because users sense heavy-handed bias in the information source.

Fogg (2002) asserts that the perceived credibility of websites can be improved by ensuring the information is verifiable, highlights credentials of experts, provides a physical address and photo of the organization's office; contact information is displayed; there are links to credible sites; organization bios are posted; a professional design is maintained; the site is easy to use; content is updated; advertisements are clearly labeled; there are no typos; content ratings are displayed; and awards are displayed. Martin and Johnson (2010) add that visual credibility and technical credibility cannot be ignored when using a corporate blog to influence external publics; using images of products and services as well as that of the blogger influenced readers' perception of credibility.

Speaking specifically to the agency and credibility of corporate social media, Barnes and Mattson (2008, 2009) found that corporations, while slow to employ social media strategies, are annually increasing the use and types of social media—including blogs, Twitter feeds, Facebook, and podcasts (audio and video). Kang (2010) adds that corporate blogs must be knowledgeable, influential, passionate, *transparent*, reliable, authentic, insightful, informative, consistent, fair, focused, accurate, timely, and popular.

Social Media Strategies in Corporate Communication

Scholars and practitioners are also weighing in on the authentic use of social media as a corporate communication strategy. Whereas it is common practice for corporate communicators to ghostwrite materials on behalf of their organizations, scholars (Burns, 2008; Craig, 2007; Kuhn, 2007; Smuddle, 2005), and practitioners (Paisner, 2006; Subervi, 2010a, 2010b) are questioning the ethics of this practice when it comes to corporate social media applications (blogs) on the grounds of the public expectations of authenticity. Kuhn (2007) suggests the following as staples of a code of blogging ethics: "promote interactivity . . . promote free expression . . . strive for factual truth . . . be as transparent as possible . . . promote the 'human' element in blogging" (p. 33–34).

Corporate blogs are often regarded as having low credibility as sources of information because users perceive that these blogs are bias toward the corporate or commercial interest of the organization (Flanagin & Metzger, 2000, 2003; Kaye & Johnson, 2011; Metzger et al., 2010). Holtz and Demopoulos (2006) assert that corporations need to use social media to keep competitive and reach organizational stakeholders. Ylisela (2010) suggests that helping corporate leaders present themselves and the organization in the best light is a key responsibility of public relations leaders and is to be expected as social media become more prevalent and accepted sources of corporate messages both to internal and external audiences.

As companies implement corporate blogs as public relations tactics, they need to consider the following concerns: a corporate blog supports a business goal; a corporate blog should reflect the company's image and overall business strategy; as a communication strategy, the blog must be monitored and measured; the company should have a policy regarding who will blog on behalf of the organization; and corporate bloggers need to consider the legal and ethical ramifications of their communications (Carr, 2006; Kim, 2009; The Society for New Communications Research, 2007). The Society for New Communications Research (2007) reiterate that a corporate blog is a two-way, personal medium; as such, monitoring and responding to comments is just as critical as regularly posting news and information of interest to the public. In studies of *Fortune 500* and Inc. 500 companies, Barnes (2010a & 2010b) found that of companies with public-facing (corporate) blogs, only 20% of *Fortune 500* companies and 36% of Inc. 500 companies had policies governing blogging.

Researchers and practitioners are also keenly aware of the risks and liabilities of social media as a communication strategy. "Having a blog can actually make your company a more inviting target" for media and pundit attacks (Carr, 2006, p. 9). Implementing a corporate blog or allowing employees to blog about their employer poses a number of risks to the corporation (Strother, Fazal, & Millsap, 2009), including damage to the organization's reputation and customer loyalty. Legal issues that corporations might encounter through corporate blogs include intellectual property concerns such as copyright infringement, disclosure of protected corporate information like trade secrets and misappropriation of information as well as defamation concerns, invasion of privacy, and securities fraud (Klosek, 2006).

A few suggestions for reducing risks and legal concerns surrounding corporate social media include: develop and enforce a corporate social media policy; use legal disclaimers to establish corporate responsibility for content; provide training to employees who will be responsible for corporate blogs; do not reveal trade secrets and private financial information; do not criticize competitors; provide reliable and timely information; develop content with the intent of being a reliable source; monitor the competitors' use of social media; develop a social media evaluation procedure (Carr, 2006; Daraiswamy, 2008; Flynn, 2006; Klosek, 2006; SNCR, 2007; Social Media Business Council, 2011; Strother, et al., 2009; Weil, 2006). Additionally, Cox and colleagues (2008) advocate for organizations to develop ethical policies regarding the use of corporate blogs: "Ethical policies for corporate blogging must therefore address truth, authenticity, verifiability, and transparency" (p. 6).

Research Question

Corporate communicators need to understand how mass media professionals perceive the credibility of corporate blogs as potential sources of news, thus leading to the research question for this study:

RQ: What factors [a.k.a., markers] cause mainstream media representatives (reporters and producers) to perceive corporate blogs as credible news sources?

METHODOLOGY

As a critical public, journalists have the power to influence other publics (internal and external); developing an understanding of their perception of corporate social media credibility should be a benefit to the practice of public relations generally, and media relations specifically.

The primary population of this study was mainstream media representatives (journalists).

A focus group of journalists was convened to investigate perceived credibility and use of corporate social media as credible sources for newsgathering. Using a convenience sampling method, five news professionals with similar responsibilities were recruited from the major news operations representing traditional and digital newsrooms: two print journalists/editors; a radio news reporter; a television news executive; and a multi-media journalist. The questions for the session were determined from the leading concepts raised in the review of literature.

RESULTS

All participants agreed that a journalist's job today includes multi-media news production as well as specific medium skills. Questioning during the focus group centered around the tenets of perceived credibility, i.e., believability, accuracy, trustworthiness, bias, and completeness.

Credibility: The participants concluded that for a source to be credible it had to have the following characteristics: contact information (names, numbers, emails); identity of the blogger; corporate branding elements; previous contact with a member of the organization; credentials of the organization and the members communicating on its behalf; fresh information in the blog post content (responding in a timely way to current events); and a list or archive of reference documents, i.e., news releases, and SEC documents, etc. One participant summarized the group's comments by stating: "For us, this site is a starting point, not an ending point. So having ready access to people that we can make direct contact with, that's the beginning of the process."

Believability: Many of the characteristics that increased the believability of corporate social media reported by the focus group members were similar to the general credibility markers: the reputation of the person(s) communicating on behalf of the organization; the use of corporate branding elements; and content that responds to both positive and negative information regarding the organization's performance.

Trustworthiness: For the focus group members to find a corporate social media site trustworthy, they said that it must: be forthright when dealing with controversy and criticism; have more proactive posts than reactive posts; provide supporting documents and links to other credible sources on a topic (even if those sources are from competing sources); have an authentic appearance and tone; be consistent with the organization's brand and reputation; be responsive to news reporters and their deadlines; and allow reporters to connect with a person and not a drop-box email address or blank form. "If they really want to impress reporters, it [contact information] would be an office number, home number and a cell number."

Completeness: Repeating some of their earlier markers of overall credibility, the participants stated that evidence of completeness includes links to credible source materials and consistent and frequent new posts that keep information fresh.

Accuracy: When the participants discussed the construct of accuracy, they described the interaction with the corporate social media site in the same way as one might describe an interpersonal transaction. The following qualities were suggested as evidence of accuracy: knowing the reputation of the person communicating on behalf of the organization; posts that are authored (no anonymous posts by staff); responsiveness to both positive and negative information regarding the success of the organization; factually consistent information; corrections to information when new information becomes available that trumps older information; links to other credible sources that contribute or triangulate the accuracy of the corporation's information; and links to corporate artifacts including videos and photographs.

Bias: The focus group members expect corporations to use their social media presence as an extension of corporate communication efforts to present information to benefit the organization. Participants said they expect to see this bias in the tone of the post and the post's content. The participants agreed that if a corporation is willing to show both positive and negative information about the organization, this behavior increases credibility and reduces the bias of the source. To paraphrase one participant, the more bias a corporate source contains, the more work the journalist has to do to find additional information from the other side of the argument. "When it comes to a website, the bias is more often than not going to be what's not there, so it's not like you can go and point to it; it would be the information that's missing." "It's kind of the other side of the completeness coin. The more complete it is the less you would see it as bias."

Members of the focus group could not quantify the number of contacts that are made through public relations contacts (agency or organizational) or corporate social media sites. But they did agree that journalists use any means available to reach appropriate sources to complete story assignments. One participant commented:

> Our reporters are following everybody that they need to be following on their beats. They should be following them through Twitter and Facebook. They should be making daily checks with sources online, you know, looking around. Not every website is going to be reporting news, but any that is active that way, you want to be looking at that with some frequency; and I don't know if that's daily or weekly, I mean depending on what's going on. But I would expect every one of my reporters every day is using new media in multiple ways to keep in touch with their sources, but that's not your reporting end point, ever.

Members of the focus group agreed that the five tenets or constructs of perceived credibility overlapped in definition. For example, for a source to be believable it also had to provide accurate and complete information. The participants concluded that all corporate information sources are biased toward the survival of the entity providing the information. Additionally, the participants commented on the development of trust as a process between a journalist and the source.

DISCUSSION

Research question one asked what factors (a.k.a., markers) cause mainstream media representatives (reporters and producers) to perceive corporate blogs as credible news sources? Commentary from the focus group members supported findings from previous studies (Abdulla et al., 2005; Bucy, 2003; Flanagin & Metzger, 2000, 2003; Fogg, 2002; Fritch & Cromwell, 2001, 2002; Gaziano & McGrath, 1986; Johnson & Kaye, 2004; Johnson & Wiedenbeck, 2009; Kang, 2010; Kaye & Johnson, 2011; Martin & Johnson,

2011; Metzger, 2007; Metzger et al., 2010; Meyer, 1988; Newhagen & Nass, 1989; Sundar, 2008; Walthen & Burkell, 2002) regarding the identification of markers that enhance perceived credibility. The focus group of journalists validated the measures of believability, accuracy, trustworthiness, bias, and completeness as important credibility markers.

Focus group results also support the 2011 study by Middleberg and McClure that found journalists are using new media tools more now than they have in the past. The increasing use of these tools highlights the need for corporations to build credibility and trust with journalists on these sites through ethical practices. Elia (2009) stressed that corporations need to promote transparency, whereas while Fritch and Cromwell (2001, 2002) suggest that author identity is important on websites. These findings were also confirmed by our focus group members who stressed that it is important for them to know who is writing the information contained on the blog. Journalists don't want to feel like anything is hidden; they want to access all of the information they need quickly. It is also important for corporate communications professionals to remember that corporate blogging sites are viewed as a starting point for story development, and having easily accessible contact information is extremely important.

In terms of the types of messages conveyed on corporate blogs, the focus group members expected corporations to be biased in their messaging. This supports the finding by several scholars that corporate blogs are often perceived as having low credibility simply due to the fact that the information is thought to be biased (Flanagin & Metzger, 2000, 2003; Kaye & Johnson, 2011; Metzger et al., 2010). Kaye and Johnson (2011) also found that a user's disposition toward using blogs can influence credibility ratings, and this finding was also confirmed. Those in the focus group said they expected a corporate blog to present information in the best interest of the company. Because journalists are approaching corporate blogs in this way, PR practitioners should take steps to present all sides of a story, even if it may not be flattering to the company. Presenting all sides of a story can earn a corporate blog more respect from journalists. It is important to remember that an expectancy violation (Metzger et al., 2010) can occur if information posted online doesn't meet a user's expectation.

As for the design of the blog, focus group members noted that the use of corporate branding elements can immediately boost a blog's credibility. This finding confirmed the results of Walthen and Burkell's (2002) study where users judged the credibility of a website based on the physical design and organization of information.

Ethical Implications for the Practice of Social Media

As new social media tools are developed, it is fair to assume that companies will continue to adopt these technologies as corporate communication strategies. Companies that use new media tools to present a transparent and credible image of their organization to all external publics will be better positioned to influence key organizational publics and be identified as trusted and ethical organizations. One of the battles corporate communicators face is the perception of journalists that messages contained on corporate blogs are biased. It's of the utmost importance that those authoring corporate blogs identify themselves and include contact information so posted facts can be verified by journalists. Before ethical issues arise, corporate communicators would be wise to heed the advice of Cox and colleagues (2008) who advise organizations to establish policies regarding the ethical use of corporate blogs.

Public relations as a business component has long struggled with characterization of the practice of situational ethics. Bowen (2007) acknowledges that public relations has matured from the practice of sheer spin of business interests to a strategic management function that seeks to provide counsel to the organization in developing transparent two-way symmetrical relationships with stakeholders. The two leading professional organizations representing corporate communication professionals, IABC and the Public Relations Society of America, both maintain codes of ethics that together promote the values of sharing honest accurate information, facilitating respect and mutual understanding between an organization and its stakeholders, fostering the free-flow of information between an organization and its stakeholders, respecting cultural values, avoiding personal and professional conflicts of interest, providing objective counsel to their employers and clients, supporting the right of free expression, and abiding by laws and governing policies (IABC, 2010; PRSA, 2000).

In addition to applying professional (IABC and PRSA) ethical standards to the practice of corporate social media, Stevenson and Peck (2011) advocate for the evaluation of the ethical use of social media tools during the planning stages as well as once the message has been launched on the web. Stevenson and Peck suggest that the ethical use of social media satisfy three conditions:

1. The act considered separately from its unintended harmful effect is in itself not wrong.
2. The agent intends only the good and does not intend harm as an end or as a mean.
3. The agent reflects upon his/her relevant duties, considering accepted norms, and takes due care to eliminate or alleviate any foreseen harm through his/her act. (Stevenson & Peck, 2011, p. 61)

Keeping in mind the ethical guidelines outlined above, corporate communicators can create materials that are accurate, complete, authentic, and transparent—as well as perceived as credible and ethical.

CONCLUSION

It is apparent that the concept of credibility in relationship to the ethical use of social media remains a subjective perception constructed by the individual interacting with the social media. By understanding common concepts that journalists employ to determine source credibility when encountering corporate social media, corporate communicators may better counsel their clients and employers in the development of credible corporate social media. For corporate communication practitioners, using the outcomes of this study may help to improve current and future corporate blog applications. For public relations scholars this research may provide insights into the socially mediated relationship between corporations and news professionals who report on corporate activities.

This is a preliminary study and the findings are based on commentary from a focus group. These results and conclusions represent a snapshot of current media representatives' opinions and cannot be generalized to all media professionals. It should be kept in mind that all members of the focus group represented one geographic area and because of this some geographic bias may be present.

Discussion Questions

1. Is ghostwriting corporate blog posts an ethical public relations practice? Why or why not?
2. What criteria do you use when you judge something to be credible? Do you agree with the credibility markers outlined in this chapter?
3. Will the use of corporate blogs continue to rise? If so, what could be some of the ethical implications?

SUGGESTED READINGS

Drushel, B. E., & German, K. (2011). *The ethics of emerging media: Information, social norms, and new media technology.* New York: Continuum Books.

Holtz, S., & Demopoulos, T. (2006). *Blogging for business: Everything you need to know and why you should care.* Chicago: Kaplan Business.

Li, C., & Bernoff, J. (2011). *Groundswell: Winning in a world transformed by social technologies.* Watertown, MA: Harvard Business School Publishing.

Postman, J. (2009). *SocialCorp: Social media goes corporate.* Berkley, CA: New Riders.

Wollan, R., Smith, N., & Zhou, C. (2011). *The social media management handbook: Everything you need to know to get social media working in your business.* Hoboken: John Wiley & Sons.

REFERENCES

Abdulla, R. A., Garrison, B., Salwen, M. B., Driscoll, P. D., & Casey, D. (2005). Online news credibility. In M. Salwen, Garrison, B., & Driscoll, P. (Ed.), *Online news and the public* (pp. 147–163). London: Lawrence Erlbaum Associates.

Barnes, N. G. (2010a). *The Fortune 500 and social media: A longitudinal study of blogging, Twitter and Facebook usage by America's largest companies.* Retrieved from http://sncr.org

Barnes, N. G. (2010b). *The 2010 Inc. 500 update: Most blogs, friend and tweet but some industries still shun social media.* Retrieved from http://sncr.org

Barnes, N. G., & Mattson, E. (2008). Social media in the Inc. 500: The first longitudinal study. *Journal of New Communications Research, III*(1), 74–78.

Barnes, N. G., & Mattson, E. (2009). The *Fortune 500* and blogging: Slow and steady. *Journal of New Communications Research, IV*(1), 123–133.

Bowen, S. A. (2007). *Ethics and Public Relations.* Retrieved from http://www.instituteforpr.org

Bucy, E. P. (2003). Media credibility reconsidered: Synergy effects between on-air and online news. *Journalism and Mass Communication Quarterly, 80*(2), 247–264.

Burns, K. S. (2008). The misuse of social media: Reactions to and important lessons from a blog fiasco. *Journal of New Communications Research, III*(1), 41–54.

Carr, N. (2006, July 18). Lessons in corporate blogging, *Business Week Online,* 9. Retrieved from http://www.businessweek.com/stories/2006–07–17/lessons-in-corporate-blogging

Constant Contact (2011, April). *Constant Contact spring 2011 attitudes and outlooks survey key findings.* Retrieved from www.constantcontact.com/small-business-week/survey.jsp

Cox, J. L., Martinez, E. R., & Quinlan, K .B. (2008). Blogs and the corporation: Managing the risk, reaping the benefits. *Journal of Business Strategy, 29*(3) 4–12.

Craig, D. A. (ed.) (2007). Cases and commentaries. *Journal of Mass Media Ethics, 22*(2–3), 215–228.

Doraiswamy, U. D. (2008). Corporate blogging. In Kelsey, S. & Amant, K. (Eds.) *Handbook of research on computer mediated communication,* 731–739. Hershey, PA: Information Science Reference/GI Global.

Edelman (2011a). *2011 Edelman Trust Barometer executive summary.* Retrieved from http://www.edelman.com

Edelman (2011b). *2011 Edelman Trust Barometer findings.* Retrieved from http://www.edelman.com

Elia, J. (2009). Transparency rights, technology, and trust. *Ethics and Information Technology, 11*(2), 145–153.

Flanagin, A. J., & Metzger, M. J. (2000). Perceptions of internet information credibility. *Journalism and Mass Communication Quarterly, 77*(3), 515–540.

Flanagin, A. J., & Metzger, M. J. (2003). The perceived credibility of personal web page information as influenced by the sex of the source. *Computers in Human Behavior, 19,* 683–701.

Flynn, N. (2006). *Blog rules: A business guide to managing policy, public relations, and legal issues.* New York: AMACOM.

Fogg, B. J. (2002). *Stanford guidelines for web credibility.* Retrieved from http://www.webcredibility.org/guidelines

Fritch, J. W., & Cromwell, R. L. (2001). Evaluating Internet resources: Identity, affiliation, and cognitive authority in a networked world. *Journal of the American Society for Information Science and Technology, 52*(6), 499–507.

Fritch, J. W., & Cromwell, R. L. (2002). Delving deeper into evaluation: Exploring cognitive authority on the Internet. *Reference Services Review, 30*(3), 242–254.

Gaziano, C., & McGrath, K. (1986). Measuring the concept of credibility. *Journalism Quarterly, 63,* 451–462.

George Washington University and Cision (2009). *2009 social media & online usage study: Top line findings.* Retrieved from http://us.cision.com/journalist_survey_2009/

Gogoi, P. (2006). Wal-Mart vs. the blogosphere. *BusinessWeek Online,* 10. Retrieved from http://www.businessweek.com/stories/2006–10–17/wal-mart-vs-dot-the-blogospherebusinessweek-business-news-stock-market-and-financial-advice

Grossman, L. (2007). The price of anonymity. *Time, 170*(5), 47–49.

Heires, K. (Nov. 1, 2005). The blogosphere beckons: Should your company jump in? A low-cost, high-impact channel would seem to have no downside. But it pays to look before you leap. *Harvard Business Review,* 3–5.

Holtz, S., & Demopoulos, T. (2006). *Blogging for business: Everything you need to know and why you should care.* Chicago: Kaplan Business.

International Association of Business Communicators. (2010). International Association of Business Communicators code of ethics for professional communicators. Retrieved from http://www.iabc.com/about/code.htm

Irwin, T. (2011 May 18). Schwab launches corporate blog, *Media Post News.* Retrieved from http://www.mediapost.com/publications/?fa=Articles.show Article&art_aid=150721&nid=126863

Johnson, K. A., & Wiedenbeck, S. (2009, Summer). Enhancing perceived story credibility on citizen journalism web sites. *Journalism and Mass Communication Quarterly, 86*(2), 332–348.

Johnson, T. J., & Kaye, B. K. (2004). Wag the blog: How reliance on traditional media and the internet influence credibility perceptions of weblogs among blog users. *Journalism and Mass Communication Quarterly, 81*(3), 622–642.

Kang, M. (2010). *Measuring social media credibility: A study on a measure of blog credibility.* Retrieved from http://www.instituteforpr.org

Kaye, B. K., & Johnson, T. J. (2011). Hot diggity blog: A cluster analysis examining motivations and other factors for why people judge different types of blogs as credible. *Mass Communication & Society, 14*(2), 236–263.

Kim. C. (2009, June 3). 10 Steps to achieving ROI (Return on Influence) through corporate blogs. Retrieved from http://www.myragan.com/_weblog/?id=Ragan/CindyKimPR&blogid=82352

Kimmel, B. (2010, December). *Trust across America.* White paper available online: http://www.trustacrossamerica.com

Klosek, J. (2006, Dec. 14). Corporate blogs: Handle with care, *Business Week Online,* 6. Business Source Complete, EbscoHost.

Kuhn, M. (2007). Interactivity and prioritizing the human: A code of blogging ethics. *Journal of Mass Media Ethics, 22*(1), 18–36.

Li, C., & Bernoff, J. (2011). *Groundswell: Winning in a world transformed by social technologies.* Watertown, MA: Harvard Business School Publishing.

Martin, K. N., & Johnson, M. A. (2010). Digital credibility and digital dynamism in public relations blogs. *Visual Communication Quarterly, 17*(3), 162–174.

McKinsey and Company. (2008, Fall). Building the web 2.0 enterprise: McKinsey global survey results. *McKinsey Quarterly,* 38–47. Available online: http://www.McKinsey.com

Metzger, M. J. (2007). Making sense of credibility on the web: Models for evaluating online information and recommendations for future research. *Journal of the American Society for Information Science and Technology, 58*(13), 2078–2091.

Metzger, M. J., Flanagin, A. J., & Medders, R. B. (2010). Social and heuristic approaches to credibility evaluation online. *Journal of Communication, 60*(3), 413–439.

Meyer, P. (1988). Defining and measuring credibility of newspapers: Developing an index. *Journalism Quarterly, 65,* 567–574.

Middleberg, D. & McClure, J. (2011). *2011 Middleberg/SNCR survey of media in the wired world*. Retrieved from http://sncr.org

Newhagen, J., & Nass, C. (1989). Differential criteria for evaluating credibility of newspapers and TV news. *Journalism Quarterly, 66*, 277–284.

Oriella PR Network (2011). *Clicks, communities and conversations: The state of journalism in 2011: Oriella PR Network digital journalism study*. Retrieved from www.oriellaprnetwork.com

Paisner, J. (January 2006). The principles of corporate blogs: Make your blog an asset to your brand. *Public Relations Tactics, 13*(1), 17.

Public Relations Society of America (2000, October). *PRSA Member Code of Ethics 2000*. New York: Public Relations Society of America.

Rubel, S. (2010). The age of media agnosticism. Retrieved from http://www.edelman.com/.../Rubel_The%20Age%20of%20Media%20Agnosticism%20FINAL.pdf

Shockley-Zalabak, P., Ellis, K., & Cesaria, R. (2000). *Measuring organizational trust: A diagnostic survey and international indicator*. San Francisco: International Association of Business Communicators.

Shockley-Zalabak, P., & Morreale, S. (2011). Communication and the high-trust organization. In Gillis, T. L. (Ed.) *The IABC handbook or organizational communication, second edition* (pp. 41–53). San Francisco: Jossey-Bass.

SmartBrief and Summus Limited (2010). *The state of social media for business: Select themes 2010*. Available online: www.summuslimited.com

Smith, G. (2009, August 31). Petrobras brandishes its corporate blog. *Business Week Online*, 2. Retrieved from http://www.businessweek.com/bwdaily/dnflash/content/aug2009/db20090830_428592.htm

Smuddle, P. M. (Fall 2005). Blogging, ethics and public relations: A proactive and dialogic approach. *Public Relations Quarterly*, pp. 34–38.

Social Media Business Council. (2011). *Disclosure best practices toolkit*. Retrieved from http://www.socialmedia.org/wp-content/uploads/Disclosure-Best-Practices-Toolkit1.pdf

Society for New Communications Research (2007 March). Corporate blogging best practices, *Best Practices Tip Sheet*. Retrieved from http://sncr.org

Stevenson, S. E., & Peck, L. A. (2011). "I am eating a sandwich now": Intent and foresight in the Twitter age. *Journal of Mass Media Ethics, 26*(1), 56–65.

Strother, J. B., Fazal, Z., & Millsap, M. (2009, September). Legal and ethical issues of the corporate blogosphere. *IEEE Transactions on Professional Communication, 52*(3), 243–253.

Subervi, A. (April/2010a). Is it right to ghostwrite? *Public Relations Tactics*, p. 6.

Subervi, A. (June/2010b). What's in a name? The ethics of anonymous blog comments. *Public Relations Tactics*, p. 6.

Sundar, S. S. (2008). The MAIN model: A heuristic approach to understanding technology effects on credibility. In Miriam J. Metzer and Andrew J. Flanagin (Eds.) *Digital media, youth, and credibility* (pp. 73–100). Cambridge, MA: MIT Press.

Walthen, C. N., & Burkell, J. (2002). Believe it or not: Factors influencing credibility on the Web. *Journal of the American Society for Information Science and Technology, 53*(2), 134–144.

Weil, D. (2006). *The corporate blogging book: Absolutely everything you need to know to get it right*. New York: Portfolio.

Welch, D. (2005). The blog from the rust belt. *BusinessWeek*, (3919), 12.

Whalen, P. (2005). *Corporate communication from A to Z: An encyclopedia for public relations and marketing professionals*. San Francisco: IABC.

Ylisela, J. (2010, January 19). How to edit your boss without getting fired. Retrieved from http://www.ragan.com/ME2/Audiences/dirmod.asp?sid=&nm=&type=. ...04A35879BEC18DDF69424&AudID=3FF14703FD8C4AE98B9B4365B978201A

13 Authority Crisis Communication vs. Discussion Forums

Swine Flu

Päivi Tirkkonen and Vilma Luoma-aho

INTRODUCTION

Public relations is said to be the conscience of an organization. Legally the role of public authorities is to secure the safety of citizens and therefore also be able to give orders, or use power over citizens in order to prevent harm. That power in democracies is given to authorities through social contract (Rousseau, 1762/2003) and authorities should represent the general will of the people. Therefore, it is vital for democracy that citizens perceive authority actions as ethical. In the social media era publics are using the Internet as a collective memory when evaluation the success of authority communication and actions (Lee, 2009).

Public authorities in Finland enjoy high citizen trust due to the efficient welfare system and uncorrupted society (Transparency International, 2011). Although traditionally in the Western countries, social contracts have enabled trust in society (Hobbes, 1651/2010), we argue that the recent changes are pushing public authorities traditionally based on the Kantian (Kant, 1758/1956) ethics of duty and responsibility toward egoism and utilitarism, where citizen demands take central stage. This emergence of self-mass communication (Castells, 2009) and social media platforms provides a possibility to publicly criticize authorities' actions. Moreover, social media is adding pressure on authorities to adopt an attitude of dialogue and collaboration.

Crisis communication activities aim at saving the organization and its publics from potential damage (Coombs & Holladay, 2007), and traditionally crises have been seen as linear events of three consecutive phases: before, during, and after a crisis. Effective crisis communication is understood to be two-way, interactive, supportive, and emphatic (Boano & Lund, 2011; Seeger & Reynolds, 2009): the societal purpose of crisis communication is to prevent and reduce harm and damage. Crisis communication should also include dialogue on perceived risks and recovery (Palttala & Vos, 2011).

Various public groups are targeted in crisis communication, and the diversity of their needs should be taken into account. The ways the media frames crises also affects citizens' perceptions (Seon-Kyoung & Gower, 2009) and even response activities (Thierney, Bevc, Kuligowski, 2006).

Moreover, after the emergence of social media or mass self-communication (Castells, 2009), information flows move freely and crisis communication has entered into an era of direct interaction between organizations and their publics.

Our study contributes to the understanding of how ethics in action affect authority communication. The chapter moves beyond the legalistic approach of referring to codes of conduct and proposes how, in practice, a new, common communication environment could be built on shared understanding and therefore led to a more ethical relationship. The chapter is organized as follows. First, we discuss crisis communication leadership during an era of social media. Second, we distinguish five dilemmas guiding authority communication during crises. Third, using the TARES-framework, we analyze how authority communication, departing from the traditional Kantian ethics meets the new utilitarian mass self-communication (Castells, 2009) by studying citizen reactions to authority communication during the Swine Flu Crises in 2009 in Finland. To conclude, we discuss the implications for public relations and propose discourse along the principles of communitarianism as an ideal for authority communication during crises.

LITERATURE REVIEW

Crisis Communication in an Era of Social Media

Effective leadership is a prerequisite for success in crisis communication. Crises call for a contingency approach to leadership; different crisis require different leadership styles (Ulmer, Sellnow, & Seeger, 2011). Devitt and Borodzicz (2008) list four key functions required for effective crisis leadership; task skills (strategic thinking, quick adaption, delegation, and decision making), interpersonal skills (emotional intelligence, interaction skills), personal attributes (credibility, ethical, confident), and stakeholder savvy (engagement with media and politics, meeting the needs of stakeholders). In addition, for crisis communication to succeed, leaders have to remain open for feedback, portray empathy (Ulmer et al. 2011), and communicate clearly (Alexander, 2004). As crises often surprise, cause threat, and call for urgent management (Ulmer et al. 2011), management procedures at the strategic and operational level have to be clarified well before the crisis hits (Seeger, 2006; Boin & McConnell, 2007; Comfort, 2007).

Communication can contribute to crisis management throughout the different phases. In the pre-crisis phase, crisis management focuses on monitoring the environment, making scenarios and response plans according to them (Boano & Lund, 2011, Boin & McDowell, 2007). Communication at this stage includes monitoring public perception of risks and public preparedness, producing educational messages and preparedness campaigns, as well as establishing a dialogue on risks and early warnings signals. Crisis communication is no longer a monopoly of authorities. Crises are co-created in interaction, not only by the organization itself, but also by politicians, media, activists, consumers, experts, and citizens giving statements on the crisis (Frandsen & Johansen, 2010). Social media is one of the arenas for that discussion.

The emergence of social media has enabled both publics and organizations to operate better during crises (Veil, Buehner, & Palenchar, 2011). For organizations, social media offer a chance to monitor citizens' opinions and perceptions. Instead of the traditional one-way informing of facts, public sector organizations are learning to listen and find the relevant issue areas, and topics being discussed (Luoma-aho & Vos, 2009). By following discussions online, authorities could better adapt their crisis communication messages according to citizens' expectations.

Authority crisis communication in the social media era should focus on preventing a crisis from escalating and helping citizens cope with exceptional circumstances (Palttala & Vos, 2011), with the help of various media. A central prerequisite for effective dialogue online is transparency (Heath & Palenchar, 2007). This remains a challenge for many bureaucratic public sector organizations.

Five Dilemmas: Ethical Challenges in Authority-Citizens Relationship

Contemporary crises differ from crises in the past, but many public sector organizations trying to manage them are still using old practices (Roux-Dufort, 2007). It is no longer enough to do what is "right," but self-centered citizen needs have permanently entered the authority communication sphere.

Social media has enabled dialogue between authorities and citizens, but certain ethical dilemmas are apparent. Figure 13.1 introduces five dilemmas apparent in the citizen-public sector organization relationship: Flexibility, internality/externality of communication, lack of common viewpoints, legal constraints, and stigma. These five dilemmas are next discussed in more detail.

First dilemma in the authorities-citizens relationship is bureaucracy causing inflexibility and slowness. As information is moving freely within flexible social networks (Castells, 2004), the bureaucratic public organizations with direct vertical control cannot easily respond to the new requirements: their organizational structure does not support fast actions. Authorities are not able to make decisions and communicate fast enough causing frustration among citizens and creating an impression on unprofessional crisis management. In public organizations, strict division of power, specialization, and formal rules prevent spontaneous action (Huhtala & Hakala, 2007).

Second dilemma is the blurred division between private and public causing difficulties in communication. Crises are mostly multi-actor or multi-authority situations and require input from many different actors (Boin,

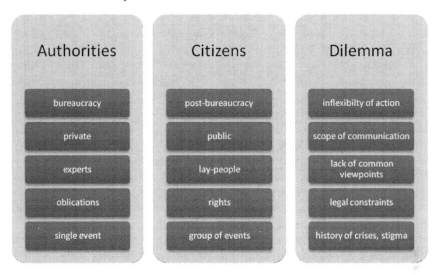

Figure 13.1 Dilemmas of authority–citizens relationship.

t'Hart, Stern & Sundelius, 2011), and require communication on both private and public arenas (private refers to authority organizations' internal communication and reality, public to the citizens' needs, (see Frandsen & Johansen, 2010). According to Frandsen and Johansen (2010), a crisis "will always extend across traditional distinctions between what is public (i.e. the public sphere of the media), semi-public (networks), or private (inside organizations)." In the publicly available social media platforms, information is easily shared between users and people can present accusations and speculations, which can be difficult to prove wrong.

Third dilemma is related to the different roles of authorities and citizens. Authorities are often experts of their field, whereas citizens are lay people, who do not have the same knowledge to evaluate the crises. Authorities have an ethical obligation to provide citizens with the information necessary for making adequate decisions (Ulmer & Sellnow, 1997) and citizens have to trust the information and guidance given by the authorities. Lack of trust towards response organizations complicates the effectiveness of crisis communication, (Veil 2008, Seeger, 2006, Coombs & Holladay, 1996); if authorities are not trusted, other sources emerge even with false, misleading, or highly subjective information (Tirkkonen & Luoma-aho, 2011). Moreover, people may believe that some factors have remained undiscovered by authorities (Sjöberg, 2001).

Several factors affect how citizens perceive crises. Therefore it is important to understand citizens' needs and the way in which people process information (Reich, Bentman, & Jackman, 2011). Sometimes publics can be afraid of issues, which are unlikely to cause danger (Seeger, 2006), and familiar hazards do not cause much worry (Renn, 2008). In fact, "the same people may be excessively concerned about some aspects of the crisis and appropriately or insufficiently concerned about other aspects" (Sandman, 2006, p. 258). Risk communication is central for crisis communication, as its purpose is to encourage citizens to self-protect (Rowan, 1991) According to Heath and Palenchar (2007) risk communication is about helping citizens mitigate consequences of risk by empowering them. Crisis management and communication should also be planned from the citizens' perspective.

Fourth dilemma refers to the tension between authority obligations and citizen rights and expectations. Citizens expect protection, yet crises question authorities' capabilities to protect (Roux-Dufort, 2007). According to attribution theory, during a time of crisis people try to understand what has happened and attribute cause, why and who is responsible (Coombs & Holladay, 1996); to make sense of the situation (Weick, 1988). If citizens feel capable, they are likely to act and contribute to crises management (Witte, 1992). Communication activities often aim at strengthening this self-efficacy of public groups. In times of crises, people resort to their closest social networks, which can be effective sources of information (Palttala & Vos, 2011), yet unchecked information can hinder crises recovery.

Fifth dilemma is the narrow perspective most organizations have on crises: they see it as a single, separate event (Roux-Dufort, 2007). Crises should be seen as processes with history: they develop, they do not happen. Crises disclose organizational problems, which have existed before. The authorities often see a crisis as a single event, but citizens may remember and associate similar cases in history and also the actions of the organization in the past. In fact, some issues or fields are stigmatized, such as products that citizens perceive to be harmful despite non-existing scientific evidence (Renn, 2008).

Research Questions

These five dilemmas lead us to the case study. Accordingly our research questions are:

RQ1:   How do citizens and authorities interact in discussion forums?
RQ2:   Are the five ethical dilemmas apparent in discussion forums?

METHOD

Case Study: Citizens and Authorities on Discussion Forums

The approach was qualitative using content analysis, with a focus on the tone and content of writing. To distinguish the organizational point of view, 73 press-releases of the National Institute for Health and Welfare (THL) as well as their website were analyzed. To get the citizen point of view, two popular discussion forums online (Iltalehti, the second biggest Finnish tabloid; and KaksPlus, a parenting magazine) were chosen due to their popularity and matching target groups. The discussions were found using the search field in the forums, and 199 discussions were found via the search engines (Google, Bing), out of which 19 contained also authority communication and were included in the analysis. In total 2,264 comments were analyzed, in average consisting of 119 comments per discussion. The majority of the discussions lasted less than two weeks (57%) and they were held between November and December 2009. The one with the most comments lasted three months and had 28 comments per day, whereas another discussion of eight months contained only 12 notes.

We propose that authority communication should meet the conditions set by Baker and Martinson (2002) on the legitimacy of ends, and asked whether swine-flu communication of the authorities served a deeper and morally based final end of keeping citizens healthy. Therefore the next step of the analysis was to find out whether understanding (the ultimate ethical goal) was reached in online discussion forums on the topic of swine flu and what ethical problems were apparent. The analysis of ethical problems based on TARES framework of ethical communication. The TARES framework consists of five principles; trustfulness of the message, social responsibility for the common good, authenticity of the persuader, equity of the appeal and respect for the persuaded.

The task of crisis communication was difficult for the Finnish authorities in the case of the Swine flu. The first media releases about the disease were sent off in the spring of 2009, referring to the disease as swine flu. However, in the summer of 2009 the WHO (World Health Organization) advised against calling the disease 'swine flu', instead proposing that only the correct term, Influenza A (H1N1), be used leaving the national institutes unable to secure the domain names associated with what citizens were already calling Swine flu. Online Swine flu—associated domain names and addresses were bought by activist groups opposing vaccinations, natural product representatives, companies and NGOs giving authorities a difficult start with crisis communication (Luoma-aho, Tirkkonen, & Vos, 2013).

RESULTS

Overall, the analysis of the data revealed that citizens were not satisfied with authority communication. Content analysis focused on the content, style, and tone. Based on our analysis, authority communication in the swine flu case can be seen both as ethical and unethical: certain aims were met whereas others were not.

Citizens with positive attitude toward authorities saw communication as ethical, whereas people with negative attitudes perceived authority communication mostly unethical. The authorities officially recommended the vaccine, and traditionally such authority recommendations in Finland have been convincing. This time, however, only approximately 50 % of Finns took the vaccine. Similar events took place in Canada, where government and health authorities were perceived incompetent to manage the crisis (Henrich & Holmes, 2011).

As persuaders, authorities succeeded only partially. Messages posted on discussion forums were written in authority jargon, using medical language, and the term H1N1 instead of understandable 'swine flu'. Also, the number of comments posted online by the authorities was small, although the presence of authority representative was publicly announced. That seemed to irritate some people and failed to enable dialogue. In fact, the dialogic nature of social media was not utilized.

Three main attitude groups emerged among the citizens online: the positive, the negative, and the neutrals. Table 13.1 summarizes all these findings. The largest group was the neutrals, then negatives and positives. Citizens with neutral distributed information gathered from the media and their social network to others by commenting facts and figures presented about the epidemic. They were either "information providers" or thirsty for knowledge. People who posted questions and asked for help were often worried or afraid of the epidemic and pondering safety of the vaccine. Authorities did not manage to convince them by their communication, and truthfulness of the message was questioned.

The second biggest group, the 'negatives' perceived authorities action as clearly unethical. They expressed openly distrust towards authorities. Citizens questioned their overall expertise and motives, safety of the vaccine, blamed them for conspiracy with pharmaceutical companies or interpreted their preventive actions are exaggeration and creation of panic. None of TARES principles were fulfilled among the negative group.

The 'Positive' group respected authorities and found their actions ethical and trustworthy, securing citizens' security by communicating and providing vaccination. People with positive attitude either expressed simply their trust in authorities and their attempts to protect citizens, or they encouraged others to take the vaccine. Thus, those people perceived authority communication as ethical. Also high education and young age have been shown to cause similar affects (VISA, 2005).

From Table 13.1 we can conclude that despite correct authority behavior, online the authorities could not convince people. The positives believed

Table 13.1   The TARES Principles and their Fulfillment in the Authority
Communication on Discussion Forums from the Points of
view of the Authorities and the Citizens

TARES Principle	Authority Communication	Citizen Expectation
Trustfulness of the message	Fulfilled in press releases	Not fulfilled (positives: partly fulfilled, neutrals: unclear, negatives: not filled)
Social responsibility for the common good	Fulfilled by authorities communicating about the epidemic, which was a risk to citizens.	Positives: partly fulfilled, negatives: not fulfilled, neutrals: unclear. Authority messages and citizens' expectations did not meet or they did not understand each other.
Authenticity of the persuader	Fulfilled by authorities keeping their role as legal body, responsible for protection of citizens.	Positives: fulfilled, neutrals: not fulfilled or unclear, negatives: not fulfilled. Negatives did not believe in sincerity of authorities action.
Equity of the appeal	Partly fulfilled as authorities were using their legal role as manager of the epidemic.	Positives: filled, neutrals: not fulfilled or unclear, negatives: not fulfilled. Especially negatives perceived disparity in the authority-citizen relationship in the sense of expertise and knowledge as well as information available.
Respect for the persuaded	Authorities fulfilled by providing information for citizens about the symptoms of the epidemic and instructions for getting vaccinated.	Positives: filled, neutrals: not fulfilled or unclear, negatives: not fulfilled. One problem might have been official and medical language used by authorities

in authorities, their action and vaccination campaign, but they were the
smallest attitude group. The negatives were skeptical on the other hand
authenticity of the persuader, credibility of their messages and felt they
were scaremongering people and trying to pressure for getting vaccinated.

DISCUSSION AND CONCLUSION

Authority communication has high moral aims, but in the era of social
media, authorities have to increasingly fight for citizen attention. This study
looked at the discussion taking place around the global pandemic Swine flu
and its vaccines in Finland in the fall of 2009, a disease and its vaccine that

caused much citizen uproar and controversy despite both global and local authority recommendations. We found that the Kantian (Kant, 1758/1956) ethics of duty and responsibility traditionally guiding authority communication have shifted in the social media era toward increased egoism and utilitarianism where citizen demands take central stage. We distinguished five dilemmas affecting communication where citizen and authority focus differs, and applied the TARES-framework to analyze both the authority communications and citizen responses in discussion forums. Strongest dilemmas affecting crisis communication of authorities appeared to be flexibility and lack of common viewpoints. Authority communication during the swine flu crisis was a challenge for the authorities and a disappointment for the citizens. The TARES principles were met only partially: the positives perceived authorities as ethical actors but the negatives questioned the authenticity and equality of the persuader.

The study has several limitations. First, it was limited to only one country, but similar results have been established elsewhere (see Henrich & Holmes, 2011). Second, the use of discussion forums for analyzing authority communication during crises limited the scope of the study, but on the other hand matched the citizens' information seeking habits.

Ethical Implications for the Practice of Social Media

Social media has brought about not only direct access to citizens but also challenges for authority communication. Traditional media was simpler than social media in its operations, as it selected issues and topics to cover according to news criteria. Authority messages of pandemics easily got through, yet in online in discussion forums, attention is more difficult to achieve. Online issues and topics are also less predictable. According to citizen expectations, authority communication now needs to include discussion with citizens. This has posed public sector organizations and their PR practitioners with several new challenges, both practical and ethical: few are well equipped to deal with citizens' direct support or criticism. Moreover, the language and procedures of public sector organizations are ill suited for social media platforms, causing further confusion and eroding trust.

Our study shows that social media is a demanding arena, where the message, role and ethics of an authority are questioned. This means public relations practitioners in authority organizations need to incorporate a new aim in their communication efforts before anything else can be communicated: getting citizen attention. In practice this means finding or establishing the right issue arenas where citizens are willing to interact with authorities. For communication to be ethical, it has to use shared language, be founded on trust, and this requires resources seldom available for authorities, such as 24–7 availability. Our results show that communication between authorities and citizens can be really two-way, but it requires long-term presence on the right issue arenas. Best practices in authority communication need to be re-negotiated, as real-time demands and emotional reactions of citizens override traditional authority principles. If authority communication fails to meet the changing citizen needs, even the legitimacy of the authorities could be at stake.

On the other hand, social media enables more ethical authority communication: listening, transparency, and collaboration. What ethical principles should authorities follow? We argue that the ethical approach called communitarianism, which is well suited for novel situations where existing rules and guidelines do not guide actions (such as pandemics and crises), should increasingly guide authority communication. Authority communication needs to focus on "social cohesion, citizen empowerment and acceptance of responsibility" (Leeper, 2001, p. 104). Individuals are responsible for their deeds and for the improvement of community (Leeper, 1996).

The benefits of social media for authority crisis communication are several: First, it offers a good tool for monitoring citizens' opinions and attitudes, vital information that could be used in communication planning. Second, new possibilities for the whole profession of authority communications emerge, as monitoring citizen attitudes enables better democracy. Third, better-planned campaigns and real-time feedback from citizens could make for savings in already cut authority budgets. Inefficiencies and unnecessary processes could be eliminated when citizens are able to voice their real needs online

To conclude, new and social media give a real opportunity for citizens to publicly question authorities' action and bring up ethical questions via discussions on various online forums. This requires authorities to engage themselves in dialogue with citizens, more transparent and openness as well as solid reasoning of decisions made in the name of crisis management. Adopting a more communitarian view for authority public relations would ensure the formation of trust between authorities and citizens. Although ideal, we acknowledge how challenging these improvements will be for public sector organizations in practice. Traditional bureaucratic culture often apparent in the public sector will remain dominant possibly also in the future. In the name of citizen rights, however, we call for more transparency and discourse between authorities and citizens, as that will be the only ethical foundation on which future trust in authorities in crisis situations can be built.

Discussion Questions

1. What ethical problems have you as a social media user noticed?
2. How do ethical issues differ between the public and private sector?
3. In your opinion, how has social media changed ethical requirements for public relations professionals in their practice?

SUGGESTED READINGS

Coombs, W. T., & Holladay, S. J. (eds.) (2009). *Handbook of crisis communication.* Hoboken, NJ: Wiley- Blackwell.
Fitzpatrick, K., & Bronstein C. (eds.) (2006). *Ethics in public relations. Responsible advocacy.* Thousand Oaks, CA: Sage Publications.
Hobsbawm, J. (ed.) (2010). *Where the truth lies. Trust and morality in the business of PR, Journalism and Communications.* (2nd edn.) London: Atlantic Books.
Parsons, P. J. (2008). *Ethics in public relations: A guide to best practice.* (2nd edn.) London: Kagan Page Ltd.
Seeger, M. W., & Sellnow, T. L. (Eds.) (2013). *Foundations in communication theory: Theorizing crisis communication.* Somerset, NJ: Wiley Blackwell.

REFERENCES

Alexander, D. E. (2004). Cognitive mapping as an Emergency management training exercise. *Journal of Contingencies and Crisis Management, 12*(4), 150–160.
Baker, S., & Martinson, D. L. (2001). The TARES test: Five principles for ethical persuasion. *Journal of Mass Media Ethics, 16*(2&3), 148–175.
Boano, C., & Lund, R. (2011). Disasters, crisis and communication: A literature review. In M. Vos, R. Lund, Z. Reich & H. Harro-Loit (Eds.) *Developing a crisis communication scorecard. Outcomes of an international research project 2008–2011.* Jyväskylä Studies in Humanities 152. Jyväskylä: Jyväskylä University Press.
Boin, A. t'Hart, P. Stern, E., & Sundelius, B. (2011). *The politics of crisis management: Public leadership under pressure.* Cambridge: Cambridge University Press.
Boin, A., & McConnell, A. (2007). Preparing for critical infrastructure breakdowns: The limits of crisis management and the need for resilience. *Journal of Contingencies and Crisis Management, 15*(1), 50–59.
Castells, M. (2004). *The network society. A cross-cultural perspective.* Cheltenham: Edward Elgar Publishing Ltd.
Castells, M. (2009). *Communication power.* Oxford: Oxford University Press.
Comfort, L. K. (2007). Crisis management in hindsight: Cognition, communication, coordination, and control. *Public Administration Review, 67,* 189–197.
Coombs, W. T., & Holladay, S. (1996). Communication and attributions in a crisis: An experimental study in crisis communications. *Journal of Public Relations Research, 8*(4), 279–295.
Coombs, W. T., & Holladay, S. (2007). Unpacking the halo effect: Reputation and crisis management. *Journal of Communication Management, 10*(2), 123–137.
Devitt, K. R., & Borodzicz, E. P. (2008). Interwoven leadership: The missing link in multi-agency major incident response. *Journal of Contingencies and Crisis Management. 16*(4), 208–216.
Frandsen, F., & Johansen, W. (2010). Crisis communication, complexity, and the cartoon affair: A case study. In W. T. Coombs & S. Holladay (Eds.) *The Handbook of Crisis Communication.* Hoboken, NJ: Wiley-Blackwell.
Heath, R. L., & Palenchar, M. J. (2007). Strategic risk communication: Adding value to society. *Public Relations Review, 33,* 120–129.
Henrich, N., & Holmes, B. (2011). What the public was saying about the H1N1 vaccine: Perceptions and issues discussed in on-line comments during the 2009 H1N1 pandemic. *PLoS ONE, 6*(4), 1–12.
Hobbes, T. (1651/2010). *Leviathan: Or the matter, forme, and power of a common-wealth ecclesiasticall and civil.* Edited by Ian Shapiro. New Haven: Yale University Press.

Huhtala, H., & Hakala, S. (2007). *Kriisi ja viestintä*. Helsinki: Gaudeamus.

Kant, I. (1758/1956). *Groundwork of the metaphysic of morals*. Translated by H. J. Paton. New York: Harper & Row.

Lee, K. (2009). How the Hong Kong government lost the public trust in SARS: Insights for government communication in a health crisis. *Public Relations Review, 35*, 74–76.

Leeper, K. A. (1996). Public relations ethics and communitarianism: A preliminary investigation. *Public Relations Review, 22*(2), 163–179.

Leeper, R. (2001). In search of a metatheory for public relations. An argument for communitarianism. In R. L. Heath (Ed.) *Handbook of public relations* (pp. 93–104). Thousand Oaks, CA: Sage.

Luoma-aho, V., Tirkkonen, P., & Vos, M. (2013). Monitoring the issue arenas of the swine-flu discussion. *Journal of Communication Management, 17*(3), 239–251.

Luoma-aho, V., & Vos, M. (2009). Monitoring complexities: Nuclear power and public opinion. *Public Relations Review, 35*, 120–122.

Palttala, P., & Vos, M. (2011). The crisis communication scorecard: supporting emergency management by authorities. In M. Vos, R. Lund, Z. Reich & H. Harro-Loit (Eds.) *Developing a crisis communication scorecard. Outcomes of an international research project 2008–2011*. Jyväskylä Studies in Humanities 152. Jyväskylä: Jyväskylä University Press.

Reich, Z., Bentman, M., & Jackman, O. (2011). A crisis communication guide for public organizations. In M. Vos, R. Lund, Z. Reich & H. Harro-Loit (Eds.) *Developing a crisis communication scorecard. Outcomes of an international research project 2008–2011*. Jyväskylä Studies in Humanities 152. Jyväskylä: Jyväskylä University Press.

Renn, O. (2008). *Risk governance. Coping with uncertainty in a complex world*. London: Earthscan.

Rousseau, J. J. (1762/2003). *On social contract*. New York: Dover Publications Inc.

Roux-Dufort, C. (2007). A passion for imperfections. Revisiting crisis management. In C. M. Pearson, C. Roux-Dufort, & J. A. Clair (Eds.) *International handbook of organizational crisis management*. Los Angeles: Sage Publications. 221–251.

Rowan, K. (1991). Goals, obstacles, and strategies in risk communication: A problem-solving approach to improving communication about risks. *Journal of Applied Communication Research, 19*, 300–329.

Sandman, P. (2006). Crisis communication best practices: Some quibbes and additions. *Journal of Applied Communication Research, 34*(3), 257–262.

Seeger. M. (2006). Best practices in crisis communication: An expert panel process. *Journal of Applied Communication Research, 34*(3), 232–244.

Seeger, M., & Reynolds, B. (2009). Crisis communication and public health. Integrated approaches and new imperatives. In M. Seeger, T. L. Sellnow & R. R. Ulmer (Eds.) *Crisis communication and the public health*. New York: Hampton Press.

Seon-Kyoung, A. & Gower, K. K. (2009). How do the news media frame crises? A content analysis of crisis news coverage. *Public Relations Review, 35*, 107–112.

Sjöberg, L. (2001). Limits of knowledge and the limited importance of trust. *Risk Analysis, 21*(1), 189–198.

Thierney. K., Bevc, C., & Kuligowski, E. (2006). Metaphors matter: Disaster myths, media frames and their consequences in Hurricane Katrina. *The Annals of the American Academy, 604*, 57–81.

Tirkkonen, P., & Luoma-aho, V. (2011). Online authority communication during an epidemic: A Finnish example. *Public Relations Review, 37*, 172–174.

Transparency International. (2011). Corruption Perception Index. Retrieved from http://cpi.transparency.org/cpi2011/results/

Ulmer, R. R., & Sellnow, T. L. (1997). Strategic ambiguity and the ethic of significant choice in the tobacco industry's crisis communication. *Communication Studies, 48*(3), 215–233.

Ulmer, R. R., Sellnow, T. L., & Seeger, M. W. (2011). *Effective crisis communication. Moving from crisis to opportunity.* (2nd edn) Thousand Oaks: Sage Publications.

Veil, S. R. (2008). Civil responsibility in a risk democracy. *Public Relations Review,* 34 (4), 387-391.

Veil, S., Buehner, T., & Palenchar, M. (2011). A work-in-process literature review: Incorporating social media in risk and crisis communication. *Journal of Contingencies and Crisis Management, 19*(2), 110–122.

VISA (2005). Valtionhallinnon viestinnän seuranta- ja arviointijärjestelmä. Valtionhallinnon viestintä 2007–hanke. Osa II: Tutkimusraportit. Valtioneuvoston kanslian julkaisusarja 4/2005.

Weick, K. (1988), Enacted sensemaking in a crisis situation. *Journal of Management Studies, 25,* 305–317.

Witte, K. (1992). Putting the fear back into fear appeals: The extended parallel process model. *Communication Monographs, 59,* 329–349.

14 Government Gone Wild
Ethics, Reputation, and Social Media

Kaye D. Sweetser

INTRODUCTION

Today, everyone is online. From grandmothers to governments, the number and variety of users has clearly pushed the Internet past the tipping point of ubiquity. A key component of Internet use over the past five years has been the group of applications called social media. Once intended only to be a way to connect two people, social media has quickly grown into an organizational tool used to create a more human face and foster a relationship with stakeholders (Sweetser, 2010; Smith, 2012). As with any organizational communication tool, social media is heavily intertwined with reputation—it can create it, it can improve it, and it can damage it all at the speed of a data connection.

Sanders (2011) suggested that the management of government communication involves consideration of reputation. Looking at Walker's (2010) definition of the key attributes of reputation, the literature posits that reputation is: (1) based on perception (which may not be factual); (2) the aggregate perception of all stakeholders; (3) inherently comparative to other institutions; (4) potentially positive or negative, and (5) established through time. Given the speed at which social media operates and connects users, it is widely accepted that social media can impact reputation be it in the short-term or with longer lasting effects. As such, public communication and activities from the government to constituents are likely able to impact reputation. When those publics perceive an action from the institution as being unethical, it can potentially damage reputation.

An artifact of reputation is institutional trust. The 2012 Edelman Trust Barometer, which measures the public's trust in different institutions internationally, showed a sharp decrease in trust in the government. Comparing 2011 data to 2012 data, the report cited a 55% decrease in trust of government officials noting that only 8% of informed publics trust these sources. While every category of potentially credible spokespeople had decreased over the year, government officials showed the largest decrease and the lowest overall trust score. Looking at government as a whole, this trend of decreasing trust continued. Comparing government to other institutions such as business, media, and non-governmental agencies (NGOs), government was the least trustworthy among both informed and uniformed publics. The largest areas of decreasing trust for government lie in people believing that the government is not operating in a transparent and open manner (decreased 50%), and that government does not communicate frequently and honestly (decreased 49%).

At the same time trust in government is decreasing, trust in social media has grown, according to Edelman. Trust in social media as an information source grew at a greater rate than any other source (e.g., traditional media, corporate, various online sources). An often-cited benefit of social media is that it provides institutions the ability to operate in a more transparent manner.

Given these changes in trust, it seemingly would behoove government to become more involved in social media not just as an institutional voice, but also as a way to create conversation among publics as they talk to one another. And indeed, the federal government has adopted social media all the way from the White House down to local offices of federal agencies and small military units. For the most part these social media activities are managed as professional communication interfaces, run by public affairs and public information officers. Yet just as corporate organizations face competition from other departments within their same organization (i.e., human resources, information technology) in the desire to manage sub-brand social media accounts (e.g., HR department's own Twitter or IT department's own Facebook page), government social media presences are complex as well. Furthermore, the use of government contractors in the communication realm may actually complicate the process and output of government information in that it leads to a decentralized communication approach where social media is used outside of concerted public affairs efforts. This may of course flatten and accelerate the sharing of information, but it can also create confusion among stakeholders and potentially impact the institution's overall reputation.

This case study will examine the reputation of the government, and specifically the military, based on three current social media wartime engagements of specific adversaries. In the first and third examples, social media activity by those outside of public affairs showcases ethical concerns that have demonstrated reputation-tarnishing reactions from stakeholders, and the second example highlights public affairs-directed communication making information spaces a true battlefield. Using a case study approach to analyze media coverage and user comments on media articles for all three cases, this chapter examines the reputational impact of activities framed by ethics.

LITERATURE REVIEW

Government Public Affairs

The primary purpose of government public affairs and public information is to facilitate information flow about government activities to taxpayers.

Traditionally public affairs officers have done this through information subsidies such as press releases and media embarks to military activities (Sweetser & Brown, 2008). Just as practitioners at corporations have begun adopting social media to engage their publics, government public affairs officers have also begun communicating through popular social networks such as Facebook and Twitter. These government-run social media sites have typically become an extension of other public affairs activities and in some cases been heralded as creating truly interactive opportunities for its publics.

Traditionally, and in some cases by statute, U.S. military communication with non-domestic publics, especially in time of war to adversary combatants and civilian populations in the war zone, has been conducted outside of public affairs as part of Military Information Support Operations (MISO), previously known as Psychological Operations (PSYOPS). The distinction between communication with domestic and foreign publics audiences is significant in determining the types of communication activities authorized by law. For instance, military attempts to persuade or influence the behavior of publics is almost exclusively restricted to non-domestic realm, as is collection of military intelligence by monitoring the communication activities of publics. This distinction between domestic and foreign audiences blurs when considering social media and becomes problematic ethically if not legally.

Social Media as Organizational Communication

Because social media is arguably the most public type of communication an institution can publish, it is often assumed that all social media sites are run by communication professionals. Even in corporate public relations, the desire of components within the organization to publically host their own profiles (i.e., human resources, information technology) has created friction and set the stage for a fight over who really owns social media. From the public relations and public affairs perspective, the argument is clear: The public will assume all of an institution's social media content is the official face for that organization.

Whether public relations/public affairs should have control over all of an organization's social media presence is not the question here. Instead, this chapter focuses on the message frames and reputation impact of what happens when a non-public affairs entity operates.

METHOD

Using a variation of Plowman's (1998) case study data analysis process, three scenarios involving government use of social media were examined. This method has been applied in other government communication case study analyses, including a review of online campaigning strategic management (Levenshus, 2010). The process in this case study involves reviewing media coverage, coding items in such a way to determine themes and issues, comparing those themes to the themes of the general public (as gauged through user-posted comments on the news articles, this replaces the traditional use of interview data to determine the public's reaction), then summarizing implications with a focus on legal and ethical expectations.

Three scenarios were selected for this case study. In all three cases the scenarios were covered in both traditional online news type articles and several of these articles had the option for readers to leave comments in response. Both the media content and the user-posted comment content were analyzed using the coding scheme described above. The news articles represented the classic media portrayal, and the user-posted comments represented what is more traditionally gathered through interview data.

Created for the purposes of this case study, the researcher identified a frame theme typology that was coded categorically for one dominant frame. The dominant frames were skeptical, technical, ethical, and tactical. The skeptical frame referred to portrayal as being a skeptical view of either the program, its intent, or uses. The technical frame referred to a focus on technology used in the program. The ethical frame referred to discussion about whether the program was ethical and/or the ethical implications. The tactical frame referred the program as being portrayed as a battle tactic.

Working also with the Kiousis, Popescu, and Mitrook (2007) explication of the Reputational Quotient index by Harris Interactive and the Reputation Institute, the cases were also examined for the attributes associated with:

1. Products and services
2. Financial performance
3. Workplace environment
4. Social responsibility
5. Vision and leadership
6. Emotional appeal

The first scenario examines the intelligence community's much-publically discussed contracting call for proposals for creating "sock-puppet" accounts aimed to engage and root out terrorists online as well as track how conversations proliferate through social media. There were two programs occurring in 2011 in particular within this scenario: the Epidemiological Modeling of the Evolution of Messages (or e-meme, as it was called in the media) and the Integrated Crisis Early Warning System (or ICEWS). In both programs media coverage explained that these activities would have limited applications to non-American citizens yet reader comments on these articles questioned the ethics involved. In this scenario the programs were said to be from the intelligence community. In military terms, this scenario would certainly support information operations, or MISO, rather than public affairs efforts, and will therefore be referred to as the information operations scenario.

The second scenario examines how public affairs engaged combat adversary-run Twitter accounts as a part of their overall communication. After an insurgent attack near a NATO base and the U.S. Embassy in Kabul in September 2011, the command headquarters for the war assumed a more active stance of engaging the Taliban through Twitter. In this scenario the official command tweets were a public affairs activity. The International Security Assistance Forces-Afghanistan (or ISAF) Twitter account @ISAF-media tweeted both conversation-starting messages and responses to a series of accounts self-proclaimed as run by the Taliban, including their official Twitter account. While the command had engaged the Taliban on Twitter previously, from time-to-time, the Kabul siege spurred a noticeably more tactical and sustained effort from the war's public affairs office. Subsequent media coverage of this example often framed this use of social media as "groundbreaking" and as a new means of warfare. This scenario is referred to here as confrontational communication, and although it supported the combat objectives, it clearly was not expected to be restricted to adversarial or foreign publics since it took place via a social media channel used to communicate with both domestic and non-domestic publics.

The final scenario occurred in early 2012. As in the intelligence software scenario it involved a government contract for communication, however the targets of the operation were United States-based journalists who cover the military and defense industry. In this scenario, government contracting company Leonie Industries was alleged to have waged a misinformation "smear" campaign against two *USA Today* journalists who had written articles criticizing the military's information operations efforts, and specifically the lucrative government contracts meant to support those efforts in Afghanistan. In retribution, Leonie was reported to have created fake Twitter accounts and websites for the journalists, populating these online accounts with criticism about their reporting and journalistic ethics. The *USA Today* reported that the Pentagon had launched an informal investigation among the information operations contractors but that all contracting companies had denied involvement. The websites were taken down after the inquiry, however, and the social media accounts were removed due to a violation of terms of service. A Pentagon spokesman went on the record saying that they were not aware of the websites but stressed that such activity (smear campaign against journalists critical to military operations) would be inappropriate. This scenario is referred to here as misinformation operations.

RESULTS

Media coverage and public response across each of the three scenarios examined here was unequal. The confrontational communication scenario received the most media coverage and user-response, followed by the misinformation operations scenario then lastly the information operations scenario.

Scenario 1: Information Operations

The overall tone of the items analyzed was negative toward the program. The overall theme of this scenario was technical, as the media articles focused on the technical aspects of the call for proposals and the programs being implemented. The media articles were short and tended to resemble general informational releases, explaining the programs, the functions, the countries that the programs would be used in, etc. A key function discussed in the media coverage was the potential of this software to be able to predict political uprisings prior to their occurrence, drawing on the recent so-called Arab Spring in 2011 as a political event that the programs could potentially identify as creating the conditions for a possible event. Conversely, the user-posted data instead focused on how this program would be used as opposed to its technical abilities. Users questioned to some degree the ethics of such programs. Some users pointed to "big brother" type listening worldwide while others posted fears that these abilities and uses had long been adopted and this was nothing new.

Looking at the reputation attributes, not all attributes were represented. For example, there were not many mentions of financial performance or workplace environment, as one might imagine with a government program. The products and services category was discussed regularly with regard to historical context (when governments had deployed sock-puppet type identities before in history or were likely already "listening" intently to online chatter) and this conversation from users was extremely negative. There was some, although minimal, discussion of the product and service being innovative but this was balanced against the feeling that this program was a waste of time and money. In the emotional appeal category, the public comments analyzed showed that response to the program was negative with regard to how people felt about the government, that the program did not inspire admiration or respect and that it in fact made the public wary of the government and their intentions. With regard to social responsibility, the program was frequently painted as being unethical and the public questioned that the data would be used against them (i.e., performing information operations against American citizens).

Looking at the issue-specific attributes that emerged, the software programs were nearly equally asserted as intelligence activity (which it was) and as a public affairs program (which is was not).

Based on this analysis, it becomes clear that the public does not have a strong understanding of how the program is being used, and has a great lack of trust in the government's operation of the program. The finding that there were nearly equal assertions of the program being a public affairs program as an intelligence collection or information operations program is quite troubling. Evidently the public instinctively worries about such software programs because of the potential for these information operations to be deployed against Americans—and with these online communications one can't be sure of where a message is originated (it could be an American citizen in Cincinnati pretending to be an extremist in Cairo). The lack of transparency inherent to intelligence activity and information operations raises suspicion of potential misuse.

Scenario 2: Confrontational Communication

The media coverage and user response to the so-called "Twitter war" in Kabul in September 2011 had the greatest number of items out of all of the scenarios. The dominant frame of the coverage was tactical, portraying this event as a battlefield tactic against the insurgency. The overall the tone of the items was neutral toward the event.

As with the previous scenario, there were scant mentions of products and services and financial performance. There was some minor discussion about workplace environment, with the media mostly being interested in *who* was tweeting under the @ISAFmedia account. In these cases the media was attempting to frame the officials composing the tweets as young people, presumably because social media is a popular tool for that that demographic. The dominant reputational category represented in this scenario was vision and leadership. Here the media very much portrayed the government as innovative and quoted military officials as referring to Twitter as yet another battle space in which to engage the enemy. In fact, the media coverage almost seemed to portray the government program here in a heroic manner. The public response was less overly supportive and impressed with the government's action, and many displayed a negative response to the Twitter war. In some cases the public response was that the military should focus on kinetic engagements, not virtual ones; in other cases the public felt that the government was giving the insurgents credibility and publicity by engaging them. The social responsibility aspect was only a small part of the online conversation, but when present the public assessed the government program negatively. With regard to emotional appeal, there was nearly equal representation of the public saying the program inspired trust and respect as with those who said it did not.

With regard to issue-specific attributes, the majority of the items discussed the effectiveness or ethical nature of the government communication. Mention of the exchanges between the Taliban and the military were made in many of the items. Several items used the term "Twitter war" and many mentioned the Taliban spokesman or quoted him. A small number of items said that the government was trying to provoke the enemy.

In this scenario, it is interesting to see how caught up in the Twitter war the media became. Interestingly, the media narrative was not one that the military command was communicating as it had engaged the Taliban on Twitter before. The media portrayed the event as bubbling over as a result of the Kabul siege, showing a virtual response to a kinetic battle. Public reaction to the Twitter war contained a greater degree of critical analysis.

The media did portray the event as a public affairs operation (which it was), although many of the public responders classified it as an information operation (which it was not). Despite the transparency of this confrontational communication, mistrust still was present.

Scenario 3: Misinformation Campaign

The coverage of this scenario was, without a doubt, overwhelmingly negative, and the dominant frame focused on the unethical nature of the smear campaign (as it was called several times in the media). Interestingly, however, the negativity and blame varied based on the audience unit. In the media articles, the wrong appeared to be squarely placed on the contracting company and nearly every media item took the time to quote the government officials who noted that such a misinformation campaign was inappropriate. This is not to imply that the media gave the government a free pass in accountability, because it did not—one article mentioned that Leonie had more than $90M in government contracts yet a history of unethical behavior within those contracts and general operations. The commenters however shifted blame to the government. Overwhelmingly the comments pointed to what they saw as historic trends of the government engaging in misinformation campaigns as well one other American journalist in Afghanistan accusing (in the comments section) that the same had happened to him with a government-initiated smear campaign using Wikipedia, Twitter, and other social tools.

As expected based on the previous two cases, the reputation categories of products and services and financial performance were not over in this scenario. That said, there was more discussion of these categories than previously although because of the allegation that a high-priced government contractor had engineered the misinformation campaign. In both cases for these reputation categories, the negative commentary was focused on the contractor as opposed to the government, although subtext of failure by the government to hold the contractor accountable could be interpreted as negative toward the government. Primarily discussion with regard to reputation focused on emotional appeal, manifesting in negative reactions toward the government among the public, a very vocal lack of trust communicated by the public, and many calls questioning the ethical and legal nature of the campaign.

DISCUSSION

All of these cases use the same communication tool, all presumably do it from the same organization (the government), yet these uses are so varied both in terms of intended effects and ethics. The finding that audiences have trouble distinguishing between professional communicators (public affairs) and information operations is a disturbing wake up call to the government on the complexity of using these online platforms. In generations past the government could drop propaganda leaflets, broadcast radio programs, and communicate through psychological operations to a very specific target. Those distinctions between foreign and domestic publics do not exist online, and certainly not in social media. What an individual or organization communicates via social media is broadcast to all, or at least has the potential to be shared beyond the intended publics In the case of information operations and intelligence collection, it is difficult if not impossible to ensure that no American citizens participate in the communication.

Beyond the legal questions raised by the blurring of these distinctions, the use of social media for military efforts other than public affairs confuses the American public. This case study illustrates that it is difficult for many people to distinguish between an intelligence or information operations effort and a public affairs effort. In the first two scenarios the line was very blurry among those who commented on the two cases.

These cases are at best unclear, at worst ethically questionable social media activities sully government reputation to an extent that mars the good that occurs every day on the many well-managed government social media accounts. For an example from the military itself, the U.S. Navy's Facebook account is known to be engaging and informative to their audience. Following a devastating flood in Millington, Tennessee in the summer of 2010, the public affairs staff on the base used social media a primary communication tool to connect with and provide customer service to the many impacted sailors and their families. Their use of social media during a crisis has become a textbook example of how organizations can harness existing social media tools during crises. Although Facebook is primarily a public affairs tool for sharing positive information, the service has also posted releases of more controversial policy changes (such as the ban of smoking on submarines) in an effort to encourage two-way communication both positive and negative. The Navy is one of many government entities ethically managing their account and attempting to foster genuine two-way communication. The credibility of those efforts suffers, however, when unethical use of social media is associated with government activity as in the case of the misinformation campaign examined here.

Ethical Implications for the Practice of Social Media

In its early days social media ethics were likened to the "wild, wild west" where organizations were experimenting with tactics and not held accountable for potential ethical missteps (Sweetser, 2008). Those days have passed. Organizations have come to know that social media is not a free-for-all space, but rather it is an extension of their brand. As such, organizations must maintain the same standards online as they do in their traditional communication programs. For government communicators, this need for transparency is even greater as publics expect and in some cases demand information digitally (Sweetser, 2011). Although online spaces have typically enabled organizations the opportunity to experiment and push the envelope of their brand through humanizing communication and two-way interactions (Kelleher & Miller, 2006), the cases presented here make it clear that such can be the case as long as tactics do not undercut basic good ethical practice (regardless of medium transmission). In these cases, the communication approaches taken by government communicators were either appropriate (even if unorthodox) in any media vehicle (e.g., press release, television interview, etc.) or equally inappropriate regardless of the media vehicle. As such, communicators should not get overwhelmed by the novelty of the technology when testing out new tactics, rather they should focus first on whether the tactic is, at its base, in-line with the organization's code and its publics' expectations.

CONCLUSION

Moving forward, communicators must realize that social media lacks discretion in terms of intended audience. There is no target audience—everyone is your audience, whether intended recipients or not. Communicators must express to other internal entities using social media tools (i.e., the intelligence community) that when something is posted online regardless of the origin or intent, it becomes attributable to the organization as a whole. As such, rogue use of social media and certainly questionable campaigns must be discouraged as they can have devastating effects on reputation.

Discussion Questions

1. How can organizations, especially government, dispute what they believe is misinformation in an ethical and professional manner?
   a. Which case studies present appropriate and ethical tactics?
   b. Which cases studies present inappropriate and unethical tactics?
   c. If a supervisor had provided an unethical solution, how would you communicate a better and more ethical approach to that supervisor?
2. What ethically questionable tactics have you seen online recently from government communicators?
   a. What might the communicators have done differently?
   b. How much of this questionable behavior might be an artifact of the newness of tool and inexperience in understanding what is ethical?
   c. How did key publics react, and was that an over-reaction or an under-reaction?
3. Think historically of different media technology when it was considered "new" (such as television or radio). What examples come to

mind of how organizations acted unethically (keeping in mind at the time it may not have seemed wrong)?

a. Who corrected the questionable behavior (e.g., society and time, competitors, government action)?

b. Should the communicators have known better?

ADDITIONAL READINGS

Bean, H. (2011). No more secrets: Open source information and the reshaping of U.S. Intelligence. Praeger Security International: Santa Barbara, Calif.

Edelman (2013). Edelman Trust Barometer. Retrieved from http://www.edelman.com/insights/intellectual-property/trust-2013/

Grupta, R. & Brooks, H. (2013). Using social media for global security. Indianapolis: John Wiley & Sons.

Munene, M. (2008). The media, ethics, and national interests. *Journal of Language, Technology & Entrepreneurship in Africa*. Retrieved from http://www.ajol.info/index.php/jolte/article/viewFile/41766/9029

U.S. Department of Defense (n.d.). U.S. Department of Defense Social Media Hub (an online resource with policy, training, examples). Retrieved from http://www.defense.gov/socialmedia/

U.S. Department of Defense (n.d.). Department of Defense Joint Ethics Regulation (DoD 5500.7-R). Retrieved from http://www.dtic.mil/whs/directives/corres/pdf/550007r.pdf

REFERENCES

Kelleher, T., & Miller, B. M. (2006). Organizational blogs and the human voice: Relational strategies and relational outcomes. *Journal of Computer⬛Mediated Communication, 11*(2), 395–414.

Kiousis, S., Popescu, C., & Mitrook, M. (2007). Understanding the influence on corporate reputation: An examination of public relations efforts, media coverage, public opinion, and financial performance from an agenda-building and agenda-setting perspective. *Journal of Public Relations Research, 19*(2), 147–165.

Levenshus, A. (2010). Online relationship management in a presidential campaign: A case study of the Obama campaign's management of its Internet-integrated grassroots efforts. *Journal of Public Relations Research, 22*(3), 313–335.

Plowman, K. D. (1998). Power in conflict for PR. *Journal of Public Relations Research, 10*, 237–261.

Sanders, K. (2011). Political public relations and government communication. In J. Stromback & S. Kiousis (Eds.) *Political public relations. Principles and applications* (pp. 293–313). New York: Routledge.

Smith, B. G. (2012). Public relations identity and the stakeholder-organization relationship: A revised theoretical position for public relations scholarship. *Public Relations Review, 38*, 838–845.

Sweetser, K. D. (2008, September). *Ethics and relationship issues for organizations*. Paper presented at UGA Connect Social Media Conference, Athens, GA.

Sweetser, K. D. (2010). A losing strategy: The impact of nondisclosure in social media on relationships. *Journal of Public Relations Research, 22*(3), 288–312.

Sweetser, K. D. (2011). Digital political public relations. In J. Stromback & S. Kiousis (Eds.) *Political public relations. Principles and applications* (pp. 293–313). New York: Routledge.

Sweetser, K. D., & Brown, C. W. (2008). Information subsidies and agenda-building during the Israel-Lebanon crisis. *Public Relations Review, 34*(4), 359–366.

Walker, K. (2010). A systematic review of the corporate reputation literature: Definition, measurement, and theory. *Corporate Reputation Review, 12,* 357–387.

15 Understanding the Ethical and Research Implications of Social Media

Shannon A. Bowen and Don W. Stacks

INTRODUCTION

The role of social media practice and research in public relations continues to press the envelope of ethical use and reporting. This chapter seeks to extend our knowledge of the ethical practice of social media and the research used to evaluate it, and to explicate a move toward standardizing the ethics of research in social media. There are a number of different ways to approach this topic. The chapter first reviews ethical theory, then introduces the reader to an ethical approach to public relations as espoused by Bowen (2004, 2010, 2012; Bowen, Rawlins, & Martin, 2010). It is integrated with Stacks and Michaelson's (Michaelson & MacLeod, 2007; Michaelson & Stacks, 2011; Stacks, 2011; Stacks & Michaelson, 2010) contention that research should be conducted in an ethical manner, leading to both more ethical practices and an approach to ethical research standards.

Bowen (2013) advocated 15 ethical practices when conducting public relations in social media. These practices are based in her interpretation of *deontology* (Kant, 1785/1964) as it relates to public relations social media practices. The chapter begins by reviewing the deontological/utilitarianism dichotomy of reasoned analysis and provides two mini-case studies of ethical/unethical public relations social media use. "Reasoned analysis" is a term from moral philosophy used instead of best case practices, experience, or gut reaction because it provides a superior means to arrive at consistent and ethical decisions. This chapter then focuses on the ethical research *process*—and social media research processes in particular—based on Bowen and Stacks (2013), Stacks (2011), Stacks & Michaelson (2010), Michaelson and Stacks (2011), and Michaelson, Wright, and Stacks (2012) to explicate social media research from an ethical standardization.

The chapter ends with a discussion of how the profession can move towards an ethical standardization of public relations social media research. It will propose several ethical research standards based on a deontological approach focused on social media research.

LITERATURE REVIEW

Establishing Ethical Standards for Social Media Research

One of the major uses of the Internet in public relations is to gather information. Another major use is to establish and maintain relationships among stake- and stockholders. A common denominator among all Internet uses in public relations, however, is research. The use of that research, or the gathering of what may be called "research," has ethical implications for the practice of public relations above and beyond how people actually use social media as a function of a public relations campaign. Here we are talking about the gathering, evaluating, and disseminating of information to target publics and to specifically targeted audiences. The assumption is that what we see, read, hear, ask about, and respond to in social media is authentic, reliable information transmitted to the user in a clear and non-deceptive communication. Obviously, as practice has illustrated over and again, there are many social media practices that raise ethical questions or appear to be an unethical use of communication for a client.

In a perfect world everyone would be ethical. In some ways the proverbial Golden Rule *would* rule. However, perception being what is how we view ethics colors our interpretation of what is ethical and unethical. Basically, if that perfect world existed, our ethics would be deontological—we would do nothing that impacts negatively on others, we would be in a rational, objective, and consistent world in which all decisions were made the same way by all people, maintaining respect for all others. This world exists in theory and is known as the *kingdom of ends* (Kant, 1785/1964), but is hardly found in modern public relations practice. Instead, research has found that public relations professionals take several common approaches to ethics. Many take the "enlightened self interest" approach, which is part of an overall materialistic paradigm. That approach, linked to egoism, selfishness, and Randian objectivism, maximizes the decision for the individual making it, but does little to further ethical interests beyond the self. Therefore, although common in practice, enlightened self-interest is an extremely limited approach to ethics. Martinson's (1994) research found that this approach fails as a guideline for ethics in public relations. Although enlightened self-interest was found to be fairly common among public relations professionals, it is not an advanced, normative, or solid ethical framework because selfishness can be argued to be morally and logically flawed; something more conscientious is needed.

There are other schools of moral philosophy that offer more rigor and reliable logic. Wright (1985) found that many public relations professionals begin their careers using utilitarian ethics then move to using deontology as their careers advance. Those systems both require a bit of explanation, but they do provide a more rigorous or systematic means of ethical examination than relying on self-interest, objectivism, or enlightened self-interest.

A brief overview of utilitarianism and deontology provides a consistent approach to the ethics of social media, whether it is used for research or to further communication goals.

Overview of the Main Ethical Paradigms

In the absence of using a self-interested approach to ethics, we must have another means through which one can determine what is ethical. We may take one of two polar-opposite stances on ethics: (1) *utilitarian*, where the consequence (or potential outcome) determines ethicality and good outcomes are to be maximized, or (2) *deontological*, where principle or moral duty and good intention determine what is ethical, based on rationality and moral autonomy (or independence). An overview of each will illustrate their differences and strengths relative to each system's weaknesses.

Consequentialist: Utilitarian Ethics

Consequentialist ethics seeks to determine an ethical course of action based on the potential outcomes of that action (i.e., for the good of the client). Although there are different types of consequentialism, utilitarian is probably the most prevalent form. Utilitarian seeks to maximize the greater good for the greatest number of people affected by an action (DeGeorge, 2010). In general, utilitarians agree that the outcome of a decision and how it affects publics are what determine its ethicality. Utilitarianism seeks to minimize negative consequences or harms while maximizing decisions for the greater good or in the public interest. Decisions creating more positive outcomes than negative outcomes are then deemed ethical choices. According to Singer (2011) who is known for animal rights but is a leader of modern utilitarian philosophy, this maximization of the good and minimization of the bad is known by moral philosophers as *the utilitarian calculus*. Utilitarianism is a consequentialist theory in which the majority benefit always wins the argument, despite arguments of moral principle, or right or wrong (Talbot, 2012). The greater good for the greatest number is always served. It is an intuitive theory because most people understand a cost-benefit projection of potential outcomes. However, it is not concerned with justice, principle, truth, or the rights of individuals. In fact, a primary weakness of utilitarian ethics is that this school of thought can be (and often is) misinterpreted to the point that a "cost-benefit analysis" for the decision maker is used to sanction whatever he or she wants to maximize in their *personal* good outcomes, as opposed to maximizing the greatest good for the greatest number or in the public interest. That "ends justifies the means" approach is really a self-interested calculation, not a utilitarian one; it completely fails most ethical tests. A true utilitarian approach seeks to maximize the good in the public interest for the greatest number of people.

Creating the greatest good/happiness for the greatest number of people is the ethical guide by which utilitarian ethics operates. However, there are a few weaknesses of the paradigm that should be borne in mind. Many ethicists object to the reduction of human beings to numbers in utilitarianism, out of individualism or the *prima facie* respect for the value of life. Others object out of a fear of suppressing the rights of a minority, with the majority always being deemed ethical—the critique is obvious given the activism and changes in social movements. Others argue that utilitarianism does not examine moral principles, rights, duties, or justice; it only examines creating beneficial outcomes rather than morals. It is difficult to know what the "truth" is under utilitarian theory; again, only numbers in creating the greatest good are involved, and those numbers shifting can also change the morality of a decision. Finally, our most practical concern with utilitarianism is that it is an *inductive* field that requires one to predict the future with some degree of accuracy. Predicting the reactions and interactions of various publics in public relations is notoriously difficult and highly inaccurate. Utilitarian ethics in public relations should be limited to areas in which the goal is clearly to work on behalf of the public interest goals commonly found in government and non-profit organizations but are not excluded from corporate responsibility.

In today's social media public relations practices, it would appear that an attempted utilitarian or consequence-based ethics is most predominant. This outcome is especially true in the research of a social media public relations campaign, where the use of new "tools" (e.g., blogging, Tweeting, "Liking") present ethical dilemmas in gathering and presenting data or communications. More problematic is that instead of creating the maximum good for the most number of people it is misapplied or forgotten in favor of a self-interested cost-benefit analysis.

Such misapplication of utilitarianism is not a form of normative ethics, so we label it *source-oriented* practice. It often leads to the excuse that "we are on the leading edge," or "we are in new ground," or "the client's ends justify the means by which we communicate." These arguments are misapplied, based on self-interest rather than the public interest.

Non-consequentialist: Deontological Ethics

Non-consequentialist ethics is an approach to moral decisions that rests on principled argument alone, rather than on consequences. There are different schools within this paradigm that offer varying approaches to determining moral principle, such as Aristotle's virtue ethics, stoicism, and Kant's emphasis on rights, and duty, (and some philosophers, such as Rawls, would add justice). Deontology is the leading school of thought in non-consequentialist ethics. It offers the most unassailable theoretical backing and the most practically accessible form of non-consequentialist ethics that we can apply to social media.

Deontological ethics is derived from the work of mathematician and moral philosopher Immanuel Kant in the late eighteenth century. Kant focused on ethics as the practice of moral principle and duty, a counterpoint to the utilitarian/consequential approach, which tries to predict consequences based on outcomes. Becoming a morally autonomous agent, or objective, is a central theme of deontology, as is upholding one's duty to the moral law out of rationalistic obligation. Self-interest alone (egoism) must be ruled out in the decision making of deontology, as all factors are considered equally. That perspective allows bias to be minimized and decisions to be based upon the duty to uphold moral principle as a rational decision-maker.

Kant disagreed with other philosophers, such as Mill utilitarians and the Hume school of passion, that maximizing happiness was the goal of ethics. He held, instead, that upholding one's duty to the moral law was the purpose of ethics. Reverence for the moral law made one worthy of happiness but in no way guaranteed it (Sullivan, 1989). To make his moral theory more accessible, Kant created three moral tests (or forms), known as the "categorical imperative" (1785/1964).

> *Form 1, Duty:* "Act only on that maxim through which you can at the same time will that it should become a universal law." (p. 88).
>
> *Form 2, Dignity and Respect:* "Act in such a way that you always treat humanity, whether in your own person or in the person of any other, never simply as a means, but always at the same time as an end." (p. 96)
>
> *Form 3, Intention:* "All maxims as proceeding from our own making of law ought to harmonize with a possible kingdom of ends." (p. 80).

Kant offered guidelines through which one could reason through a decision and the moral principle involved. Any potential decision or action must meet *all* three forms of the categorical imperative in order to be considered ethical.

Duty, asks the decision maker to contemplate whether the action could become a universal law. Again, consequences do not come into play in deontology any more than other considerations do: decision should be based on an underlying moral principle that all rational agents could agree to be ethical. For a simple example, take the principle of honest disclosure of information. We could say that all rational decision-makers would consider honest disclosure of information a universal law applicable for everyone; it allows us to conclude that if all people in all places and times would agree that a decision is ethical, it has enough moral worth and subjected to the next two forms of the test.

Dignity and respect obligates the decision maker to treat others as having value in themselves, not simply as a means to achieve an end (such as a simple public relations objective). In other words, the person is valued is having inherent dignity by means of being a rational agent, and any decision must respect those who would be affected by an order to be ethical. To continue with the preceding example, the honest disclosure of information would maintain the dignity and respect of those who need that information, as well as the other parties involved in the issue (regulatory agencies, the organization, the self, and so on), therefore, the concept passes Form 2 of the test. If a potential action meets the test of Form 2, the final form of the categorical imperative is used.

Intention, is arguably the toughest form of the categorical imperative. It holds that only actions taken from good intentions (for the right reason) are ethical. Harmonizing with Kant's kingdom of ends is a normative, or abstract test. The kingdom of ends is a place in which all moral agents act according to their duty and rational, ethical reflection; therefore, everyone acts out of a good will. Kant believed that a good will was the only thing that is good in and of itself. In essence, believing something is the morally right thing to do is the only quality that makes it an ethical action, not a desire to help a client, look good in front of one superior, generate increased sales, and so on. Returning to the example, the honest disclosure of information would be deemed ethical when the action was taken out of an intention to do the right thing. The same honest disclosure of information that would *not* be deemed ethical if it were merely taken out of and intention to make a company or client look good.

Passing all three forms of the categorical imperative result in a rigorously analyzed and defended ethical decision; Using deontology results in consistent decisions. The ethics of those decisions can then be understood from a rational perspective, even by those who may disagree with the decision. The result of a deontological framework for ethics is that organizations can build more satisfying, longer-term relationships with both internal and external publics.

Further, it allows the organization to be known and create expectations, such as an ethics statement or statement of core values that it then actually uses in decision-making. As Bowen and Stacks (2013) noted, the categorical provides a wonderful backing for an ethics statement because it asks the autonomous moral decision maker to do three things (see also: Bowen, 2004, 2010, 2012; Bowen et al. 2010). Each becomes a standard for evaluating the ethics of the position in that decisions are (1) universal, meaning that anyone could understand the ethics of the solution or action; (2) treating with dignity and respect, meaning that the action or solution should "value others as morally-autonomous individuals;" and (3) intentionally based on good will that overrides all other considerations.

Kant's idea that moral action is superior to any other type of action is a powerful one. There are few weaknesses with deontology; the analysis relies on having or gathering accurate information and having a degree of moral independence or autonomy from the organization or client that some public relations professionals have yet to achieve (Bowen et al., 2006, 2008).

Standards for Social Media and for its Use in Research

Next we turn to current thought on research and social media ethics, lead-ing to the two mini-cases chosen to highlight social media ethics and how ethical frameworks could have changed decisions. Finally, we discuss the implications from both the public relations professional and targeted audi-ence perceptions of the ethical use of social media research in the practice.

Establishing Standards for Research

Three articles published in *Public Relations Journal* (Michaelson & Stacks, 2011; Michaelson et al. 2012; Bowen & Stacks, 2013) have begun the pro-cess of establishing for the first time a set of standards that public rela-tions research should be evaluated against. Michaelson and Stacks (2011) focused on the standards associated with the collection, assessment, and evaluation of data, providing a model against which excellent research can be judged. Michaelson et al. (2012) extended that work to setting both standards and a model for evaluating excellent public relations program-ming or campaign evaluation.

Bowen and Stacks (2013) focused on setting ethics standards for public relations research and focused on 5 principles and 18 core values derived from a deontological emphasis on research ethics. They also reviewed the ethics codes and statements of 14 public relations-related associations, 11 professional, and 3 academic associations (see Table 15.1). Their findings were surprising and informative, leading to a proposed statement to guide research public relations:

> *Research should be autonomous and abide by the principles of a uni-versalizable and reversible duty to the truth, dignity and respect for all involved publics and stakeholders, and have a morally good will or intention to gather, analyze, interpret, and report data with veracity.* (p. 20; emphasis in original)

Ethical Guidelines for Using Social Media

Bowen (2013) studied the use of social media by public relations profes-sionals. She noted, based on an analysis of four landmark public relations cases in social media, that ethical missteps are common and there are few, if any, ethical guidelines to govern the arena of social media. Although general ethical principles still apply, social media combine many fast moving forms of communication and more specific guidance is needed. Indeed, although unreported in Bowen and Stacks (2013), only three of the 14 academic and research associations' ethical codes or statements dealt with the "Internet," and those that did for the most part simply pasted "Internet" or "social media" in their statements or codes. This

Table 15.1 Research Ethics Standardization Grid[1]

Association*	Association Ethics Statement	Code of Conduct	Stated Positively or Negatively	Enforcement Statement	Formal Research Ethics Statement	Intellectual Context	Fairness	Dignity	Disclosure	Respect for all Involved	Autonomy	Independent Rights	Fairness	Balance	Duty	Law and Rule	Honesty	Not using misleading data	Fair disclosure	Disclose	Judgement	Promises of proprietary data	Harm or risk weighing	Good intention	Avoid putting the welfare	Tell results	More coverage & sensitivity	Other
(P) American Academy of Advertising / Audit Opinion Research (AAPOR)	Yes	No	Positively	No	Yes	Yes	Yes	Yes	Yes	Yes	Yes	Yes	Yes	Yes	Yes	Yes	Yes	Yes	Yes	Yes	No	Yes	Yes	Yes	Yes	No	No	Yes
(P) American Marketing Association (AMA)	Yes	No	Positively	Yes	Yes	No	Yes	No	Yes	Yes	No	No	No	No	No	No	No	No	No	No	No	No	No	No	Yes	Yes	Yes	Yes
(A) Association for Education in Journalism & Mass Communication (AEJMC)	Yes	No	Positively	No	Yes	Yes	Yes	Yes	Yes	Yes	Yes	Yes	Yes	Yes	Yes	Yes	Yes	Yes	Yes	Yes	Yes	Yes	No	Yes	Yes	No	Yes	Yes
(P) Council of American Survey Research Organizations (CASRO)	Yes	Yes	Positively	No	Yes	No	Yes	Yes	Yes	Yes	Yes	Yes	Yes	No	Yes	Yes	Yes	Yes	Yes	Yes	Yes	Yes	No	Yes	Yes	No	Yes	Yes
(P/A) ESOMAR International Code on Market and Social Research	Yes	Yes	Negatively	No	Yes	Yes	Yes	Yes	Yes	Yes	Yes	Yes	Yes	Yes	Yes	Yes	Yes	Yes	Yes	Yes	No	Yes	Yes	Yes	Yes	No	No	Yes
(P) Institute for Public Relations Measurement	Yes	No	Positively	No	No	No	No	No	No	No	No	No	No	No	No	No	No	No	No	No	No	No	No	No	No	No	No	No
(P) International Association for Business Communicators (IABC)	Yes	Yes	Positively	Yes	No	No	No	No	No	Yes	Yes	No	No	No	No	Yes	No	No	No	No	No	No	Yes	No	No	No	No	Yes
(A) International Communication Association (ICA)**	Yes	No	Positively	No	No	No	No	No	No	No	No	No	No	No	No	No	No	No	No	No	No	No	No	No	No	No	No	No
(P) International Public Relations Association (IPRA)	Yes	Yes	Negatively	Yes	No	No	No	No	No	No	No	No	No	No	No	No	No	No	No	No	No	No	No	No	No	No	No	No
(P) Marketing Research Association (MRA)	Yes	No	Positively	Yes	Yes	Yes	Yes	No	No	Yes	No	No	No	No	No	No	No	No	No	No	Yes	No	No	No	Yes	No	No	Yes
(A) National Communication Association (NCA)	Yes	No	Positively	No	No	No	No	No	No	No	No	No	No	No	No	No	No	No	No	No	No	No	No	No	Yes	No	No	Yes
(P) Professional Marketer Association (PMA)	Yes	No	Positively	Yes	No	No	No	No	No	No	No	No	No	No	No	No	No	No	No	No	No	No	No	No	Yes	No	No	Yes
(P) Public Relations Society of America (PRSA)	Yes	Yes	Positively	Yes	No	No	No	No	No	No	No	No	No	No	No	No	No	No	No	No	No	No	No	No	Yes	No	No	Yes
(P) Qualitative Research Consultants Association (QRCA)	Yes	No	Positively	No	Yes	Yes	Yes	Yes	Yes	No	No	No	No	No	No	No	No	No	No	No	No	No	No	No	Yes	No	No	Yes

Notes

1. Associations chosen that deal primarily with public relations/corporate communications
2. Principles are clearly articulated statements
3. Core values are expressed in terms analogous to those listed.
   YES = Found in research-specific statements
   Yes = Found in general ethics statements
4. Determination of positively or negatively stated based on being at least 51% of statements.
* (P) = Professional Association; (A) = Academic Association
** No specific comprehensive code of conduct or practice.

laxity in coverage prompted Bowen (2013) to post 15 ethical guidelines for public relations use of social media:

1. Be prudent: Potentially libelous, slanderous, or defamatory statements should not be made.
2. If it is deceptive, do not do it.
3. If an initiative warrants secrecy, that is a red flag that something needs ethical examination.
4. Paid speech should be transparently identified as such by "(Endorsement)" or similar.
5. Personal, individual speech and opinion, versus speech as representative of the organization, should be clearly identified.
6. Use a rational analysis examining the message from all sides. How would it look to other publics, and how could it potentially be misconstrued?
7. Does the message maintain your responsibility to do what is right?
8. Is it reversible—How would you feel on the receiving end of the message? Is it still ethical then?
9. Does the communication maintain the dignity and respect of the involved publics?
10. Is the intention behind the communication morally right?
11. Emphasize clarity in your communication, even if you think the source or sponsorship is clear . . . make it clearer.
12. Emphasize transparency in how the message came about. Disclose.
13. Verify sources and data. Rumor mongering destroys your credibility—do not traffic in rumor and speculation.
14. Consistency of messages across time is good because it allows publics to know and understand you, and you can meet their expectations. Consistency builds trust.
15. Encourage the good. (p. 4)

Integrating Social Media use and Research Ethical Standards

It should be apparent by now that many of the "misuses" in social media are tied to the ethical statements and core values identified by Bowen and Stacks (2013). Combining these with Bowen's (2013) ethical use of social media demonstrates an overlap that should not be surprising. The creation of a social media campaign is based on research and an understanding of the targeted publics or audiences. As observed in Bowen's 15 use guidelines, all involve the 5 ethical research principles as identified by Bowen and Stacks' (2013) analysis: *intellectual honesty, fairness, dignity, disclosure*, and *respect for all*. Further, the use guidelines contain all 18 research core values either outright or inferred: *Autonomy, respondent rights, fairness, balance, duty, lack of bias, honesty, not using misleading data, full disclosure, discretion, judgment, protection of proprietary data, public responsibility, intellectual integrity, good intentions, valuing truth behind the numbers, reflexivity,* and *moral courage.*

How these principles and core values are evaluated depends on what ethical paradigm the public relations professional takes. From a utilitarian perspective, decisions governing social media will be seen from a consequences approach; the decision should maximize the greater good for the greatest number of people. From a deontological perspective, the principles and core values form the core of Kant's three categorical imperatives: duty, dignity, and respect, and intention or a good will. In the next section two short public relations social media research and use cases and analyses are presented.

MINI-CASES

Edelman Worldwide Public Relations has been at the forefront of social media public relations campaigns. As a front-runner, it has had successes and failures. Its successes in social media space have been many. However, what Edelman may be most remembered for are two cases involving the ethically questionable use of blogs (weblogs).

Edelman Wal-Mart Blog walmartingacrossamerica.com

As part of a campaign for Wal-Mart, Edelman Worldwide created a program of blogs for its client that lead to one of the first criticisms for misleading a client's publics (Terilli, Driscoll, & Stacks, 2009). What Edelman attempted to do was to create a blog by Wal-Mart visitors who were traveling across the U.S. as part of an organization called, "Working Families for Wal-Mart." The couple was billed as an average couple on a recreational vehicle trip, recording great experiences at Wal-Marts along the way. What was not revealed is that they were not an average couple, but two professional journalists hired to "pose" as a couple and blog about Wal-Mart under those pretenses.

The blog campaign, launched September 27, 2006, did not last long as Wal-Mart critics quickly pounced on the fake blog labeling them a "flog" (Staff, 2006). Scott Karp (2006) of Publishing 2.0 noted that

> It's inevitable that a PR firm like Edelman would create a phony blog for one of its clients. . . . For all the hype over "conversation" as the new media paradigm, no one has yet figured out how to use conversation to reliability achieve any business objectives. So Edelman naturally fell back on the approach that has worked for decades—control the conversation by manufacturing it, because if you can't control the conversation, then you can't make it do what you want. Edelman wanted to make consumers think that Wal-Mart is a hip place that you'd want

to use as the anchor point for a road trip. The problem is that it's not. And because blogging is not a control-based medium, Edelman couldn't make Wal-Mart appear to be something it's not. It rang false, and they got caught. (¶1)

The actual blog was written under the direction of and by Edelman, which has a reputation for being a 'cutting edge' social media company. Indeed, Edelman CEO, Richard Edelman, responded in his own October 16, 2006, blog entitled, "A Commitment," saying

> For the past several days, I have been listening to the blogging community discuss the cross-country tour that Edelman designed for *Working Families for Wal-Mart*.
> I want to acknowledge our error in failing to be transparent about the identity of the two bloggers from the outset. This is 100% our responsibility and our error; not the client's.
> Let me reiterate our support for the *WOMMA* guidelines on transparency, which we helped to write. Our commitment is to openness and engagement because trust is not negotiable and we are working to be sure that commitment is delivered in all our programs. (¶1–3)

In Edelman's response, WOMMA stands for the Word of Mouth Marketing Association, who had publically censured Edelman over the incident. *Business Week* wrote exposé stories condemning the behavior of Edelman, and activist websites already primed against Wal-Mart seized upon the issue as another example of corporate betrayal. The ensuing crisis for both Edelman and Wal-Mart provided a fruitful learning ground for ethics in social media.

Were transparency and the lack of disclosure the only ethical standards and core values violated in this case? Richard Edelman responded from a utilitarian approach—that is, arguing that the agency had made mistakes and that it was learning as it employed campaign strategies utilizing cyber tools such as social media to drive "conversation" and ultimately return *on the client's investment* in social media public relations campaigns (Hamilton, 2006; Sullivan, 2006; emphasis added). In other words, Edelman argued that the harms caused by a few "mistakes" were outweighed by the greater good created in using social media to promote "conversation."

An Ethics Analysis

From a utilitarian perspective, Edelman's claims ring false. They misapplied the utilitarian calculus to their client's own ends rather than the good of the greater number of people in society as a whole. The public good was not maximized; Wal-Mart's own interests were maximized in this case. Members of society did not have greater happiness due to the false conversations on behalf of Wal-Mart perpetuated by Edelman Digital. In fact, in the utilitarian framework of creating the greatest good for the greatest number of people, Wal-Mart had not created good through true conversation, but created harm by employing false or deceptive speech. That action does not maximize the greater good in the public interest nor minimize negative outcomes, so the case fails a utilitarian test of ethics. They used what we labeled earlier a source-orientation that misapplies the utilitarian calculus to selfish ends rather than to maximizing public good.

When a more rigorous deontological test is applied, the case obviously fails to meet any of the ethical standards espoused in the categorical imperative. The very act of concealing the true identities of the blog writers is one of deception. Deception takes away the moral autonomy of the audience to judge a situation based on rationality, logic, and merit; it is also unethical because it denies them the dignity and respect due rational people. It fails to uphold the duty to behave honestly under the moral law, and it fails the test of good intention because the blog was based on deception and concealment, not honesty, transparency, or truth.

How could Edelman have handled this situation more ethically? They could have revealed the true identities of the writers—a professional journalist and photojournalist—and their mission to chronicle visits to Wal-Mart. Would the persuasive power have been lost of the message were made ethical? Or would the ethical nature of the communication have added to the credibility and legitimacy of the blog? We will never know the answer to those questions in a conclusive way. What we do know is that both Wal-Mart and Edelman left the deceptive situation with tarnished reputations and a loss of credibility in the eyes of their publics.

Edelman Microsoft Vista OS Campaign

One tool used by public relations professionals is the so-called "third-party endorser" strategy in which a respected source, an agenda-setter, or an opinion leader says or endorses a client's product or service (Stacks, 2011; Stacks & Michaelson, 2010, 2011). The strategy is to provide the endorser with the information necessary to evaluate and then speak to his/her followers about the product or service, providing not only influence but also credibility. We see this strategy in editorial endorsements, positive reviews by well-known journalists, and positive "mentions" in the various media. This is another source-based orientation and obviously courts problems with transparency and disclosure. However, in social media, where almost anyone can be an expert endorser, are there ethical rules to guide the use of this strategy?

About three months after Edelman's flogging campaign for Working Families for Wal-Mart was exposed, a second social media transgression was reported, this time in a third-party endorser strategy for client Microsoft and the introduction of its Vista operating system through Edelman's

Me2Revolution office (O'Brien, 2007; Are Freebies A Blogosphere Taboo?, 2007). The campaign strategy was to get influential, high-profile social media bloggers to use the Vista operating system and then publish product reviews. However, as part of the campaign the operating system was accompanied by a free Acer notebook computer. As Terilli et al. (2009) pointed out, "Although Edelman 'covered all disclosure bases,' the outcry in the blogosphere was fast and furious with bloggers criticizing the attempt to post positive reviews of the operating system (p. 542)." As B. L. Ochman (2006) critiqued in her *What's Next?* Blog, "Edelman Has New Ethics Scandal Brewing with Microsoft's Blogger Bribe Campaign,"

> A group of high-profile bloggers started getting gifts several days ago. Robert Scoble quipped, "Talk about Pay Per Post." The article added: **The reason is simple.** If you've ever tried to add a new Microsoft OS to an existing computer, you know you can't do that without totally fucking [sic] up your computer. The only way to switch to a new Microsoft OS is to start with a new computer. And, of course, to wait a year or two while they get the kinks out. . . . They [Microsoft] gave the computers as gifts instead of lending them to the bloggers for review, which the norm when dealing with traditional journalists. (¶2) (Emphasis in original)

Ochman went on to quote APC News Editor Dan Warne:

> This is a PR disaster for Microsoft. Within a few days it'll be in every newspaper and tech publication in the world; I guarantee it. It's bizarre for one of the world's largest PR companies, Edelman, to think it could get away with this. Perhaps they don't know bloggers as well as they thought they did . . . Whatever the subtleties of the offer were, it comes across as nothing more than a bribe, and that is a very bad look for Microsoft. (¶4)

Was this a strategic mistake? Another ethical blunder? Or both? Following up on the Wall-Mart flogging problem, did Edelman learn from its prior ethical mistake? Additionally, are bloggers "journalists" and should they be approached differently when asked to serve as third-party endorsers?

An Ethics Analysis

In this case, Edelman again considered only the action that would maximize outcomes for its client, Microsoft, rather than acting to serve the greater good. The consequences of the strategy described before were to ignore the greater good in favor of the good of a few bloggers and the client, at the cost of damage to the reputations of both Microsoft and Edelman. Working to maximize the public good would have explored the merit of the new Vista operating system with honesty and candor, not with the overshadowing of "pay per play" messages. By valuing the outcome of the public good, Edelman could have been maximally transparent on why a new computer was needed to test Vista, and paid for return shipping of the Acer at the blogger's convenience. Edelman should have avoided using a source-orientation prioritizing its own selfish interests and should have used a utilitarian or deontological framework for analysis.

A deontological duty to truth, dignity and respect, and good will were also neglected in this case. If Vista was truly a valuable operating system, the bloggers would have borne that out in testing, were they given the respect and moral autonomy to do so. Edelman seemed not to proceed with a good intention to discover and support the truth, but to further only the selfish interest it had in promoting the client. Good intention, dignity and respect, and a duty to the truth could have been maintained in this case if more careful attention had been given to the way in which the bloggers were treated, the computers were loaned (not given) and free moral autonomy to a honest review were encouraged. Sadly, Edelman fell far short of these considerations and damaged the reputations, credibility, and relationships that it had built with the tech blogger community.

This case introduced the additional concern of whether bloggers are journalists and should be treated similarly. More importantly, bloggers are human beings with autonomous moral compasses that warrants dignity and respect, just as do journalists and all other members of publics with whom public relations professionals interact. Maintaining a high ethical standard, such as that offered in deontology, allows one to see past labels and temporary situations, and even industry-specific codes of ethics, to evaluate the moral principle involved had Edelman taken that step, their introduction of Vista would have undoubtedly gone smoother and would not have encountered the ethical critiques of the blogosphere. Even referring to the more simply-stated ethical guidelines for social media use (Bowen, 2013) could have helped Edelman avoid costly mistakes in both of the aforementioned cases. Can you add other steps, outcomes, or considerations that could have resulted in a better, more ethical strategy for Edelman?

DISCUSSION & CONCLUSION

Ethical Implications for the Practice of Social Media

As demonstrated in the two mini-cases, there was a lack of research into how audiences perceive public relations strategies, what the values of those audiences were (such as the bloggers), or how they perceived the ethics of the communication in each case. Further, it is questionable as to whether whatever research was conducted met the ethical standards we should expect public relations professionals to adhere to when collecting data of any sort, whether on social media or other communication channels. The 5 core values and the 18 ethical principles, (see Table 15.1) as well as the statement to guide the research industry on ethical behavior could be instrumental in conducting research on and in social media (Bowen & Stacks, 2013).

Research could have helped to prevent the ethical missteps of Edelman in both of the aforementioned cases. Good research, adhering to the ethical standards for research discussed earlier in this chapter, could have identified the potential clash of values between Edelman's self-orientation (focusing on client interests) and the expectations of publics (focusing on truth and fair play or on the public interest).

Research should be undertaken in a manner that has good intention or good will behind it, or what we used to label a symmetrical worldview. Kant's *kingdom of ends* should be upheld, meaning that we do not do research in order to selfishly exploit or manipulate, but to seek truth and real understanding in order to solve problems, provide information, and collaboratively engage in dialogue with publics. Research allows one means of understanding the values of publics so that their ideas and beliefs can be incorporated into strategy—respectfully (as opposed to as a means to our own ends).

This expectation for employing social media to create a true ethical engagement between organizations and publics is a normative one. But it is an ideal that also *does* happen in practice: We would just like to see it happen more often and at the instigation of the public relations professional. Using the 15 guidelines (Bowen, 2013) for social media is one place to start creating a more ethical and responsible atmosphere for engaging with social media.

Further, both utilitarian and deontological ethics provide powerful frameworks through which public relations strategies and tactics can be considered. Bearing in mind the weaknesses of utilitarian ethics and the detailed nature of deontology, it is probably best to use both forms of analysis when planning social media engagement. The preceding cases on social media and its misuse through deception or "buying" positive feedback offer but two examples. Many positive examples also exist, and through the use of both (or combined) utilitarian and deontological ethical analyses, we expect positive examples to outnumber negative ones. Exactly when that ethical evolution happens lies in the hands of the many public relations professionals who use social media.

CONCLUSION

No social media public relations campaign should begin without a thorough review of the intended target audience. That research should meet the standards set by Michaelson and Stacks (2011) for the gathering and evaluation of that data and the actual campaign standards established by

Michaelsonet al. (2012). Before gathering that data, however, the ethicality of not only research, but also the campaign should be analyzed against what Bowen and Stacks (2013) and Bowen (2010; 2013) set forth as the standards for ethical professional practice of public relations, especially with the "new" tools and unprecedented access to target publics and audiences. Both make the ethical decision-making process perhaps more important than ever.

Discussion Questions

1. What are the ethical responsibilities of bloggers when it comes to public relations?
2. There are a lot of bloggers on the Internet who do not check facts or report accurately. What should the profession do to such people and the organizations they work for?
3. As evidenced in the two mini-cases, some public relations agencies are riding the "wave" in terms of using social media for clients. From your reading of this chapter, how would you talk to a client about social media strategies as ethical responsibility?

SUGGESTED READINGS

Bowen, S. A. (2013). Using classic social media cases to distill ethical guidelines for digital engagement. *Journal of Mass Media Ethics, 28,* 119–133.
Michaelson, D., & Stacks, D. W. (2011). Standardization in public relations measurement and evaluation. *Public Relations Journal, 5,* 1–22.
Michaelson, D., Wright, D. K., & Stacks, D. W. (2012). Evaluating efficacy in public relations/ corporate communication programming: Towards establishing standards of campaign performance. *Public Relations Journal,* 6. Retrieved from http://www.prsa.org/Intelligence/PRJournal/Documents/2012Michaelson.pdf
Stacks, D. W., & Michaelson, D. (2010). *A practitioner's guide to public relations research, measurement, and evaluation.* New York: Business Expert Press.

REFERENCES

Are freebies a blogosphere taboo? (2007, January 12). *PR Week,* 18. Retrieved from http://www.prweek.com/uk/news/627124/News-Analysis-freebies-blogosphere-taboo/?DCMP=ILC-SEARCH
Bowen, S. A. (2004). Expansion of ethics as the tenth generic principle of public relations excellence: A Kantian theory and model for managing ethical issues. *Journal of Public Relations Research, 16,* 67–92.
Bowen, S. A. (2008). A state of neglect: Public relations as corporate conscience or ethics counsel. *Journal of Public Relations Research, 20*(3), 271–296.
Bowen, S. A. (2010). The nature of good in public relations: What should be its normative ethic? In R. L. Heath (Ed.), *Handbook of public relations* (pp. 569–583). Thousand Oaks, CA: Sage.

Bowen, S. A. (2012). The ethical challenges of pre-crisis communication. In B. A. Olaniran, D. E. Williams, & W. T. Coombs (Eds.) *Pre-crisis planning, communication, and management: Preparing for the inevitable* (pp. 57–78). New York: Peter Lang.

Bowen, S. A. (2013). Using classic social media cases to distill ethical guidelines for digital engagement. *Journal of Mass Media Ethics, 28*, 119–133.

Bowen, S. A., Heath, R. L., McKie, D., Lee, J., Agraz, F. & Toledano, M. (2006). *The business of truth: Communicating ethics in public relations.* San Francisco: IABC.

Bowen, S. A., Rawlins, B., & Martin, T. (2010). *An overview of the public relations function.* New York: Business Expert Press.

Bowen, S. A., & Stacks, D. W. (2013). Toward the establishment of ethical standardization in public relations research, measurement and evaluation. *Public Relations Journal, 7*(3), np. Retrieved from: http://www.prsa.org/Intelligence/PRJournal/Documents/2013_StacksBowen.pdf

Chan, C. (2012, July 25). Did Chick-fil-A pretend to be a teenage girl on Facebook? (Updated). Retrieved from: http://gizmodo.com/5928926/chick+fil+a-got-caught-pretending-to-be-a-fake-teenage-girl-on-facebook

DeGeorge, R. T. (2010). *Business ethics, 7*th edn. Boston: Prentice Hall.

Edelman, R. (2006, October 16). A commitment. 6 a.m. Retrieved from http://www.edelman.com/p/6-a-m/a-commitment/

Hamilton, N. (2006, October 23). Edelman acknowledges mistakes in blog matter. *PR Week*, 3.

Kant, I. (1785/1964). *Groundwork of the metaphysics of morals* (H. J. Paton, Trans.). New York: Harper & Row. (Original publication 1785).

Karp, S. (2006, October 15). Edelman, Wal-Mart and the loss in controlled media. Publishing 2.0. Retrieved from http://publishing2.com/2006/10/15/edelman-wal-mart-and-the-loss-of-control-in-media/

Martinson, D. L. (1994). Enlightened self-interest fails as an ethical baseline in public relations. *Journal of Mass Media Ethics, 9*(2), 100–108.

Michaelson, D., & MacLeod, S. (2007). The application of "best practices" in public relations measurement and evaluation systems. *Public Relations Journal, 1*, 1–14.

Michaelson, D., & Stacks, D. W. (2011). Standardization in public relations measurement and evaluation. *Public Relations Journal, 5*, 1–22.

Michaelson, D., Wright, D. K., & Stacks, D. W. (2012). Evaluating efficacy in public relations/ corporate communication programming: Towards establishing standards of campaign performance. *Public Relations Journal, 6*(5), Retrieved from http://www.prsa.org/intelligence/prjournal/documents/2012michaelson.pdf

O'Brien, K. (2007, January 8). Edelman defends ethics of Vista PC gifting tactic. *PR Week*, 6. Retrieved from: www.highbeam.com/doc/1G1-157030909.html

Ochman, B. L. (2006). Edelman has new campaign ethics scandal brewing with Microsoft's blogger bribe campaign. What's Next? Blog. Retrieved from: www.whatsnextblog.com/2006/12/edelman_doesnt_give_a_crap_what_you_think_about_their_ethics/

Singer, P. (2011). *Practical ethics, 3*rd edn. Cambridge: Cambridge University Press.

Stacks, D. W. (2011). *Primer of public relations research, 2*nd edn. . New York: Guilford.

Stacks, D. W., & Michaelson, D. (2010). *A practitioner's guide to public relations research, measurement, and evaluation.* New York: Business Expert Press.

Staff. (2006, October 16). Wal-Mart, Edelman Flogged for blog. Retrieved from http://www.webpronews.com/walmart-edelman-flogged-for-blog-2006–10

Sullivan, L. (October 30, 2006). Hard-lessons-always: Wal-Mart's cybereducation. *Information Week*, 17.

Sullivan, R. J. (1989). *Immanuel Kant's moral theory*. Cambridge: Cambridge University Press.

Talbot, M. (2012). *Bioethics: An introduction*. Cambridge: Cambridge University Press.

Terilli, S. A., Driscoll, P. D., & Stacks, D. W. (2009). Corporate bloggers and the commercial speech legal blog. Proceedings of the 9th International Public Relations Research Conference (pp. 542–562). Retrieved from: http://195.130.87.21:8080/dspace/bitstream/123456789/766/1/Corporate%20Bloggers.pdf

Wright, D. K. (1985). Can age predict the moral values of public relations practitioners? *Public Relations Review, 11*(1), 51–60.

Contributors

Marcia W. DiStaso, (Ph.D., University of Miami, 2007), is an assistant professor of public relations in the College of Communications at Pennsylvania State University. Her research has been published in a variety of journals including *Journal of Public Relations Research, Public Relations Review, Public Relations Journal, Mass Communications & Society, Journalism Studies, Journal of Social Media in Society, Global Media Journal–Canadian Edition, Digithum;* in several different books; and through the Institute for Public Relations. DiStaso is a Page Legacy Scholar and Senior Research Fellow with the Arthur W. Page Center and is chair-elect of the Public Relations Society of America (PRSA) Educators Academy. Her professional experience includes work for T. Rowe Price, American Red Cross, Ketchum, and social media consulting. She is a past recipient of the Ketchum Excellence in Public Relations Research Award and was recognized as both a Promising Professor and an Emerging Scholar by the Association for Education in Journalism and Mass Communication. She won a 2013 Silver Anvil Award of Excellence, a 2013 Platinum Hermes Creative Award, and was a finalist for a 2013 IPRA Golden World Award for her campaign to improve trust in banks. She is an associate editor for the Science of Social Media Research Center, chair of the PRSA Financial Communications Section, Co-Chair of the PRSA National Research Committee, member of the PRSA Speakers Bureau, and an advisory board member of the International Public Relations Research Conference.

Denise Sevick Bortree, (Ph.D., University of Florida, 2007), is an associate professor of communication in the department of Advertising and Public Relations at Penn State University. Her research focuses on ethical dimensions of communication in a number of contexts including nonprofit organizations, environmental responsibility, and new media. She has authored more than twenty five peer-reviewed journal articles published in journals such as *Journalism and Mass Communication Quarterly, Journal of Public Relations Research, Nonprofit Management and Leadership, Public Relations Review, Public Relations Journal,* and the

International Journal of Nonprofit and Voluntary Sector Marketing, among others. Bortree is a Page Legacy Scholar and Senior Research Fellow with the Arthur W. Page Center, and she has held numerous leadership roles in the public relations division of the Association for Education in Journalism and Mass Communication. Before joining academia she worked for over a decade for organizations including BellSouth, Alltel Communications, and Modis. In 2011 she consulted for the United Nations on the State of the World's Volunteerism study, and she is a board member with the association/nonprofit division of the Public Relations Society of America where she has been a member for nine years.

Kati Berg, (Ph.D, University of Oregon, 2006), is assistant professor of public relations in the Diederich College of Communication at Marquette University. Her research has been published in the *Journal of Mass Media Ethics, Public Relations Journal, PRism,* and in different edited books. She is a past chair of the Media Ethics Division of the Association of Educators in Journalism and Mass Communication. Her professional experience includes work in non-profit and agency public relations.

Thomas H. Bivins, (Ph.D., University of Oregon, 1982), is a professor and John L. Hulteng Chair in Media Ethics and Responsibility at the School of Journalism and Communication, University of Oregon. His research focuses on media ethics. He has authored numerous articles in *Journalism and Mass Communication Quarterly, Journal of Mass Media Ethics, Journal of Business Ethics, Public Relations Review,* and *Business and Professional Ethics Journal.* He is the author or co-author of five books on media ethics, public relations writing, newsletter publication, advertising design, and publication design and writing. He has worked in broadcast journalism, corporate public relations, and advertising, and as an editorial cartoonist.

Shannon A. Bowen, (Ph.D., University of Maryland, 2000), is an associate professor in the School of Journalism and Mass Communications, at the University of South Carolina. Her research focuses on ethics, issues management, strategic public relations, and the social media. Bowen is joint editor of *Ethical Space: The International Journal of Communication Ethics.* She authored or co-authored numerous chapters in books, co-authored *An Overview of the Public Relations Function,* and published in the *Journal of Public Relations Research, Public Relations Review, Journal of Public Affairs, Journal of Communication Management, International Journal of Strategic Communication, Journal of Applied Communication Research, Journal of Mass Media Ethics, PR Tactics, Journal of Business Ethics, and PR Journal.* Her professional experience includes work for Congressman Floyd D. Spence, and work as an analyst at a research firm for numerous political candidates and corporate clients. She is a member of the Arthur W. Page Society, the IPR Commission on Public Relations Measurement and Evaluation, is a past chair of the Media Ethics Division of the Association for Education in Journalism and Mass Communication, and serves on the Board of Directors of the International Public Relations Research Conference. Bowen is the 2011 winner of the Jackson Jackson & Wagner Behavioral Science Prize for her research program in ethics.

Yoon Y. Cho, (M.A., University of Missouri, 2005), is a doctoral student in the School of Journalism at the University of Oregon. Her dissertation focuses on consumers' pro-social versus pro-self motivation behind environmental behaviors and the role of environmental advertising on consumers' skepticism toward greenwashing. She has presented several papers at leading conferences, such as the Association for Education in Journalism and Mass Communication, Marketing and Public Policy, and American Academy of Advertising. Her professional experience includes work for McDonald's Korea as a media planner at LG Ad, an advertising agency in South Korea. Cho is a Page Legacy Scholar.

Renita Coleman, (Ph.D., University of Missouri), is associate professor and Graduate Studies Committee Chair at University of Texas–Austin. Her research focuses mainly on visual communication and ethics. She has studied the effects of photographs on ethical reasoning, the role of images in agenda setting, and the moral development of journalists and public relations practitioners, among other topics.

W. Timothy Coombs, (Ph.D., Purdue University, 1990), is a full professor in the Nicholson School of Communication at the University of Central Florida. His research areas include crisis communication, activist use of the Internet to pressure organizational change, and issues management. His articles have appeared in a variety of journals including in the *Journal of Public Relations Research, Public Relations Review, Journal of Public Affairs, Management Communication Quarterly, Journal of Business Communication, Journal of Communication Management International Journal of Strategic Communication., Journal of Promotion Management, and Corporate Reputation Review.* His book chapters have appeared in major works in the field of public relations including the *Handbook of Public Relations* and *Encyclopedia of Public Relations.* His crisis books include the award winning *Ongoing Crisis Communication, Code Red in the Boardroom,* and co-edited *The Handbook of Crisis Communication* with Sherry Holladay. His other books include *Public Relations Strategy and Application: Managing Influence, Managing Corporate Social Responsibility: A Communication Approach* the award winning *It's Not Just PR* (all co-authored with Sherry Holladay). He has twice been Chair of the Public Relations

Division of the National Communication Association. Dr. Coombs has worked with consulting firms in Norway and Belgium on ways to improve crisis communication efforts for their clients.

Tiffany Derville Gallicano, (Ph.D., University of Maryland, 2007), is an assistant professor of public relations in the School of Journalism and Communication at the University of Oregon. Her research areas are relationship management and social media. She has authored peer-reviewed journal articles that have been accepted for publication in the *Journal of Public Relations Research, Public Relations Review, Journal of Communication Management, Public Relations Journal, PRISM, Teaching PR,* and *Communication Teacher.* Gallicano is a Page Legacy scholar and serves as the social media co-chair for the Public Relations Division of the Association for Education in Journalism and Mass Communication. She has worked for Senator Kennedy's campaign and political action committee, in addition to a nonprofit health association, Ketchum, Hill & Knowlton, and the University of Maryland. She has served on the board of directors for the Cameron Siemers Foundation for Hope since the organization was established in 2007.

Homero Gil de Zuñiga, (Ph.D. in Politics at Universidad Europea de Madrid; Ph.D. in Mass Communication at University of Wisconsin–Madison), is associate professor at the University of Texas at Austin, where he directs the Digital Media Research Program within the Annette Strauss Institute. He has participated in summer doctoral programs at the National Communication Association and the University of Oxford. Since 2010, he was appointed Nieman Journalism Lab Research Fellow at Harvard University. Generally, his research addresses the influence of new technologies and digital media over people's daily lives, as well as the effect of such use on the overall democratic process. He has published several books, book chapters, and over 30 articles in academic peer-reviewed journals such as *Communication Research, Journal of Communication, Journal of Computer Mediated Communication, New Media & Society,* etc. He has also obtained a number of grants and awards as principal investigator, co-principal investigator or executive committee member totaling close to 2 million dollars.

Tamara L. Gillis, (Ed.D., University of Pittsburgh, 1997), is a professor of communications in the Department of Communications at Elizabethtown College. Her research interests include organizational development, change management communication, public art as communication, and the impact of new media on corporate communication strategy. She has written numerous book chapters, articles and books on organizational communication; her most recent works include the second edition of *The Handbook of Organizational Communication* (Jossey-Bass, 2011) and *The Essentials of Employee Communication* (IABC Knowledge Centre, 2008). She was recognized as a Lifetime Friend of the International Association of Business Communicators Research Foundation in 2004 and continues to serve as a consultant with the Foundation and to IABC's Executive Accreditation program at Royal Roads University. She is also a Page Legacy Scholar. Dr. Gillis holds the designation of accredited business communicator through the IABC. Her professional experience includes work with Pennsylvania Psychological Association, Memorial Healthcare Corporation, the University of Pittsburgh, and Cooper Wright Consulting.

Kirsten A. Johnson, (Ph.D., Drexel University, 2007), is an associate professor in the Department of Communications at Elizabethtown College. Her research focuses on web credibility and citizen journalism. She has co-edited a book titled *News with a View: Essays on the Eclipse of Objectivity in Modern Journalism*; written book chapters including, *Gatekeeping in the Digital Age: A New Model for a Post-Objective World*; and *Citizen Journalism in the Community and the Classroom*. She has also written articles in peer-reviewed journals including *Journalism and Mass Communication Quarterly*, and *Learning, Media, and Technology*. She has served as the Chair of the Civic and Citizen Journalism Interest Group as part of the Association for Education in Journalism and Mass Communication. She worked for nearly a decade in radio and television, including, KRNT radio in Des Moines, Ia., WOI-TV in Des Moines, and WGAL-TV in Lancaster, Pennsylvania.

Thomas J. Johnson is the Amon G. Carter Jr. Centennial Professor in the School of Journalism at the University of Texas at Austin. Johnson has written or co-edited five books, more than 55 refereed journal articles published or in press, 19 book chapters, and presented more than 100 papers at international, national, and regional conferences.

Vilma Luoma-aho, (Ph.D., University of Jyvaskyla, Finland, 2005), is a researcher and lecturer of organizational communication and public relations at the department of Communication, University of Jyvaskyla as well as an adjunct professor (docent) at the University of Helsinki and at the University of Vaasa. Her research focuses on stakeholder relations (primarily in the public sector), intangible assets, and social media. She has authored many book chapters and online publications along with peer-reviewed journal articles published in *Public Relations Review, Business Ethics: A European Journal, Electronic Journal of Business Ethics and Organization Studies, Corporate Reputation Review, Business History, Corporate Communication, International Journal of Public Sector Management,* as well as *Management Research Review* and *Ethical Space.* She is the leader of the research group WEM- What is Expected of the Media in a Reputation Society?, and is the head of the Intangible Assets division in the cross-disciplinary research group Organizational Evolution and Dynamics. She has developed the Reputation Barometer for Finnish Ministry of Social Affairs & Health, and is a requested speaker on topics such as reputation, social media, and trust in the public sector. Her previous work experience consists of agency work and information officer duties in the public sector, as well as post-doc research at Annenberg School for Communication, USC, Los Angeles (2006) and at H-Star, Stanford University (2008–2009).

Angela M. Lee, (M.A., University of Pennsylvania, 2009), is a Ph.D. student in the School of Journalism at the University of Texas at Austin. Her research has been published in peer-reviewed journals such as *Communication Research, Journal of Broadcasting & Electronic Media, Digital Journalism, The Social Science Journal,* and *#ISOJ–The Official Research Journal of the International Symposium on Online Journalism,* among others. She is a William Powers Jr. Graduate Fellow, and was vice president of the Communication and the Future division in the National Communication Association in 2012. She is also a member of Phi Kappa Phi (UT-Austin chapter), Phi Beta Kappa (UCLA chapter), International Communication Association, and Association for Education in Journalism and Mass Communication.

Nneka Logan, (doctoral candidate, 2012), is pursuing a Ph.D., in public communication in the Department of Communication at Georgia State University. Logan holds a master's degree in mass communication from Georgia State University and a bachelor's degree in journalism from the University of Georgia in Athens. Her research focuses are public relations, rhetorical studies, corporate discourse, and diversity. She has published an article in the peer-reviewed *Journal of Public Relations Research* and is the James Woodruff, Jr. Research Fellowship in Ethics 2011–2012 award winner. She has taught public relations and human communication courses. She also has professional experience in public relations and corporate communications. Logan has worked for Cox Enterprises, Fox Broadcasting Company and as a freelance music and entertainment writer for local and national print and online publications. She brings a unique combination of rigorous academic training as well as professional experience to her research and pedagogical endeavors. In addition, she has won several awards for her academic and professional work.

Tina McCorkindale, (Ph.D., University of Miami, 2006), is an associate professor of public relations at Appalachian State University. Her research has been published in *Public Relations Review, Journal of New Communications Research, Public Relations Journal, Journal of Social*

Media in Society, Journal of Hospitality and Leisure Marketing, Teaching Public Relations Monograph, Global Media Journal–Canadian Edition, Feedback, and in several books. McCorkindale serves as the chair for the Public Relations Society of America (PRSA) Educators Academy, co-chair of PRSA's National Research Committee, a member of PRSA's MBA Initiative committee, a member of PRSA's Awards and Honors committee, a member of the Commission for Public Relations Education, research advisory board member for the International Public Relations Research Conference, and an associate editor for the Social Science of Social Media Research Center. Her research broadly focuses on social media with specializations in authenticity, transparency, and reputation.

Marcus Messner, (Ph.D., University of Miami, 2009), is an assistant professor of mass communications in the School of Mass Communications at Virginia Commonwealth University. His research agenda explores the adoption and use of social media platforms in journalism and public relations. His research has been published in *Mass Communication & Society, Newspaper Research Journal, Journalism Studies, Journalism Practice, Public Relations Journal, Digithum* as well as in many books. Messner has been named an Emerging Scholar and a Promising Professor by the Association for Education in Journalism and Mass Communication and a Page Legacy Scholar with the Arthur W. Page Center. He is a past head of the AEJMC Communication Technology Division and an editorial board member for the Newspaper Research Journal. He serves as academic director of an annual Social Media Institute for the U.S. State Department, which designs social media campaigns for non-profit organizations, and as Director of Research and Teaching for the Center for Media + Health at Virginia Commonwealth University.

Kim Bartel Sheehan, (Ph.D, University of Tennessee, 1995), is professor of advertising at the University of Oregon, as well as the Director of the Master's program in Strategic Communication and the Director of the Honors program. She has published in numerous journals including the *Journal of Advertising*, the *Journal of Advertising Research*, the *Journal of Public Policy and Marketing*, and the *Journal of Computer Mediated Communication*. She currently serves as President of the American Academy of Advertising. Her professional experience includes more than 12 years of experience in advertising and marketing in which she held leadership positions at agencies in Boston, Chicago, and St. Louis, and has consulted with numerous companies including People Magazine and Laura Ashley.

Hilary Fussell Sisco, (Ph.D., University of South Carolina, 2008), is an assistant professor of public relations at Quinnipiac University. Her research focuses on social media use, nonprofit organizations and crisis communication. She has published numerous articles in peer-reviewed academic journals, including *Journal of Public Relations Research, Public Relations Review, and Public Relations Journal, Social Media in Society* among several others. She is research chair of the Public Relations Society of America (PRSA) Educators Academy, member of the PRSA Research Task Force, and Vice Chair of the PRSA Work, Life and Gender Committee.

Brian Solis is principal at Altimeter Group, a research firm focused on disruptive technology. A digital analyst, anthropologist, and futurist, Solis has studied and influenced the effects of emerging technology on business, marketing, and culture. Solis is also globally recognized as one of the most prominent thought leaders and published authors in new media.

Don W. Stacks, (Ph.D., University of Florida, 1978), is a full professor of public relations and corporate communication in the School of Communication at the University of Miami. His research focuses on research and measurement, strategic public relations, crisis communications, biosocial communication, reputation, social media processes and evaluation, and persuasive processes. He has authored or co-authored over 20 chapters in books and has authored or co-authored eight books—to include two PRIDE award winners in *Primer of Public Relations Research*, 1ˢᵗ Ed., and with David Michaelson, *A Practitioner's Guide to Public Relations Research, Measurement, & Evaluation*. Stacks is the editor of the *Dictionary of Public Relations Research and Measurement*, and He is editor of the *Journal of the Association for Communication Administration* and has edited two other journals and has served on over 11 editorial boards. Stacks has published in such journals as the *Journal of Applied Communication Research, Journalism & Mass Communication Quarterly, Public Relations Review, PR Tactics, Communication Monographs, World Futures, Communication Education, Journalism Educator, Communication Quarterly*. He has professional experience with Sears, Allstate Insurance, Columbia Energy Company, IBM, and other top *Fortune 500* companies. He is currently the Director of the International Public Relations Research Conference and has served as a Board of Directors on several academic and professional associations. He has received the PRSA Outstanding Educator, Jackson Jackson & Wagner Behavioral Science Prize, Pathfinder, and SuPRstar awards, in addition to a number of University of Miami awards. He is a member of the Arthur W. Page Society and has served as Public Relations Division head for the Association of Education in Journalism and Mass Communication.

Kaye D. Sweetser, APR, (Ph.D., University of Florida, 2004), is an associate professor of public relations at the University of Georgia. Her research focuses on the use of social media in public relations and political communication contexts. She has more than 15 years of professional public relations experience and is an accredited public relations practitioner (APR+M). Since 1996, she has been practicing military public affairs–first as an active duty enlisted Navy mass communication specialist and then as a commissioned Navy Public Affairs Officer, and continues to do so today. In 2007, she worked as media officer on a campaign that earned PRSA's highest honor, the Silver Anvil, in the government crisis communication category. In 2011, she won a second Silver Anvil as the advisor for the iCount campaign. It is of worth to note that Dr. Sweetser is also a battle-tested public relations practitioner having served as a mobilized Reservist at the headquarters for the war in Afghanistan for seven months in 2011. As an academic, Dr. Sweetser has more than 30 publications in communication and public relations journals, such as *Journalism & Mass Communication Quarterly* and the *Journal of Public Relations Research*. In 2010, she advised the winning team of students in PRSSA's Bateman Case Study Competition. She was named a Research Fellow for the Society of New Communications Research in 2008, served as a Lilly Fellow at the University of Georgia from 2007–2008, and won the Russell Award for Undergraduate Teaching at the University of Georgia in 2011.

Natalie T. J. Tindall, (Ph.D., University of Maryland, 2007), is an assistant professor in the Department of Communication at Georgia State University. Her research focuses on diversity in organizations, specifically the public relations function, and the situational theory of publics and intersectionality. She has authored many book chapters and online publications along with peer-reviewed journal articles published in *Journal of Public Relations Research*, *Public Relations Review*, *Public Relations Journal*, *Howard Journal of Communications*, *PRism*, and the *International Journal of Strategic Communication*. She is the chair of the Public Relations Society of America Diversity Committee, member of the Public Relations Society of America Work, Life & Gender Task Force, and Vice Chair-Elect for the Public Relations Division of the Association for Education in Journalism and Mass Communication.

Päivi M. Tirkkonen, (MA, University of Jyväskylä, 2008), is a doctoral student at University of Jyväskylä, Finland and Tallinn University, Estonia; and lecturer of organizational communication and public relations at Tallinn University. Her research focus is on risk and crisis communication, social media and authority-citizens relationship. Her articles have been published in *Public Relations Review* and *Journal of Communication Management*. She is a member of the research group Organizational Evolution and Dynamics. She has been working developing Crisis Communication Scorecard for public authorities within international

Index